Digital Photography Essentials

Digital Photography Essentials™:
Point, Shoot, Enhance, Share

ERICA SADUN

SAN FRANCISCO | LONDON

SYBEX®

Associate Publisher: Dan Brodnitz
Acquisitions and Developmental Editor: Bonnie Bills
Editor: Marilyn Smith
Production Editor: Kylie Johnston
Technical Editor: Eric Bell
Production Manager: Amy Changar
Cover, Interior, and Technical Illustration Designer: Caryl Gorska
Icon Illustrator: Tina Healey Illustrations
Compositor: Maureen Forys, Happenstance Type-O-Rama
Proofreaders: Laurie O'Connell, Nancy Riddiough, Sarah Tannehill, Monique van den Berg
Indexer: Ted Laux
CD Coordinator: Dan Mummert
CD Technician: Kevin Ly
Cover Designer: John Nedwidek, emdesign
Cover Photographers: John Nedwidek, emdesign; Erica Sadun; Definitive Stock

An earlier version of this book was published under the title *Digital Photography! I Didn't Know You Could Do That!* Second Edition © 2001 SYBEX Inc.

LIBRARY OF CONGRESS CARD NUMBER: 2002108067

ISBN: 0-7821-4177-3

Dear Reader,

Thank you for choosing *Digital Photography Essentials*. This book is part of a new wave of Sybex graphics and digital photography books, all written by outstanding authors who know their stuff—and know you, their audience. It's also the fifth Sybex book from author Erica Sadun. Erica has a gift for writing books that are practical and fun. *Digital Photography Essentials* is a great example, with practical advice on choosing and caring for your digital camera, fixing image problems, and processing and sharing your photos, plus fun projects at every turn.

At Sybex, we're committed to producing a full line of quality digital photography books. Other titles on the horizon include two full-color books from acclaimed author Mikkel Aaland: *Photoshop Elements 2 Solutions: The Art of Digital Photography* and *Shooting Digital: Pro Tips for Taking Great Pictures with Your Digital Camera.*

With each book, we're working hard to set a new standard for the industry and for ourselves. From the paper we print on, to the designers we work with, to the visual examples our authors provide, our goal is to bring you the best graphics and digital photography books available.

I hope you see all that reflected in these pages. I'd be very interested in hearing your feedback on how we're doing. To let us know what you think about this or any other Sybex book, please visit us at www.sybex.com. Once there, go to the product page, click on Submit a Review, and fill out the questionnaire. Your input is greatly appreciated.

Best regards,

Daniel A. Brodnitz
Associate Publisher
Sybex Inc.

Dedication

For Mom and Dad, who put up with me until adulthood, with respect and gratitude, especially now that I've got kids of my own.

And in memory of Mamma, who will sorely be missed and who always had her head on her shoulders just right.

Acknowledgments

This book could not have been written without the generosity and skill of others. I am deeply grateful for the assistance offered so freely by so many kind people. No book is ever truly the work of one person. I would like to thank everyone who has given of their time, help, advice, and information. I humbly beg the forgiveness of any person I have overlooked.

I wish to thank, in particular, Sherry Bonelli, formerly of Sybex, and Neil Salkind of Studio B. I cannot express how marvelous it was to work with both of them. In fact, all of the wonderful folks at Sybex and Studio B made this a project of particular joy and pleasure. I would also like to thank Bonnie Bills, Kylie Johnston, Liz Burke, Amy Changar, Siobhan Dowling, Maureen Forys, Judy Fung, Molly Glover, Nancy Guenther, Christine Harris, Don Hergert, Tony Jonick, Chuck Larrieu, Lucienne Loh, Kevin Ly, Dann McDorman, Keith McNeil, the amazing Dan Mummert, Jill Niles, Laurie O'Connell, Ceola Richardson, Ann Rogers, Kara Schwartz, Marilyn Smith, Colleen Strand, Jangshi Wang, Kris Warrenburg, and Nathan Whiteside. Sybex is truly a kinder, gentler publishing company. The entire production team did a fabulous job. Thank you.

I want to thank all of the companies and Web sites that have graciously granted permission for their software and services to be included in this book. In particular, Adobe generously allowed me to package PhotoDeluxe on the CD-ROM that accompanies this book. In addition, thanks to those people whose outstanding courtesy helped this process enormously. These include the simply incredible Mike Wong, formerly of Lexar; Mary Kuch-Nagle, of Digimarc; The Altamira Group, especially Carolyne Walton and Sid Fish; Steve Berezin of Berezin 3-D; Ceiva and Richard Attenberg; Jeff Kelling of FotoTime; JP Wollersheim, Bridget Thornton Padilla, and Lisa Marshall of PhotoLoft; Rachel Branch of Sony; Abe Schoener of eFrames; Chris Johnson and Lylia Lammens of PhotoPoint; Tara Poole of Shandwick, International; Avi Shmidman; Bill Martin; Patty Thompson, Peter Hanisch, Patrick Sagisi, Mark Dahm, Alan Williams, John Nack, and Scott Wellwood of Adobe; the good folks at Ulead, especially Travis White and Pam Swartwood; ClubPhoto; eFrames, especially Abe and Michelle; Jackie Zide of Manning, Selvage, and Lee for eMemories; Dick Paulson of EZ Prints; Ofoto, especially Jeremy Pepper; PhotoChannel, especially Joseph Bach and David Bremner; Dawn Weissman of PhotoPoint; GatherRound.com's Mollie Lupinacci; Marc Holmquist of PhotoDex; Laura Shook of Cerious Software; Dennis Curtin of Short Courses; Michael Bartosh and Bo Turney of Apple; Jenny Menhart of Ahead; Kris Konietzko of TSI Communications WorldWide; Gerald of Seattle FilmWorks, aka PhotoWorks; Shelly Sofer of MGI; Stephanie Xavier and Molly Fitzpatrick of Access Communications; Kari Day of Real Networks; Sean Wright of Dell, Inc.; JASC; CompuPic; and PhotoIsland. Thanks also to Jim Dielschneider and Hyung Lim of LizardTech; Sandy Kensinger of Fisher Price; Frank Weber of Orasee; Kerry Reuer of NixVue Systems; Bill Strum of Imageatics.com; Kim Agricola of PhotoParade; Larry Wooden of 3D Creations; Paul Talbot of Rocky Mountain Memories; Jessie Chew of FlipAlbum; Simone Souza of Roxio/MGI; Bruce Gee of Gee Three; Chris Hart of XAT; Derek Bump of Dreamscape Software; Jaime Cornelison of Pegasus Tools/JPG.com; and Dawn Ginn of Spinwave.

Finally, let me thank Hayden Starr, Barbara Liebman, Sally Stieglitz, and everyone else who provided moral support.

CONTENTS AT A GLANCE

Contents

Introduction

A couple of nights ago, we took the kids out for ice cream, and I noticed a big advertisement hanging above the counter. It said, "Bring in your digital photographs. We'll put them on ice cream cakes." I found the manager and asked what was involved. "It's simple," she said. "Just bring in the picture on a disk or CD, and they'll make the cake for $7 above the normal price." They print the pictures using a special printer with edible food dyes on edible paper, and then lay it flat on the ice cream cake. It was then I knew. Digital photography isn't up and coming; digital photography is here. If you can bring your digital images into the corner ice cream shop for a cake, then you can use digital pictures almost anywhere.

The digital camera has been a common business tool for several years. With a digicam and a Web site, more and more people are moving their local shops online. Digital photography can quickly put a store's inventory in front of a huge audience of shoppers. Insurance adjusters and real estate agents think of digital cameras as one more necessary tool in their arsenal, like cell phones.

Within the last year or two, most barriers that kept digital cameras from home use have fallen away. Prices have dropped; optics have improved. For just a few hundred dollars, you can buy a camera with excellent zoom and superb picture quality. And now, you can even take your digital pictures to Wal-Mart or the corner drugstore and walk away with prints in an hour, for about the same cost as film developing. Receiving pictures in e-mail is now an everyday experience.

For me, the pervasiveness of digital photography is absolutely thrilling. I love to see that people are discovering the same excitement I felt when holding a digital camera in my hand for the first time.

Despite the growing popularity and ordinariness of the technology, digital photography hasn't lost a single bit of the art. The techniques for taking good pictures taught in traditional photography classes are just as applicable to digital photography. Additionally, image-editing software offers many ways to improve your pictures and use them in novel ways.

This book (which is based on *Digital Photography! I Didn't Know You Could Do That,* Second Edition) offers ways for you to learn how to go beyond "point and shoot" and expand your creativity. It doesn't matter if you're familiar with digital photography or just starting out. Inside each of us lies the potential for great pictures. If this book allows you to discover that potential in the field of digital photography, then it has done its job. Enjoy your camera and take a lot of digital pictures.

What's in This Book?

Digital Photography Essentials: Point, Shoot, Enhance, Share covers the range of digital camera basics to advanced digital photography techniques. Each chapter contains a mix of background and how-to material. Topics range from snapping high-quality photographs, to editing your photographs with image-editing programs, to sharing your pictures as prints or on the Web. You'll find many step-by-step instructions to guide you through sample projects.

Here's a chapter-by-chapter summary of what you'll find in this book:

Chapter 1, "Composition, Lighting, and Posing: Some Tried-and-True Advice" Learn how to take excellent photos, light your scenes, set up a portrait studio for under $20, and pose your subjects. This chapter contains plenty of photos to illustrate how you can take better pictures.

Chapter 2, "Digital Camera Equipment" Discover how to power your camera, add image memory, transfer your pictures to your computer, and use filters and lenses. The types of batteries and memory you use for your camera can make the difference between capturing that special moment or missing it because you ran out of power or storage.

Chapter 3, "An Introduction to PhotoDeluxe" Acquire the essential Adobe PhotoDeluxe skills that will help you improve and manipulate your images. Many of the projects covered in this book make use of this software, which you'll find on the *Digital Photography Essentials: Point, Shoot, Enhance, Share* CD.

Chapter 4, "Digital Photo Editing" Learn how to use image-editing software to improve your pictures and make the most of your images. In this chapter, you'll learn how to fix image flaws such as poor contrast, low light, and red-eye. You can even get rid of unwanted background elements and improve your subject's complexion.

Chapter 5, "New Viewpoints: Postprocessing Your Images" Find a different view within your photos. You'll learn how to stitch together panoramas, assemble three-dimensional pictures, and blow up images to poster size.

Chapter 6, "Digital Photo Printing" Explore the process of making prints from your digital photographs. You'll learn how to print your photos at home on your own printer, as well as how to prepare your digital photos to send to a photo-finishing service for producing silver-halide prints.

Chapter 7, "Photos on CDs and DVDs" CDs, DVDs, and Video on CD (VCDs) offer great ways to distribute your pictures to play back on computers and television. Learn how to author interactive slide shows for these media.

Chapter 8, "Share Your Pictures" Learn how to distribute your photos over the Internet. You can send photos by e-mail, create and share online photo albums, and use a digital photo frame to send pictures to those without Internet connections.

Chapter 9, "Digital Camera Versatility" Discover all the weird, wacky, and wonderful ways your digital camera can help you remember, document, and see things. The ideas presented in this chapter range from the serious (taking shots at the scene of an accident) to the silly (playing Face Bingo).

Chapter 10, "Digital Camera Crafts" Learn how to create craft projects with your digital images. From fashion wear to window decals, digital photo projects are fun, easy, and make great gifts.

Chapter 11, "Photo Transformation Projects" Use your digital photos to create animated slide shows, coloring book pages, calendars, and more. These projects are easy and put your photos to good use.

Chapter 12, "Just For the Fun of It: Digital Photo Projects" Learn how to warp images, morph between photos, make photo montages, and create other photo fantasies. You'll have a lot of fun with the Web site–based and PhotoDeluxe projects covered in this chapter.

Digital Photo Sampler Throughout the book, you'll see many digital photos illustrating the concepts and projects covered here. However, the black-and-white pictures cannot do justice to the full range of color and tone that you can capture with your digital camera. This 16-page color insert presents photos that show how you can use your digital camera to produce fun, interesting, and artistic images.

In addition, you'll find an appendix and a glossary at the back of this book. The "Field Guide to Online Finishing and Album Sites" appendix lists the top online digital photo-finishing and album sites. Use this handy reference to decide where and how you'll post and process your digital snapshots on the World Wide Web. If you're unfamiliar with any of the terms you see in this book, check the glossary for the definition.

What's on the Accompanying CD?

The CD-ROM that accompanies this book is jam-packed with demos and shareware that you can use with your digital images. But the best part is that it contains a licensed copy of Adobe's PhotoDeluxe software for Windows. Yes, you read that correctly. PhotoDeluxe is included free with this book. This edition offers the new 4.1 version, just released in summer 2002.

With PhotoDeluxe, you'll be able to see, manipulate, and edit your images with wonderful control and precision. Make sure to read through Chapter 3, "An Introduction to Photo-Deluxe," and Chapter 4, "Digital Photo Editing," of this book to learn more about how to use this powerful photo-editing software.

In addition to PhotoDeluxe, you'll find quite a few commercial demonstration software packages. These packages "expire" after a period of time, usually ranging between 15 and 30 days. Take advantage of this free time to test the programs, kick the tires, and see if they are worth your monetary investment to purchase a license. These are truly excellent packages that you'll probably want to make part of your digital photographer's toolkit. Mac users will be particularly interested in the 30-day free trial version of Photoshop Elements on the accompanying CD-ROM. You can do nearly everything with Photoshop Elements that you would with PhotoDeluxe. It's a terrific piece of software and well worth further investigation. If you're interested in learning more about Photoshop Elements, I'd recommend Mikkel Aaland's excellent book, *Photoshop Elements 2 Solutions* (Sybex, 2002).

Finally, you'll find a number of shareware programs. Unlike PhotoDeluxe and the commercial demos, these packages are not free. Instead, they allow you to try the product before you buy it. Shareware works only when people take personal responsibility and pay for the software they actually use. Be responsible. If you like the software, send the requested fee to the developer. This helps keep shareware alive and available for the rest of us.

CHAPTER 1

Composition, Lighting, and Posing: Some Tried-and-True Advice

Whether you're using a traditional film camera or a fancy new digital one, composition, lighting, and posing play important roles in your photos. Taking pictures is as much an art as a science. Learn from the classics. The basic rules of portraiture and landscape art are as applicable to digital pictures as they are to traditional canvases. As you will discover in this chapter, it's important to think about how you should place your subjects, light them, and frame them with your camera. The time-tested techniques and tips described here will help you create better, more professional snapshots, while taking advantage of the special features provided by your digital camera. Learn to combine the traditional with the state-of-the-art, and you'll be richly rewarded by the results.

This chapter covers the following topics:

- **Compose your shot with care**
- **Use light effectively**
- **Understand depth of field**
- **Achieve natural poses**
- **Focus sharply**
- **Tips of the trade**

Compose Your Shot with Care

Do you remember that joke about Mozart (the one in which he is busy decomposing)? In photography, composition doesn't mean creating music. Instead, it refers to the way that the photographer places all of the visual elements of a picture. Good pictures don't happen by accident. Good pictures result from planning and following the basic rules of composition; the better the composition, the better the photograph. If you think that you take pretty good pictures now, you'll be astonished how quickly your snapshots improve when you apply the basic rules of photographic composition.

Get Closer...Much Closer!

Do you know the single worst mistake that amateur photographers make? They shoot pictures from too far away. They think they need to capture the whole scene instead of just the real point of interest. This one bad habit makes many bad photos.

You can easily improve your photos with one quick fix: Move closer. The closer you get to your subject, the better your photos will turn out. Some people operate under the mistaken impression that you need to take pictures of an entire landscape or an entire person—including all the hair, limbs, clothes, and so forth—in order to create a memorable shot. On the contrary, your photos should focus on a point of interest. For example, when your subject is a person, think of the eyes as the most important part of your photo. The more you concentrate on a person's face—and, particularly, a person's eyes—the better your photo will turn out.

Consider the three photos shown in Figure 1.1. With each photo, the camera moves in toward the subject. See how the pictures improve with each step? Getting closer creates snapshots that focus more narrowly on the subject while creating a sense of intimacy between the subject and the viewer.

Figure 1.1

Don't be afraid to close in on your subject.

From too far away, the subject is completely lost in the picture. The real center of interest occupies only about one-sixth of the total photo.

Moving closer improves the picture, but the ratio of background to subject is still too high. At this distance, a picture taken in portrait mode would work better than one in landscape orientation.

Use the Rule of Thirds

Long ago, in ancient Greece and Egypt, philosophers noticed a strange feature of beauty. Many things we find attractive incorporate a natural ratio of approximately 3:2, which they called *Phi* (rhymes with *tie*). This ratio came to be known as the golden ratio, or even the divine ratio. The ancients used this ratio to create art and architecture to mimic the beauty one finds in nature. The idea is this: Compositions that are split into thirds, with some feature placed about two-thirds of the way across the scene, look good. It's as simple as that.

Artists and, later, photographers picked up on this ratio to form the rule of thirds, which we use in composition. This involves placing visually interesting points along imaginary lines at one-third and two-thirds of the way across a picture. But the adherence to using Phi goes further than that. Even the most common print sizes (3.5×5, 4×6, 5×7, and so forth) approximate the golden ratio between their width and their height.

You can improve your photos by using this rule of thirds. Just imagine two pairs of lines. One pair runs horizontally across your picture at one-third and two-thirds of the height. The other pair runs vertically, again at one-third and two-thirds of the width. When framing your image through the viewfinder or on your camera's liquid crystal display (LCD) screen, place the most important features of your picture along one of these lines. Whether you shoot your pictures in landscape or portrait mode, this rule will improve your picture's composition.

Most digital cameras now ship with both a traditional viewfinder and an LCD screen. While some people prefer using the viewfinder to "point and shoot," others like the convenience and preview features of the LCD screen. Whichever feature you use, remember to frame your pictures carefully before pressing the shutter release.

Finally, close enough for a great picture.

If you're not comfortable "imagining" the lines, you can actually place them onto your camera's LCD screen. Simply cut out some transparent plastic, draw your lines on it, and apply it to your camera's display. Plastic used for making viewgraphs or transparencies works particularly well for this purpose. If static electricity doesn't keep your plastic attached to the LCD screen, use a little transparent tape to fasten it.

The illustration shown in Figure 1.2 shows the differences between images composed with and without using the rule of thirds. Notice how both portrait and nature shots improve when this rule is applied.

When using the rule of thirds, it doesn't matter on which of the lines you choose to set your visual focus point. Use any of the four lines or four points (where the lines intersect). Your photos will improve.

Simplify Your Background

One of a photographer's biggest goofs is to allow the background to be too cluttered with objects and people. Busy backgrounds distract the eye from your main subject, drawing attention away from what you should really be looking at. Contrast the pictures in Figures 1.3 and 1.4. See how the picture works better with less happening in the background?

Figure 1.2

The rule of thirds will improve your shots.

Composed without using the rule of thirds, a picture is not visually interesting.

Positioning the eyes on the top line improves the picture.

The horizon rests directly in the middle of the picture.

By shifting the horizon down to the bottom line, the rule of thirds improves the picture.

Figure 1.3

A complicated background detracts from your portrait.

Figure 1.4

A simple background allows your picture to emphasize your subject.

You can easily solve the busy background problem. Consider these hints:

Avoid busy scenery. The simplest solution is the most obvious. Take pictures away from cluttered areas. Choose a plainer backdrop for your snapshots.

Move the camera. Sometimes you can avoid visual clutter by adjusting your viewpoint. Try walking around your subject with your camera until you find a more flattering angle.

Move closer. The more subject the picture contains, the less background your picture shows.

Drop down. By shooting up at your subject, you can sometimes avoid a lot of eye-level clutter.

Take a portrait. Turn your camera 90 degrees and shoot in portrait mode rather than in landscape mode. Portrait shots limit the amount of background and show more of your subject.

Frame It!

Shooting your picture through a natural frame can add elegance to your pictures. Natural frames include windows, doors, and tree limbs, as well as other overhanging features. Adding a frame to your picture can make it look better. This works by directing the eye toward the subject. Figure 1.5 shows an example of how you can shoot a "framed" shot.

Watch out for your depth of field—make sure that both your frame and your subject stay in focus! Frames don't work well if either they or the subjects slide into fuzzy obscurity. See the "Understand Depth of Field" section later in this chapter for details.

Figure 1.5

Keep your eyes open to find natural frames for your shots.

Choose the Best Camera Angle

Did you know that your point of view could dramatically change the way that you perceive a subject? When a camera shoots down, we tend to think a subject looks smaller and humbler. When the camera looks up, we think the subject looks bigger and stronger. These camera angles mimic the way that we have learned to look at things and people during life. Consider the viewpoint of an adult looking down at a child or a child looking up at an adult, and you can understand how the direction of a photo can resonate with personal experience. You can take advantage of the way that we naturally interpret these angles to add meaning and effect to your pictures.

Downward Angles

You can make your subjects seem smaller and more appealing by shooting down. This angle can make a young girl look more demure. It can make a child seem more childlike or an adult less imposing. Downward angles emphasize eyes and cheeks, while minimizing chins. Large cheeks and small chins correlate with the way we view children. Figure 1.6 shows a person shot at a downward angle.

You can use a downward angle for good or for evil. Many political photographers shoot down when they want to humiliate or minimize a politician or public figure. Because we identify downward shots with an adult viewpoint, these pictures can make people look less important.

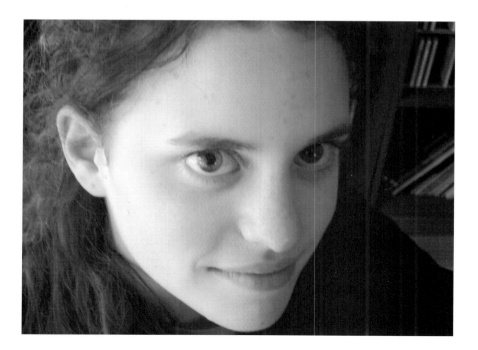

Figure 1.6

Downward angles emphasize cheekbones.

Downward angles also make pictures feel more closed and complete than other angles do. When taking photos of the outdoors, a downward shot where the horizon appears high in the picture will produce a feeling of limits and claustrophobia. You can also use a downward angle to hide an ugly, overcast sky, as in Figure 1.7.

Upward Angles

You can make your subjects appear bigger, more imposing, and more demanding of attention just by lowering your camera and looking up. Use this camera angle to flatter your subjects and make them seem more important. You need not limit this technique to photos of people. Take an upward-pointing picture of your dog to show how strong and fierce he is. Take a picture from the bottom of a statue to emphasize its height and majesty.

The upward angle lends prominence and strength to both the subject and to your photos. This technique particularly emphasizes the chin, lending a sense of power to your subject. Figure 1.8 shows an example of a person shot at an upward angle.

Upward angles open up pictures by lowering the horizon, as in Figure 1.9. They lend a feeling of spaciousness and freedom without limits or restrictions. When shooting outdoor photos, use an upward shot to draw in the sky and capture the full magnificence of nature.

Figure 1.7

A downward angle hides the sky and creates a sense of enclosure.

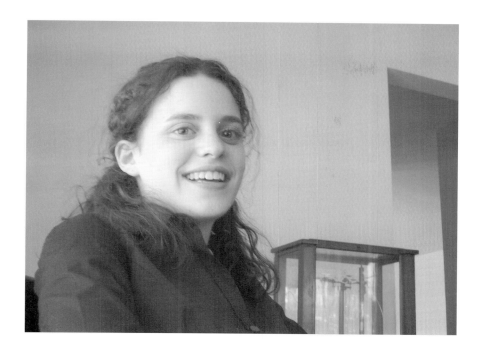

Figure 1.8

An upward angle emphasizes a subject's importance and authority.

Figure 1.9

An upward shot creates a sense of openness and possibility.

Figure 1.10

A straight-on shot creates a direct connection between your subject and the camera.

Straight-on Shots

The most common shot—the straight-on, neutral shot—forms the bread and butter of photography. This shot creates plain and undistorted portraits of your subject, as you can see in Figure 1.10. Use this angle when you're not trying for artistry or special effects. It's straight, honest, and simple. It may be boring, but it works for almost all of your photography needs.

Horizontal or Vertical Orientation?

As you've probably noticed, photos tend to come in one of two orientations. In the vertical portrait shot, the height exceeds the width. In the horizontal landscape shot, the width exceeds the height.

Horizontal and vertical compositions create different effects. Vertical photos capture individuals and small groups best, at the expense of the background. Horizontal shots, in contrast, are best for large group shots and general photography of people and nature. Figure 1.11 shows how using a vertical shot can improve a portrait photo.

Because of its more generalized nature, the typical camera creates horizontal shots by default. To take a vertical picture, just turn the camera on its side and shoot. Many tripods allow you to mount your camera for either vertical or horizontal shots.

Figure 1.11

Vertical composition improves a portrait.

Horizontal composition includes too much background for a portrait.

Vertical composition captures more of the individual.

Face Your Subject to the Center

The way a person faces, called a *leading look*, can direct attention into the picture or out of it. Looking out of the picture produces photos that don't quite work, as you can see in Figure 1.12.

Ask your subjects to look toward the center of your photographic frame, or move the camera and your composition until their pose works.

Figure 1.12

A leading look can ruin a pose.

Avoid Unwanted Background Elements

Sometimes we forget to look at the background. We become so fixated on our subject's great expression or adorable pose that all sorts of unwanted visual details pop into our photos, unannounced. Often we don't notice the other elements until too late, when the moment has already gone, and then we're stuck with pictures that have little "problem" items all over the place.

You can learn to break out of the whole subject-fascination trance and avoid the pitfalls of unwanted elements in your photos. Start by thinking before snapping your photos. Take a good, long look at the whole picture. What items don't belong? What can you improve simply by moving an item—or yourself—to another location? It's easy to get rid of unsightly details. The problem is noticing them in the first place! The pictures in Figure 1.13 show the difference between just shooting a photo and noticing the background first.

The worst offender for this sort of photography is the classic "tree growing out of someone's head" shot, seen in Figure 1.14. By concentrating on your subject, rather than the background, you may end up with a telephone pole, sign, or tree sprouting from a head. Remember the basic rule: Stop, look, and if necessary, move! Only then should you snap.

Figure 1.13

Plan your shots.

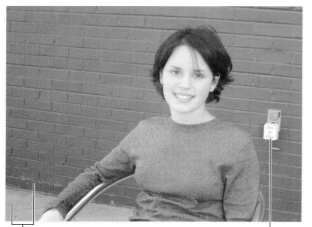

This photo will work better without seeing the contrast between the brick wall and the ground.

This electrical outlet is distracting.

The photo is greatly improved without the background elements.

Figure 1.14

If you don't notice the background, your subject may end up with a tree growing out of her head.

In some cases, you can fix background problems by using photo-editing program tools. For some suggestions, see Chapter 4, "Digital Photo Editing."

Use Light Effectively

As a digital photographer, you need light. For obvious reasons, without light, you cannot take pictures. And without good lighting, you cannot take good pictures. Good lighting makes the difference between drama and melodrama, between splendor and ordinary, and between memorable and dull.

Sunshine can be your best friend, or it can be your worst enemy. While you're letting it fill your camera with brilliant colors and images, remain wary. Learn to tame and control it. Make it do what you need it to do. Natural sunlight creates the most dramatic and colorful scenes. It can also fool your camera. It can make your pictures harsh and unflattering. It can bleach images to near whiteness or hide your subject in an artificial dark.

You can improve your digital photography by learning to use light effectively. By following simple guidelines, you can ensure that your pictures turn out the best they can be—whether you're shooting indoors or outdoors, or in bright light or near dark.

Avoid Backlight

Backlight occurs when the sun (or, for that matter, any other light source) shines too close to your subject's back. Backlight tricks your camera into thinking it is taking a picture of a very bright object. Your camera adjusts its light levels too high. Instead of picking up the light levels from your subject, it picks them up from the scenery. While the scenery appears beautiful and well lit, your subject looks awful—usually as a silhouette against a bright and colorful background.

To avoid backlight, keep the sun behind you and in front of your subject. This allows your camera to properly interpret your exposure settings.

You may need to physically move yourself and your camera to find the proper lighting. If you cannot reverse direction completely, such as when you are taking a picture of someone standing outside a famous monument, move in a circle around your subject until you find a happy compromise.

Some digital cameras automatically "handle" backlight, usually by turning on the flash. You can, too. Set your camera to use its flash and ignore the ambient lighting. The pictures in Figure 1.15 show how the flash will compensate for backlighting. However, even though using the flash will fill in your subject, this method does not produce particularly wonderful pictures. Your subject's features will appear "flatter" than in natural light. Instead, try to avoid backlit conditions completely whenever possible.

Use Indirect Light

A face full of sunshine is about as flattering as mud. Sunshine fills a face with harsh, unpleasant shadows. People look haggard, tired, and old. Every wrinkle is brought into full prominence. Shadows on the neck add an extra chin or two. Add squinting eyes into the mixture, and you have the lighting environment from hell.

Figure 1.15

Backlight can ruin a picture.

With the sun behind her, the subject's face is dark.

When you cannot avoid backlighting, use the flash to fill in your subject's features.

Fortunately, there's a quick fix: Move your subject into the shade. Look for a tree, an over-hang, or a trellis. Wait for a cloud to cover the sun, or shoot your pictures on a hazy or overcast day. Although most people think they need to take pictures in the brightest sunlight possible, you can snap excellent photos under covered patios or shadowed overhangs, as shown in Figure 1.16.

Unlike direct sunshine, indirect light creates soft and beautiful pictures. It flatters your subjects rather than batters them. Indirect light means exactly that. Instead of light stream-ing directly from the sun onto your subject, it bounces off the walls, the ground, and the scenery around you. You still get plenty of light, but it's a different, more playful, and far more flattering light. Figure 1.17 shows how indirect light can create a great portrait.

When you cannot avoid full sunlight, use your flash to fill in some of the harsher shadows. Set your digital camera's flash to its always-on setting and take your pictures. Although indi-rect lighting produces better pictures, your flash will counteract some of the worst shadows. On the other hand, when you have good indirect light available to you, turn that flash off!

Pick a Good Time of Day

Contrast the warm, soft colors of sunrise and sunset with the harsh noonday sun. When you take out your camera, consider how the time of day will affect the light. Choose a time that matches the mood you need. At midday, sunlight is strongest and most direct. Light appears to be at its whitest, colors at their most true and vivid. At sunrise and sunset, the color of light deepens and changes—often minute to minute. Colors are redder, kinder, and more dream-like.

Use these changes in light to your best advantage. If you plan your photo shoots in advance, consider how the time of day will affect your images. Do you want to create a romantic portrait? Perhaps you should wait until late afternoon or early evening. Are you seeking a dramatic landscape showing a lot of detail? Midday should work better. And don't forget those great sunset shots. When the last rays burn over the horizon, turning the clouds to fire, don't miss having your digital camera in hand and ready to shoot.

Figure 1.16

Use Indirect light whenever possible.

Squinting in the direct sunshine

Cooler in the shade

Step to a Window

Sunlight streaming through a window creates the most dramatic light of all. As it gently caresses your subject's face, get ready to snap terrific portraits. Nothing comes close to the beauty of the classic "sitting by the window" shot. Figure 1.18 shows an example of this type of photo.

Use all sorts of windows. Consider photographing a child playing by a sliding glass door. Take a picture of another passenger while inside your car. Go to public galleries such as museums or libraries where windowed light is plentiful. Place your subject next to the stained glass in a chapel. Be creative. Use a window with sheer curtains blowing in the wind. Examine the light streaming through Venetian blinds in bars of brightness and darkness. Have your subject look outside through the window or just sit, lost in contemplation. The possibilities are endless. Wherever you find a well-lit window, you can create beautiful and exciting pictures.

When shooting your camera directly toward a window, don't forget to turn off the flash!

Create Unnatural Light

Did you know that you can create your own portrait studio for under $20? You just need a few simple items. Most of them are probably lying around your house. The rest you can easily pick up at a local camera or hardware store. Don't let a small budget keep you from taking terrific pictures.

Figure 1.17

Indirect light avoids harsh shadows.

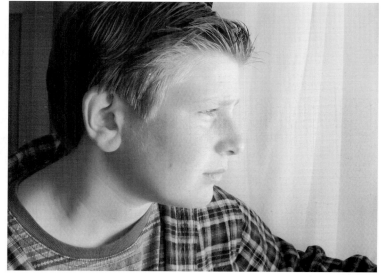

Figure 1.18

Windows provide dramatic lighting opportunities.

The Right Equipment

Here's a list of the basic equipment you need to put together your home studio:

A sheet Any sheet will do, although flat works better than fitted. You will use this sheet to create a uniform backdrop. In general, the more neutral the pattern, the better. The focus should remain on your subjects rather than the cute linen dinosaurs behind them.

Duct tape Duct tape is the home handyman's best friend. Let it become your friend, too.

Photographic-quality floodlight bulbs You'll need one or two floodlight bulbs. I use General Electric's PhotoFlood bulbs. They cost about $4 each at my local camera shop. I prefer to use the ones with blue coating, as the plain ones create light with a distinct yellowish cast. The blue bulbs avoid this problem, albeit with some loss of luminescence.

Aluminum clamp work lights You'll need one or two lights for your bulbs. You can pick these up at your local hardware store for under $5. Make sure to choose work lights that can handle the heat from your floodlight bulbs.

Various props Props make a more interesting portrait. You can use chairs, stools, hats, fake flowers, stuffed animals, and so forth.

Your Setup

Once you've done your shopping, follow these steps to get your studio up and running:

1. Pick a quiet part of the house. Try to find a room that doesn't get much traffic.

2. Duct tape your sheet to the wall. (You may want to check with your spouse or parent before you do this.) Avoid damaging your walls where possible.

3. Screw your floodlight bulb into the work light and clamp it near an outlet. (If you cannot get close to an outlet, use an extension cord.) These lights get very, very hot. Keep them away from children and any flammable objects!

4. Bounce your light off a wall or ceiling. This creates a softer and more indirect light.

5. Pose your subjects with your various props.

6. Get set, aim, and shoot!

> Photographic floodlights get very hot. Use extreme caution when placing them to avoid fire hazard. These lights can burn your skin. Keep children away from your studio when the lights are on and until they have cooled off and been put away properly! Never leave these lights on and unattended.

Figure 1.19 shows an example of a home studio setup.

Tips for the Home Studio

When you're ready to start taking pictures in your new "studio," keep these tips in mind:

Turn off your flash. Flash photography in these conditions can flatten the faces of your subjects, removing features. Instead, set your digital camera to suppress the flash and let the indirect light from the floodlights create more "natural" lighting. If you cannot figure out how to turn off your flash, tape a small piece of tissue over it. This will soften the flash instead.

Move away from the wall. Sit your subjects at least a foot or two away from your backdrop. This softens shadows and de-emphasizes the backdrop.

Turn off fluorescent lights. If fluorescent bulbs normally light your home studio, turn them off. These lights can create weird, greenish overtones in people's faces.

Use extra sheets. If your studio's walls are dark, duct-tape a light-colored sheet to a nearby wall. Bounce your floodlight off the sheet rather than off the dark wall. That way, more light will travel to your subject.

Figure 1.19

Set up your own home studio.

Backdrop held up by duct tape, under $5

Chair from around the house, $0

Lighting, under $10

Shoot in Low (or No!) Light

You can take surprisingly good digital photos in low-light conditions. Of course, your most important tool for working in the dark is your camera's built-in flash. Your flash will trigger when light conditions drop below a certain threshold. Also, some cameras allow you to take long exposures, so you can take pictures in near darkness. Keep in mind how to combat the constant enemy of flash photography—the dreaded red-eye effect—and you will be ready to start snapping your shots in the shadows.

Come to the Dark

Why not take a picture in complete darkness? I recently attended a party high up in the Colorado mountains, far from any city lights. Our host walked us back to the car, using a flashlight to guide our steps. Just as we reached the car, I decided to test my camera's flash. I had our host turn off his lantern, and I took a picture of him in the complete darkness. With only a flash to light up my shot, I was able to snap the fairly nice portrait shown in Figure 1.20.

Of course, most photo opportunities don't take place in total darkness. You may take a picture indoors during a party. You may be sitting outside during twilight. If, for whatever reasons, the ambient light is too low, use your camera's flash to help you capture the

Figure 1.20

With a flash, you can take pictures in complete darkness.

moment. Your pictures may not turn out as artistic or beautiful as those shots for which you've planned dramatic lighting, but you will not have missed the chance to capture images of a special event or person.

To use your flash, keep your camera set to automatic mode. This mode allows your camera to determine when and if a flash will be needed. Because most of us want to take pictures on the spur of the moment, it's best to leave your camera in automatic mode most of the time. When you're ready to work with lights and poses, that's the time to turn off the auto-flash feature. Until then, leave it on. You never know when a special moment will come by.

Most digital camera flashbulbs have a limited range of effect. Often, this runs to about 10 feet. As you move farther away from your subject, the light from the flash will fall off dramatically. Keep this in mind when you attempt to take shots of large objects or groups of people. However, if you get too close to your subject with a flash, your camera may overexpose, washing out fine details. Instead, if your camera supports zoom, step back a bit and use your camera's optical zoom feature to get closer.

Another feature of digital flash photography is that it does not usually brighten the whole scene uniformly. Some parts of your picture may appear darker than other parts. Typically, the center is lit more directly than objects on the periphery of the scene. If I were to let my physicist husband explain why, he would probably go on a bit about inverse squares, sines of the angle, and other rules of physics. What you really need to know is that your flash and your camera's sensors do not always produce uniform lighting in your images. Figure 1.21 show the difference a little distance can make in a flash photo.

The inverse-square law states that the amount of light from a single source falls off as the square of the distance from that source. If an object lies some unit distance away from the light and another is twice the distance, the second object will be lit only one-quarter as much as the first.

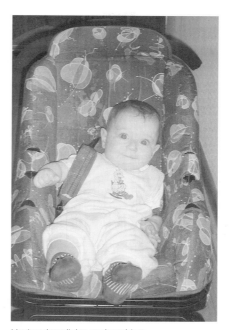

Figure 1.21

Lighting from your flash falls off quickly as distance increases.

With a flash, the center is brighter, and the rest of the scene is in shadows.

Moving closer lights up the subject.

Combat Red-Eye

Often, flash photography causes that eerie effect known as *red-eye*. Not to be confused with conjunctivitis (or pink-eye), red-eye occurs when the light from the flash bounces off your subject's retina, as shown in Figure 1.22. This causes the pupil to appear red rather than black. Let me suggest four ways to deal with this problem.

First, most digital camera manufacturers now ship their products with a built-in solution called *red-eye reduction mode*. In this mode, the camera actually flashes twice. The first flash causes people's pupils to quickly contract. This allows less light into the eye, and thus produces less reflection when the light flashes a second time to actually take the picture. Check the instructions that came with your camera to see if it supports red-eye reduction mode and, if so, how to activate it.

Figure 1.22

Red-eye can strike without warning.

It may not be apparent in this black-and-white print, but these eyes are glowing red.

Be aware, however, that red-eye reduction mode puts a higher drain on your batteries (due to the double flash), and it causes a slight delay in taking the picture, usually one or two seconds. When you're trying to take action photos, you may want to turn off this feature. It can be hard to capture the moment when time passes between when you press the shutter release and when the camera actually takes the picture.

Also, red-eye reduction mode sometimes causes people to blink. After the first flash, some people will close their eyes, so that the second flash, which accompanies the picture, creates a lovely image of your subjects with their eyes shut. (Of course, if their eyes are shut, you don't need to worry about red-eye.)

A second solution is to move the flash away from the camera. This creates a wider angle between the light, your subject, and the camera. This wider angle means that the light bouncing off someone's retinas ends up somewhere on the other side of the room and not in your camera. In just one step, you've gotten rid of red-eye. Unfortunately, few digital cameras support external flash systems, and those that do aren't the type you can slip into your pocket. The gain you make in reducing red-eye is offset by the inconvenience of carrying around an external flash system.

The third solution—and, incidentally, my favorite—is to simply take more than one picture. People's irises are not so flexible that they bounce back immediately from a flashed picture. The second and subsequent pictures will capture your subjects with more constricted pupils and less red-eye. This may not eliminate red-eye completely, as will widening the angle between the camera and the flash, but it should reduce it enough to create better pictures.

The fourth, and most obvious, solution is to bring more light into the scene. Turn on some lights or move to a brighter room. The more light, the less pupils dilate. Unfortunately, this solution is not always the most convenient one.

Did you forget about red-eye when taking your pictures? You can fix red-eye in your photo-editing program. See Chapter 4 for details on repairing red-eye.

Long Exposures

I love those long-exposure photos, where the headlights and taillights of cars form streaks of light along a cityscape. Many new digital cameras support special slow-exposure modes that allow you to create this effect in your own pictures.

You will need a tripod (or some reasonable equivalent) to take this sort of picture. Consider the images shown in Figure 1.23. In one shot, I tried to snap an image relying only on the steadiness of my hand. For the other shot, I used a tripod. Clearly, the longer the exposure, the more crucial it becomes to steady your camera.

Make sure to take your picture on a street with some regular traffic. Waiting for a car to come by can be excruciatingly boring, and you might miss the one car that finally appears. Always start the exposure before the car comes into view. This permits you to obtain long, colorful streaks. Also, I prefer to snap slow pictures on streets without (or with few) pedestrians. This way, I can focus the scene on the beams of light rather than any passerby. Keep in mind that composition is just as important in long-exposure shots as it is in short-exposure ones.

Exposure Compensation Tips

Have you ever wondered what that little button on your camera labeled +/– does? This button provides you with something called *exposure compensation.*

Your digital camera takes an average of the light of your scene before snapping a picture. This helps it figure out how to set the exposure. When your camera detects high levels of light, it reacts in one of two ways: It either takes a quicker exposure or uses a smaller lens opening, both of which let less light enter your camera. When your camera detects a low light level, it either takes a slower exposure or steps up the lens opening to allow more light in.

Digital cameras use two techniques to determine how to set exposure levels. The first, called *segment metering*, divides the image into a number of segments. The camera's light meter evaluates each segment and determines how to set the exposure for a given scene. This technique is only now coming into widespread use. The second, more popular system is *center-weighted exposure*, which places a greater emphasis on the light values measured at the center of the image. This assumes that the object you wish to photograph lies at the center of the scene. Pointing your camera at a dark object might cause the rest of the scene to overexpose and bleach out.

Figure 1.23

Use a tripod when taking long-exposure shots.

An unsteady hand ruins a long-exposure shot.

Using a tripod creates a better long-exposure picture.

No matter how your camera sets exposure levels, keep one thing in mind: Picture data in overexposed images cannot be recovered. A photo-editing program will not be able to undo the damage that overexposure causes. By using your exposure-compensation button with care, you can prevent losing your precious photos to overexposure.

For example, the exposure-compensation button can help compensate for a backlit situation. This may wash out the background, but it allows your camera to receive the proper amount of light from your subject. Similarly, if you're shooting a picture of a bright object in a dark background, you might want to reduce the exposure compensation. This can bring out the details of a pretty pair of candles on a dimly lit table.

> Techniques for operating exposure-compensation buttons vary by manufacturer. Consult your manual to see how this button works on your particular camera.

When you're unsure exactly which exposure-compensation settings to use, try taking a lot of pictures with a variety of settings. You can always free the memory used by any bad pictures. If your camera has an LCD screen, it may be able to show you how successful your exposure compensations have been. Just to be sure, it's best to play with various settings, increase the number of pictures, and hope that you have taken one or two good ones.

Understand Depth of Field

To better understand focus, you need to learn about depth of field. *Depth of field* refers to the zone in which all elements appear in focus. Any objects in this range look sharp and clear in your photo. Objects outside this range appear fuzzy and out of focus. An example is illustrated in Figure 1.24. Notice how the first flower, falling within the proper range, remains in focus, while the second flower looks blurry.

Using zoom or wide-angle settings can affect your depth of field, as illustrated in Figure 1.25. With zoom, maintaining correct focus becomes more exacting. When you move the camera, even a little, your subject may appear out of focus because of the limited depth of field. In contrast, wide-angle settings offer a much larger in-focus range. This makes your camera much more tolerant of small camera movements and shakes. Also, your subjects can move in a larger range closer to or away from the camera before the camera must refocus.

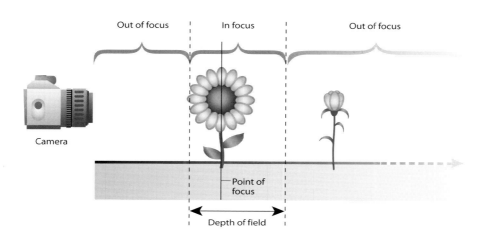

Figure 1.24

Depth of field affects focus.

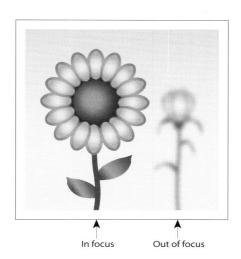

The distance that your focal point is located from the camera can also affect the depth of field, as illustrated in Figure 1.26. The nearer the focal point, the smaller the depth of field. More distant focal points offer larger ranges in which objects remain in focus. You obtain the greatest depth of field by focusing on objects in the far distance, such as clouds or mountains.

Figure 1.25

Telephoto and wide-angle settings change your depth of field.

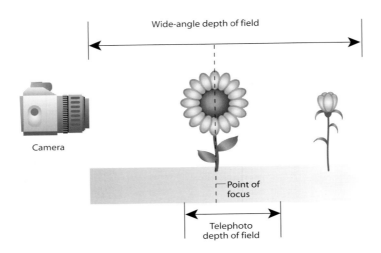

Wide-angle depth of field

Camera

Point of focus

Telephoto depth of field

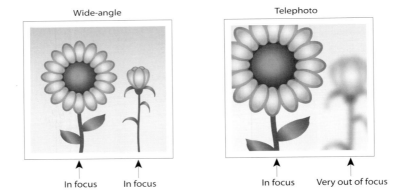

Wide-angle

Telephoto

In focus   In focus

In focus   Very out of focus

Figure 1.26

Depth of field varies with distance.

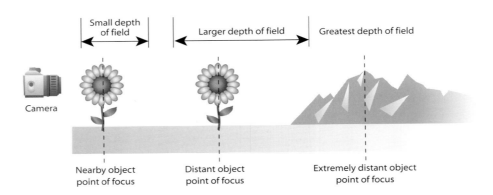

Small depth of field

Larger depth of field

Greatest depth of field

Camera

Nearby object point of focus

Distant object point of focus

Extremely distant object point of focus

While a distant focal point offers a very large depth of field, nearby subjects will still appear out of focus. Don't assume that the "greatest depth of field" means that all distances fall within your field of focus.

The aperture levels on your camera also affect the depth of field, as illustrated in Figure 1.27. The iris on your camera opens and closes to let in various amounts of light. This works just like the iris in your eye, dilating to adjust for light levels. The wider the opening, called the *aperture*, the more light flows through to your camera's detectors. Smaller apertures let in less light. Even inexpensive cameras, like my old analog video camera and my new digital camera, may allow you to set these aperture levels manually. The smaller the aperture, the larger the depth of field, and vice versa. Closing down the aperture works much like squinting your eyes.

The range of the depth of field in front of and behind the focal point is not equal, as you can see in Figure 1.28. The range of focus behind your focal point is always larger than the range in front of it. Keep this fact in mind whenever you set your focus and arrange your subjects. As a rule of thumb, about two-thirds of your field of focus lies behind and about one-third lies in front. When in doubt, always focus a little closer than farther away.

Figure 1.27

Aperture affects depth of field.

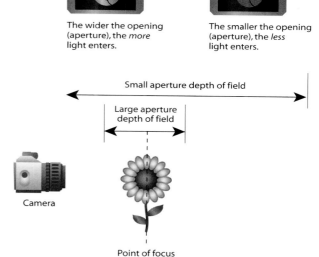

Iris lets in light.

The wider the opening (aperture), the *more* light enters.

The smaller the opening (aperture), the *less* light enters.

Small aperture depth of field

Large aperture depth of field

Camera

Point of focus

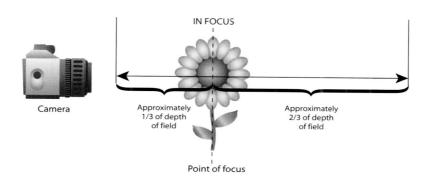

IN FOCUS

Camera

Approximately 1/3 of depth of field

Approximately 2/3 of depth of field

Point of focus

Figure 1.28

Depth of field is split unequally before and after the point of focus.

Achieve Natural Poses

Have you ever noticed how stiff and uncomfortable some people look in photos—those fake smiles and awkward postures? One of the most important techniques a photographer can develop is putting people at ease. A relaxed subject helps make a portrait more flattering and memorable. Create a relaxed atmosphere when taking your pictures. Not only will your pictures improve, but your subjects will come back again for more!

Lighten the Atmosphere

These techniques may help lighten the atmosphere and relax your subject:

Talk to your subject. As you get ready to take your pictures, start a conversation. Talking helps many people forget about posing and produces better and more natural facial expressions.

Make them laugh. Tell some jokes or silly stories. Laughter shakes people right out of their stiffness and into photographically pleasing facial expressions. A colleague relates, "If subjects know I'm going to take their picture, I like to get the camera ready but not in position, then make them laugh. I then grab a few quick shots while they're still laughing naturally, and before they're in 'posed for portrait' mode. Those are usually the best smiles."

Give them something to do. Props are great photographic tools. When people are busy doing something—anything—they tend to focus on the task and stop thinking about their facial expression. Children may enjoy playing with a toy. Adults will tend to focus on a task and forget about the camera. Show someone working on a hobby, doing a household chore, or otherwise occupied.

Take *a lot* of pictures. People can keep that silly, stiff smile on their face for only so long. The more pictures you take, the more those muscles will tire. Prepare to throw out a lot of early shots. Eventually, the awkwardness will disappear.

Move them around. Why not go to another room? You can go inside if you're outside or outside if you're inside. Each time you change locations, you get a fresh start and new facial expressions to work with.

Catch them at an off moment. This can be tricky, but it's frequently worth the trouble. Some of your best pictures will be those that were shot when the subjects didn't know that you were taking their picture. The more memory you use in your camera, the more likely you'll be able to snap an extra picture when no one expects it. Use the biggest memory cards you can afford. Sometimes these shots turn out badly, but sometimes they produce treasures. (You can learn more about memory cards in Chapter 2, "Digital Camera Equipment.")

Remember that the best images aren't always the ones that show smiles plastered on faces. In portraits, you may want to see the truest person looking out.

Take Flattering Photos

The simple truth is that some people photograph better than others do. Some are natural models; others aren't. Whether you're dealing with a double chin or a prominent nose, you can help your subjects look their best by keeping a few tips in mind. Here are some common problems and some suggestions for minimizing them:

Double chins You can minimize the prominence of double chins in your photos in two ways. First, ask your subjects to hold up their chin slightly. Second, shoot from a bit above the subject. Raise your tripod and shoot slightly down to de-emphasize the neck. Figure 1.29 shows the contrast between a flattering and unflattering shot.

Weak chins In the case of a weak chin, you want to lower your tripod to slightly below your subject's face and shoot up. This changes the emphasis toward the top of the face and away from the bottom.

Wrinkles Wrinkles show their worst in bright light. Keep your lighting as diffuse as possible. This minimizes the shadows between wrinkles and flatters the subject.

Prominent noses If a nose presents a problem, avoid profile shots. To de-emphasize a nose, have your subject face the camera directly. Keep the camera level with the face and avoid shooting up or down.

Unflattering eyeglasses In the case of thick eyeglasses or unflattering eyeglass frames, consider using the glasses as a prop. For what I call the "professor shot," have your subject hold the glasses and gesture with them. This shows more of the face and avoids distortions around the eyes from both the lenses and the shadows created by the frames. This may not work for subjects with very poor vision or those who wear their glasses constantly. The

Figure 1.29

Shoot to flatter your subject's chin.

Shooting from below emphasizes those chins.

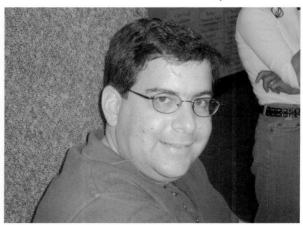

Shooting from above proves more flattering.

former may look "dopey" during the shoot because they cannot see. The latter will seem unfamiliar to friends and family because the glasses are such an intrinsic part of the person. In these cases, consider the next suggestion instead.

Reflections from eyeglass lenses You can fix this problem in a number of ways. First, you can add a polarized filter to your camera to minimize reflection from the lenses. Second, you can slide the glasses up or down the subject's nose to produce less reflection. Third, you can keep the glasses in place but move the subject's head slightly to minimize the reflection. If you still cannot find a flattering shot, consider using the glasses as a prop, as described in the previous suggestion.

Blemishes When you're dealing with facial blemishes, use diffuse lighting. Also, consider touching up the photos after the shoot in an image-processing program. An airbrush will blend away most obvious facial blemishes.

> You can reduce the impact of some unflattering features, such as blemishes, with photo-editing programs. For details, see Chapter 4.

Use Standard Poses

It helps to have a few standard poses up your sleeve. These poses can help get the ball rolling and sometimes produce the best pictures on the whole digital "roll." When you're not sure how to start, pick one of the poses suggested here.

The Angled Pose

For this first pose, you'll need a chair. Angle the chair about 20 degrees away from the camera. Sit your subject—Lela, in this example—in the chair, completely facing the way that the chair faces. Lela's legs, arms, and head should face slightly away from you. You may cross Lela's hands in her lap or place them on her hips. Next, have Lela turn her head, but only her head, toward the camera. The rest of her body—shoulders, back, feet, and so forth—remain aligned with the chair, as shown below. Tell Lela to take a few deep breaths and smile. Start shooting.

The Classic Portrait Pose

For this second pose, find a table. Place it in front of your subject (Lela again), and otherwise set up the portrait as described for the first pose, with a small angle between her body position and the camera. This time, however, when turning Lela's head, place one of her elbows on the table and support her chin with her hand. Raise your tripod and aim down toward Lela. Ask her to look up toward the camera, and then shoot the picture.

The Window Pose

For this third pose, you'll need some window cleaner. Okay, you won't need it right away, but you'll need it after the shoot to wipe off the window. Here's how it works: Have your subject (we're still posing Lela) look out of a window on a sunny day. Place one or both of her hands on the window and have her keep her eyes focused on the outside. A good way to do this is to ask Lela to talk about what she sees. This forces her to keep her attention outside and allows you to shoot your pictures from the side.

Angled

Classic

Window

Focus Sharply

The average modern digital camera ships with both manual and automatic focus options. Today's auto-focus systems provide good results for almost all of your photo needs. They eliminate the need to manually adjust the focus for each picture and generally make life much easier. Auto-focus works by shooting out an infrared beam and measuring how long it takes to bounce back. This lets your camera know the distance to your subject and, there-fore, how to set the lenses to create an in-focus photo.

Most digital cameras are built to take slightly wide-angle photos. These wide-angle set-tings produce larger depths of field. As you've learned, depth of field can be important. As it increases, your camera can take in-focus pictures over a wider range of distance. In contrast, the more you use magnification—either with a zoom or telephoto lens—the smaller the depth of field, so exact focus becomes more critical.

Even with auto-focus enabled, sometimes you still take blurry photographs. Three cul-prits account for almost all out-of-focus pictures when using auto-focus: steadiness, low light, and incorrect targeting.

Avoid Unsteadiness and Improper Light Levels

Your camera is vulnerable to shaking hands. No matter how superb the auto-focus system, unsteadiness will ruin your shot. This is where a tripod comes to the rescue. Keep your camera steady, and you may avoid inadvertently blurring your pictures. (See the "Steady Your Camera" section a bit later in this chapter for some alternatives to using a tripod.)

No matter how steady you keep your camera, a moving subject will blur. To capture a moving subject, you need a very short exposure time. Ambient light levels determine these exposure times. The lower the light, the longer the exposure. The longer the exposure, the more your subject may move and blur. To bypass this problem, avoid taking action shots in low-light conditions.

"Noise" presents another low-light problem for digital cameras. When you shoot pictures in dim lighting, you're far more likely to produce images with unintentional pixel variation. This noise, which fades to the background in well-illuminated shots, adds graininess to your low-light photos. You can reduce the noise to some degree using a photo-editing program. See Chapter 3, "An Introduction to PhotoDeluxe," for details.

Target Your Subject Correctly

Blurry pictures can also result from incorrect targeting. This focus problem occurs in two instances: off-center subjects and subjects positioned at different distances.

When you shoot pictures of an off-center subject, your camera may not focus correctly. The ultrasound beam bounces off whatever occupies the middle of the picture rather than your subject. Then it reports a meaningless value to the auto-focus mechanism. Fortunately, digital cameras support a quick fix for this problem:

1. Place your subject directly in the center of the frame.

2. Depress the shutter button halfway. The auto-focus system will set the focus correctly.

3. Keeping the shutter button halfway depressed, compose your shot.

4. With the shot composed, finish pressing the shutter button. Your digital camera will take the photo using the correct focus settings.

The problem of dealing with subjects at varying distances proves more difficult. Unless all of the subjects fall within your camera's depth of field, it's likely one or more of them will end up out of focus. You will not find an elegant solution for this problem. Instead, you must either move your subjects to more uniform distances or use a wider-angle lens with a more robust depth of field.

Tips of the Trade

Good composition, lighting, and poses will help you to produce better pictures, but there are some other steps that you can take to make sure you get the best shot at the best time. Here is an assortment of tips for the digital photographer.

Take Your Camera Along—Everywhere

No matter how well you compose, light, or pose your subjects, it won't matter if your camera is not *right there with you* when the moment strikes. As long as your camera is at hand, you can capture that moment. No camera, no moment—it's as simple as that.

Take your camera with you wherever you go. Stick it in a glove compartment, a briefcase, or a diaper bag. With your camera nearby, you'll be ready to seize the moment when the right opportunity strikes.

Steady Your Camera

The culprit for many bad pictures is unsteady hands. You can prevent the wiggles, jiggles, and bouncies that ruin pictures. All you need to do is steady your camera. Sure, you can use a tripod for dependable support. But if you don't have a tripod at hand, you can still steady your camera. Try one of these helpers:

- Rest your camera on a fence or a low wall.
- Steady your camera on a friend's shoulder.
- Use the top of a public mailbox as a camera rest.
- Pile up a stack of books and use them to hold your camera.

The possibilities are endless. Just remember the importance of keeping your camera still. Don't ruin a shot because your hand was too unsteady.

Take a Lot of Pictures

The more pictures you take, the more likely you will end up with a good one in the bunch. Load up your camera with as much memory as it can hold and keep an extra disk or memory card on hand to swap as needed.

Taking a bunch of pictures means you don't need to bet on any single picture being perfect. The worst that will happen is you get a few good shots among many bad ones. The best result will be that you get to choose from many, many wonderful pictures.

Remember to keep shooting. Take pictures from different angles and distances. Don't just seize the moment, keep seizing it. Take a lot of pictures!

Don't Be Shy

Shy photographers rarely shoot great pictures. One secret to great photography is to boldly take pictures under all sorts of circumstances.

Unless you have the camera out and you're taking pictures, you cannot catch that perfect moment. You'll miss that kiss, that laugh, that smile, that tear, and so forth, unless you're willing to jump in and photograph it. Don't be timid. Learn to let your camera into the best times in life. You'll be glad you did.

Watch Your Thumb

Don't put your fingers in front of the lens. No, I mean it. It sounds silly and obvious, but you would be surprised how easily you can ruin a shot by sticking your thumb where it shouldn't be. And dangling bits aren't limited to your digits. Keep that lens cap, that wrist strap, that handbag, and that power cord out of the way, too. Sometimes we are so intent on other matters that we forget the simplest things.

In This Chapter...

In this chapter, you've learned about making the most of your digital photo shoots. Here are some key ideas from this chapter:

- Learn about composition before you pick up the camera. The basic principles of balance, avoiding distracting elements, and so forth will help you take better pictures.

- If you don't remember any other tip about shooting pictures, remember this one: Get close. Learn to take pictures of faces rather than of people.

- Avoid backlight whenever possible. Try to move your subject or your camera to keep the light in front of your subject.

- Windows provide elegant lighting situations. If you've never done so, give window-lit shots a try.

- Depth of field will help you understand why some shots are in focus and other shots are not.

- Take flattering shots. Pictures can be (and should be) forever. Make the most of your subjects, and both you and they will be happy with the results.

- You cannot snap a picture if you don't have your camera. Make sure to take your camera with you whenever possible.

CHAPTER 2

Digital Camera Equipment

Know your digital camera, and it will serve you well. There are more hardware choices available today than ever before. Digital cameras offer so many power, memory, and lens solutions that you can easily become overwhelmed.

In this chapter, you'll learn the ins and outs of choosing and managing your digital camera equipment, including the camera itself, batteries, memory cards, photo-transfer hardware, and optical components. You'll also learn how to treat your "negatives" with care and use them in the best possible way. No digital photographer has exactly the same needs. Use this chapter to help pick the equipment that's right for you.

This chapter covers the following topics:

- Which camera should you buy?
- Your camera's batteries and power cells
- Your camera's memory
- Photo-transfer hardware
- Your camera's optical components
- Digital camera Resources

Which Camera Should You Buy?

The question I'm asked the most is, "Which camera should I buy?" There are so many excellent digital cameras on the market today that I find this question difficult to answer. Instead of recommending a particular model, or even manufacturer, I suggest that you base your camera choice on your individual needs and budget.

How you plan to use your camera directly influences the type you should buy. Will you use it primarily outdoors or in a studio setting, for a hobby or for business, and so forth? Also consider how rugged you need your camera to be. Is waterproofing important? And, of course, how much you'll spend affects your camera choice. The following sections discuss the main items to consider when purchasing a camera.

Pixel Resolution

When you shop for a camera, you'll find the term *megapixel* bandied about. This term refers to how many image elements, called *pixels*, your camera can produce in a single picture. A pixel is the smallest part of an image. When light from your scene strikes a single sensor in your camera, it creates a pixel. The total number of pixels, called *pixel resolution*, allows you to learn instantly a key fact about the general quality of your camera, because more pixels mean better pictures.

> When buying a camera, make sure you look for real resolution, not interpolated resolution. Interpolated pixels are a fake kind of selling device. The camera makes guesses about light levels that fall *between* real pixels detected by the sensors. If you see the word *interpolated*, look further, because you're not seeing the real resolution.

A 1-megapixel camera creates images with approximately one million pixels. These cameras offer basic-quality, consumer-grade pictures and should cost below $150. Middle-grade cameras provide two and three million pixels, and they cost between $200 and $800. Better-quality cameras offer 4- and 5-megapixel resolution, typically at a price of $1,000 or more.

Pixel count greatly influences image print quality. The more pixels you print per inch, the better any image will look. A resolution of 300 pixels per inch (ppi) produces the best-quality images. For a 4-inch × 6-inch picture, that comes to 1200 × 1800 pixels. If your camera does not support that resolution, don't despair. Even 100 or 150 ppi images look pretty good when printed to commercial-grade silver-halide paper by a photofinisher. That comes out to 400 × 600 or 600 × 900 pixels—less than even 1 megapixel. More pixels just give you more flexibility and quality.

> As a rule of thumb, you can always make big pictures smaller, but you cannot effectively make small pictures bigger.

If you're aiming to put pictures on the Web, you can think even smaller. Web resolution typically ranges between 60 and 80 ppi, with 72 ppi as the most common resolution. Even an inexpensive (below $100) camera provides sufficient image resolution for Web-based imaging.

Portability

Many people consider portability to be a prime element of camera selection. People like to be able to fit a camera into their pocket or handbag. Manufacturers now cater to this market, producing cameras that are ever smaller and more powerful.

Ruggedness is another aspect of portability. Water resistance, and even waterproofness, allows you to take your camera into less-civilized terrains. If you plan to take your camera camping, hiking, and snorkeling, look for one that can take the punishment you're bound to inflict on it.

A last element of portability concerns battery life. Many cameras balance weight and price with battery duration. When you take your digital camera out to the hillside or on vacation, make sure that it can support long-life batteries.

Some Component Suggestions

When you're shopping for a camera, optics are a key element to consider. The better the optics, the better your pictures will turn out. For example, the better the zoom, the more flexibility you'll have while taking pictures, both in terms of composition and depth of field. (See Chapter 1, "Composition, Lighting, and Posing: Some Tried-and-True Advice," for details on composition and depth of field.)

Look for high-quality lenses and hardware on your camera. As you would expect, you'll pay more for higher-quality components. In the long run, you'll be happy you did. Your investment will reward you with peace of mind, general satisfaction, and excellent pictures. Here are some of my recommendations for camera components:

- Look for a good, high-powered, built-in zoom that provides a wide range of zoom settings.
- Onboard LCD and flash, like zoom, are invaluable features.
- A video-out port and an A/C adapter port let you plug in your camera and save batteries.
- I like compact flash image storage, but smart media and stick memory are also popular.
- Better cameras have lens threads that allow you to easily attach filters and other components.

All of these components are discussed in more detail in this chapter.

Cost and Reviews

After sorting through camera types and determining your needs, you'll typically narrow your choices to a few models. At this point, you'll want to start a full investigation. Get on the Internet and search for those model numbers. You'll find many sites with a variety of user tests and feedback. This knowledge can prove invaluable in making your decision. I particularly like the reviews at the Digital Camera Resource page (`www.dcresource.com`). The "Digital Camera Resources" section at the end of this chapter lists other sites that offer camera information.

After settling on a model, take the time to find a good price. Some retailers, such as Sears, will match the prices of online sites. If you're willing to take the risk and order online, pick a dealer with a good reputation, such as B&H Photo (`www.bhphotovideo.com`) and make sure to pay with a credit card (to maximize consumer protection). If you're a bargain hunter, stop by the AnandTech Forums (`http://forums.anandtech.com/categories.cfm?catid=40`) to search for a good deal on your digital camera.

Your Camera's Batteries and Power Cells

Your digital camera needs good, reliable power. You should be familiar with the various types of batteries and power cells that can help your camera function at peak levels, as well as how to tend and care for your batteries. Treat your batteries right, and your camera will thank you. Remember that digital cameras are power-hungry. Feed them the finest "juice" you can.

Types of Power-Sources

You can power your digital camera in many ways. Over the past few years, new battery types have entered the marketplace. These batteries offer alternatives and features far beyond old-fashioned AA batteries. Most digital cameras accept a wide variety of battery types. This creates a broad spectrum of, ahem, "power tools" from which to choose.

> With the exception of generic batteries, most manufacturers' warranties require you to use designated proprietary power sources. Doing otherwise may void your warranty and cause problems down the road. Check that your camera's voltage and amperage requirements match your power source before you plug in and power up.

Alkaline Batteries

Alkaline batteries are a type of nonrechargeable power cell. They are the most commonly available batteries. Alkaline batteries are freely available at drugstores, groceries, and so forth, at very reasonable prices. You can expect their shelf life to run for about five years, making for excellent backup power. Consider keeping a set on hand for emergencies.

The bad news is that alkaline batteries do not perform well in most digital cameras. They drain rapidly, and you cannot recharge them. Using your camera's LCD screen means an almost-certain quick death for your alkaline cells. Alkaline batteries are not recyclable and must be disposed of with care.

> When your alkaline batteries seem to run out of juice, you can usually squeeze out an extra shot or two. Just turn off your camera and let the batteries cool down for five or ten minutes. Turn the camera back on, and you can often take one or two more photographs before the batteries truly die.

Lithium Batteries

Lithium batteries are a type of nonrechargeable power cell. They provide greater power and endurance than alkaline batteries but at a greater cost.

More and more stores have started to carry long-life lithium cells. Although they're not cheap, lithium battery prices are dropping. You can probably pick up a set at a RadioShack near you.

Lithium batteries provide excellent performance in digital cameras and will not drain quickly, as alkaline batteries do. They have an astonishing ten-year shelf life, which means that they make a superb backup power source. They give steady and dependable power output throughout the life of the battery.

Among all of the battery types, lithium batteries perform the best in cold-weather conditions. Other batteries fail at near-zero conditions; lithium batteries provide dependable power in sub-zero temperatures as low as –40 F. Environmentally, lithium batteries produce fewer hazards than alkaline batteries do. They also weigh in at the lightest weight of all of the battery types.

Unfortunately, lithium batteries are still about five to ten times as expensive as alkaline batteries. Also, like alkaline batteries, they cannot be recharged.

Nickel-Metal-Hydride (NiMH) Batteries

Looking for the digital camera power source of choice? You'll find it in NiMH batteries. NiMHs (pronounced "nimms") are a type of rechargeable cell. NiMH batteries offer the best renewable power source available today.

NiMH batteries provide environmentally friendly, reliable power for your digital camera. You can charge cells up to a thousand times, furnishing years of use. You can also recharge them after a partial drain without creating a charge-level "memory," which might otherwise limit their power capacity.

However, NiMH batteries do have a few disadvantages. They may cost slightly more than the other types of power cells. Their shelf life is limited to a few weeks, usually less than a month. Also, NiMHs can be damaged by overcharging and overdischarging. Make sure to juice up your batteries on a regular basis, following the manufacturer's instructions for maximum charge time. See the "NiMH Care" section, coming up shortly, for more information about NiMHs.

> NiMH battery packs are a good alternative to individual cells and provide hours of continuous camera use. Some people do not like the "tethered" feel of using battery packs, while others swear by them. Packs have two big advantages. First, you can use them in concert with onboard batteries in your camera. The batteries only kick in when the power pack runs down. Second, you can leave your battery pack in your pocket, keeping it warm in cold weather. This allows you to keep taking pictures when normal batteries might fail.

Nickel-Cadmium (NiCd) Batteries

NiCds (pronounced "nigh-cads") are a type of rechargeable cell. NiMH batteries have all but replaced NiCds because of worries about heavy-metal toxicity. I do not recommend that you purchase NiCd batteries now that NiMHs are freely available (even though they have better shelf life and a greater number of recharging cycles). NiCds contain the heavy metal called cadmium, so you must take special care when disposing of them. NiCds also have "memory," so if you charge a NiCd before you fully empty the battery, you can limit its power capacity.

A/C Adapters

A/C adapters allow you to plug your camera into a wall outlet. Your camera's manufacturer usually provides these adapters at an additional cost (usually a large additional cost). A/C adapters work best for studio shots and when you're sitting at your computer.

An adapter provides unlimited power. It never runs out of energy (unless you forget to pay your electric bill). A/C adapters help you conserve batteries and allow you to leave your camera powered on and unattended during image transfers.

The problem with A/C adapters is that without an electrical outlet nearby, you're out of luck. You may need to use an extension cord to reach the nearest outlet, or you may find yourself entirely too far away from an outlet to use an adapter at all. Many people do not like being tethered to a wall socket during photo shoots. Cords tangle and create tripping hazards. Sometimes the cords dangle in front of the lens and interfere with taking pictures.

Solar Power Packs

Solar power packs provide environmentally kind, "green" power for your digital camera. They allow you to take advantage of the ultimate renewable energy source—the sun. Okay, so "ultimate renewable" may not be scientifically accurate. Physicists, like my husband, will tell you in excruciating detail exactly when the sun will run out of energy and the universe will expand to ultimate entropy. Needless to say, this will not affect the average life of a digital camera.

Use your solar power pack for tripod shots and when wandering through the wilderness away from traditional power sources. If you plan on staying away from civilization for an extended period, solar power packs provide endless energy at a low weight. Some solar power packs will also charge your NiMH cells. You can pick up a solar NiMH charger for under $20 or a solar power pack that also charges NiMH cells for about $50. Solar power packs typically produce six-volt output, about the same as four AA batteries.

The main disadvantage of solar power packs is their bulk. Solar power packs are awkward to use. Additionally, these packs have an untested operational life and do not work indoors, at night, or on overcast days.

> Some camera manufacturers, notably Agfa and Kodak, now provide solar panels on some models of their cameras. These panels co-power the LCD screen and help save battery life.

NiMH Care

NiMHs are the best overall choice for your digital camera, and if you treat your NiMHs well, they'll provide years of dependable power. The following tips will help you make your batteries last.

Condition Your New Batteries

Run your new batteries through at least two, and preferably three to five, conditioning cycles. Start by treating your cells to a full charge as recommended by the manufacturer. Use the cells until you've reasonably discharged them, and then fully charge them again.

The battery manufacturers I spoke to suggested placing the batteries in your camera and taking pictures for an hour or two to produce a good discharge. You can also condition your batteries in any battery-operated device, such as a Walkman or radio.

Some battery purists recommend using special dischargers to increase the discharge and enhance conditioning. The manufacturers I spoke to said this wasn't necessary. In any case, after you pass your batteries through a few cycles of use and recharging, they will be ready for regular use. You can then recharge them after even the shallowest of discharges.

Charge and Recharge, but Don't Overcharge

Charge your NiMHs on a regular basis. It's better to charge more often rather than wait for the cells to run down; this helps your batteries last for years. Unlike NiCd batteries, NiMHs do not have memory. Recharging after a shallow discharge does not limit the battery's ability to hold a charge. Unfortunately, when you over-discharge your batteries by running them down too much, you might reduce their ability to maintain a charge.

More worrisome than over-discharging is overcharging. When you overcharge your batteries by leaving them in the charger too long, you can destroy them. Not only that, you might create a safety hazard. Some battery manufacturers now include fuses in NiMH battery packs. This allows the packs to self-destruct before they injure a passerby.

Always use and charge your NiMH batteries as a set. If you own multiple NiMH sets, do not mix and match batteries between sets. When you charge batteries at different states of discharge, you can actually damage them. Use a permanent marker to identify which battery belongs to which set.

Power Source Tips

No matter which battery type you use, you can extend the working life of the batteries by following a few simple rules:

Turn off the LCD. Your LCD eats batteries. It consumes huge amounts of power when turned on. When you don't need to use the LCD, turn it off and keep it off.

Stop the zoom. When cameras turn on, many of them automatically extend the zoom lens. Leaving your camera on but in "sleep" mode may override this behavior and help save power.

Turn off the flash. Flash photography drains your batteries. When you turn off the flash, you conserve power.

Plug in! When at home, especially when transferring pictures to a computer, plug your camera into a wall outlet and avoid using the batteries.

> Your camera's energy-conservation mode can be your friend or your foe. While it works to save energy and preserve your batteries, it might make you miss an important shot. Often, you must wait for the camera to turn back on after conservation mode kicks in. When you're in the middle of an intense photo shoot, consider turning off energy-conservation mode.

Your Camera's Memory

What film is to traditional cameras, memory is to digital cameras. Without memory, you can't capture and reproduce images. Digital "film" allows your camera to store pictures.

Manufacturers offer a wide variety of memory solutions for their various camera models. Whether you already own a camera or are considering buying one, knowing about the diverse ways that cameras store pictures may prove valuable. Today's cameras support two types of removable onboard media: memory cards and disks.

Internal Memory

Older cameras provided internal picture memory built directly into the camera. Internal memory extends the camera's capability, adding capacity for "emergency pictures" when you run out of space on your memory cards.

Internal memory is common on older digital camera models, since they do not support memory cards or any of the other media now available. You'll find internal memory on newer models, too, notably the Ricoh line.

Cameras lacking memory cards rely on cables. These cables allow you to move pictures to your computer, but cable transfer varies in speed. Serial transfer is extremely slow. USB (Universal Serial Bus) transfer can prove to be fairly quick.

Cameras that support memory cards usually allow you to copy internal memory directly to an onboard card. This bypasses the cable solution and speeds up transfers by many orders of magnitude.

Some newer digital cameras now have firmware memory (or CMOS).

Flash Memory Cards

Flash memory cards, such as compact flash, smart media, and stick memory, use solid-state memory chips to store your pictures. These chips, like elephants, do not forget. They store your pictures indefinitely and without power.

You won't find batteries onboard flash memory cards. They take their power from the camera or card reader in which they're placed. Their ATA (Advanced Technology Attachment) architecture—the same architecture used by your PC's IDE (Integrated Drive Electronics) and EIDE (Enhanced IDE) drives—allows cards to pretend to be traditional hard disk drives, complete with files and directories. Place your card in a USB card reader, connect it to your USB port, and it appears on your computer as a new drive. You can then read and write from your card as if it were simply another hard drive.

For older PCs and laptops without USB support, you can use an ATA adapter with your computer's PCMCIA (Personal Computer Memory Card International Association) port. This type of connection offers excellent transfer speed, many times faster than a typical USB connection.

Compact Flash

Compact flash (CF) cards are built from banks of flash memory and a controller embedded in thin plastic, as shown in Figure 2.1. At the time I am writing this book, compact flash cards lead all of the other media in supplying digital camera memory. They are small and rugged, and they contain a lot of memory. Flash memory combines high read and write speeds with low power consumption. Compact flash cards also have a high tolerance for shock and vibration.

Compact flash cards are smart, too. Controllers are built right into compact flash cards. This allows a compact flash card to tell its host—whether a camera, computer, or any other consumer device—how it operates and how to access its data. Stick a compact flash card into a computer (using an inexpensive adapter), and it looks and acts just like a hard drive. Stick a compact flash card into your camera or MP3 player, and it's ready to store images or music.

Compact flash cards are built in many shapes and sizes, although most digital cameras use those about 1-inch square and a quarter-inch thick. In this tiny space, they provide incredibly large memory resources.

Today, you can buy a 128-megabyte (MB) compact flash card for about $50. Prices for these cards are going down, while their memory size is increasing.

Figure 2.1

Compact flash cards are built from banks of flash memory with a built-in controller.

Smart Media

Many camera makers, most notably Olympus, support a type of electronic memory called *smart media*. The actual name for this type of memory is Solid-State Floppy Disk Cards, or SSFDC. These cards consist of a flash memory chip embedded in thin plastic, as shown in Figure 2.2. Smart media cards are small, usually about one-third the size of a credit card.

Unlike compact flash cards, smart media do not contain onboard controller chips; they have only storage chips. That means the smartest part of the compact flash cards doesn't appear on smart media cards. (Now, if the "smarts" don't actually occur on "smart media," why is "smart media" smart?)

Actually, the lack of controller chips is why smart media may be on its way out in the digital camera community. Since cameras that use smart media must provide their own controllers, newer and bigger cards eventually become incompatible with older cameras. In contrast, compact flash and stick memory (discussed next) keep their brains onboard. New cards can always tell older cameras how they work. Recently, Olympus began to ship cameras containing slots for both smart media and compact flash cards.

Figure 2.2

Smart media, a.k.a. SSFDC

You can find smart media support on many cameras. Manufacturers who provide smart media support on their products include Agfa, Ansco, Epson, Fujifilm, Minolta, Olympus, Phillips, Ricoh, Sanyo, Sega, Toshiba, and Trinus.

Stick Memory

In recent years, Sony developed its own form of flash memory called *stick memory*. You've probably seen this memory in new products. This product shares many of the same features of compact flash cards in a slightly different body shape. Memory sticks resembles a half-stick of Wrigley's gum, as shown in Figure 2.3.

Stick memory is fast. It can transfer 64MB of information in less than 10 seconds and provides a read-only toggle to protect data.

One might ask, "Why do we need another standard when compact flash works so well?" I am at a loss to explain this. Leaving that aside, Sony does have grand plans for stick memory. The manufacturer intends to use stick memory in everything from public information kiosks to music systems in automobiles. Digital cameras provide only one market for this new product.

Figure 2.3

Stick memory

PC Cards

The term *PC card* refers to any media you can stick in a PCMCIA slot in your computer. PC cards come in four types, designated type I through type IV. Although every PC card shares identical dimensions in width and length (for the curious, those dimensions are just over 3 inches by 2 inches), they vary in thickness (from about one-eighth inch to one-half inch), depending on what sort of memory has been tucked within them. Figure 2.4 shows an example of a PC card.

Only type I and type II PC cards use solid-state flash memory. A few digital cameras, including some Ricoh models, use PC cards to store photos.

MultiMedia Card

The SanDisk/Siemens AG MultiMedia Card (or MMC), shown in Figure 2.5, measures about the size of a thick postage stamp and delivers competitive storage capacities. The MultiMedia Card Association (MMCA) was founded in 1998 to promote this card as the global, open standard for removable solid-state memory. Usable in many branches of mobile electronics, the MMC has started to make an impact in digital photography as well. Most notably, the MMC offers a variety of security features. These are not very applicable to digital photography, but they do help enhance and promote the standard.

Various other memory cards linger in the digital camera world. These mostly include extinct (or almost-extinct) dinosaurs and yet-to-be-introduced wares. A good example of a dinosaur is the Intel Miniature Card. Announced in 1996, this card became an also-ran by 1998.

Figure 2.4

A PC card

Figure 2.5

The MultiMedia Card (MMC)

NOVEL USES FOR MEMORY CARDS

Memory cards aren't just camera workhorses. You can use them in some novel and interesting ways. Here are a couple of fun things you can do with your digital memory cards.

Stick Your Card into a Photo Printer

Many new photo printers, including the Kodak Personal Picture Maker, allow you to create prints directly from compact flash and smart media memory cards. This means that you don't need to load your pictures into a computer before printing them. Insert a memory card into the printer itself, as shown here. The printer reads the card and creates an index print showing thumbnails of all the images on the card. You can print all or some of the images. Choose an image by selecting its number off the index print.

Stick Your Card into a Photo Frame

Sony offers a digital picture frame called the Cyber Frame. This device, which looks just like a normal picture frame, uses stick memory. Insert your memory into the frame, plug it in, and you're ready to view your images, as shown here. You can set the frame to flip through your pictures as quickly as one picture every 15 seconds or as slowly as one picture a day.

The Sony frame understands the difference between landscape and portrait images and will automatically adjust to display the proper orientation. You can display images as large as 1600 × 1200 in this frame. You can also add sound memos to your stick memory and play them back using the built-in volume-controlled speaker. As if that were not enough, watch out Martha Stewart. You can accessorize your frame with different shells to coordinate with your decor. Current colors include terra cotta and earthy green.

At this time, you're going to pay through the nose for this toy. The retail price now runs about $700. Expect a variety of offerings and competitors to lower prices over the next few years. You can find an alternative, lower-cost solution to the Sony frame in the versatile Ceiva. Read more about Ceiva in Chapter 8, "Picture Sharing."

Disk Storage

Some digital cameras also support a variety of conventional disks. The Sony Mavica line initially used a traditional 3.5-inch floppy disk to store your pictures; newer models actually write to a mini-CD-R. Iomega and IBM offer miniature hard-disk solutions. Unfortunately, some disks do not provide the stability and trustworthiness you find in flash memory card solutions, leaving them less suitable for digital cameras. However, IBM's offerings are quite rugged and provide outstanding storage capabilities.

Clik! Disks

A true disk, the Iomega Clik! (with that irritating exclamation point, which I will now drop) offers 40MB of storage in a small package. The idea works like this: When your compact flash card grows full, you slip it into the compact Clik drive and transfer the data to a Clik disk. Clik disks cost much less than additional compact flash cards, so you don't need to buy extra cards. While they're a nice idea, Clik drives fail in the following ways:

- Many compact flash cards now exceed the storage available on Clik disks.
- Compact flash card prices are dropping rapidly. With the money you would invest in a Clik drive and Clik disks, you can buy a handful of extra compact flash cards instead.
- Clik disks and drives are bulky to carry around, whereas extra compact flash cards fit nicely in your shirt pocket.
- Clik disks are vulnerable to thumps and bumps. Compact flash cards are sturdy and less likely to lose data.

Microdrives

IBM's high-capacity, miniature hard drives come packaged in a convenient compact flash type-II shell. These microdrives offer very high capacities. Microdrives have entered the consumer market and prices continue to drop.

Microdrives have proven surprisingly invulnerable to shocks. They're quite robust. And, because they work in type II slots, they provide easy interchange with traditional compact flash cards.

Floppy Disks and CDs

Some of the most popular digital cameras on the market, Sony Mavica cameras, use floppy disks and recordable CDs (CD-Rs) to store images. You just insert a 3.5-inch floppy or blank CD-R into your camera, take your pictures, pop out the disk or CD, and stick it into your computer.

Digital Wallets

It used to be that laptop computers helped store pictures when photographers went on the road. Fortunately, you no longer need to drag around that heavy and power-hungry laptop. In the past year or two, portable-storage solutions, called *digital wallets*, have become popular with the traveling digital photographer. These devices allow you to transfer images from your smart media, compact flash, and stick memory to a small, lightweight, portable, but high-capacity disk drive. This frees your solid-state devices for easy reuse.

> Portable-storage solutions for images are offered by a variety of manufacturers, but the actual Digital Wallet brand is owned by Minds@Work (www.mindsatwork.net).

One of the more exciting trends in portable image storage is exemplified by the Nixvue Vista, shown in Figure 2.6. This unit not only allows you to store your transferred images, but also to display them using the onboard full-color LCD screen. You can use the Vista as follows:

- Connect your unit to a television screen using the composite video outputs to create a traveling slide show.
- Use the USB connectors to transfer photos back to your home computer.
- Use the optional printer jack to connect your Vista directly to a printer.

It's unlikely that the Vista will remain alone at the head of the portable storage pack. Expect competing units to hit the market over the next year or two. Already, Minds@Work has introduced the higher-end MindStor unit, which does not have an onboard LCD but does offer FireWire connectivity (see the "Cables" section later in this chapter for more on FireWire connections).

Figure 2.6

The Nixvue Vista with its onboard LCD screen

Memory Card Care

Love your memory card and treat it with care. In return, your memory card will reward you with years of faithful and dependable service. Treat your card badly, and you may lose pictures, usually at the worst possible time. Here are some tips for taking care of your memory cards:

Don't launder your memory. Avoid brain washing. As with any electronics, water can (and usually will) damage memory cards. Their small size makes them a particular laundry hazard—it's easy to put them into a shirt pocket and forget them. Keep them dry and store them away from moisture.

Don't melt or freeze your memory. Memory cards are sensitive to extremes of temperature. Unlike traditional film, your memory cards will not thrive in your refrigerator or freezer. Instead, keep them at room temperature. Avoid storing your memory in cars that may become overheated or extremely cold.

Don't fiddle with your memory. Some memory cards, especially smart media, flex naturally. Take pity on these poor cards. Do not bend or tweak them. Your cards were not designed to function as guitar picks, no matter how perfect the size and feel. And for heaven's sake, don't chew or nibble on them!

Don't scratch the contacts. You can easily ruin a smart media card by scratching the exposed gold contacts. Hold your card by the other end and avoid handling this area. If needed, gently rub off fingerprints from the contacts with a soft cloth.

Don't drop your memory. Some memory cards respond badly to rough treatment. Avoid dropping your cards, especially on hard surfaces.

Don't shock your memory. Do you work in a dry or carpeted area? Discharge any static electricity before handling your memory cards. Touch grounded metal before you touch your cards.

Format your card. Most digital memory cards work just like hard drives. Occasionally, they need preventative maintenance. Every now and then, say a few times a year, your card needs defragmenting. A fast and easy way to do this is to simply reformat your card. (Make sure you've safely removed any pictures you want to keep from them first.) You can also use a disk-scan/defragmentation utility, but it's much easier just to treat it to a fresh format.

Memory Management Tips

You can control your camera's memory or let the memory control you. Keeping on top of your memory can make the difference between getting that extra shot and searching for an extra memory card (which you may or may not have on you at the time). It's up to you to make sure that you have enough capacity to take all of the pictures you need to take.

Reduce Memory Usage

If you have limited memory resources, you can reduce memory usage in three ways:

Take smaller pictures. By lowering the resolution from 1600×1200, to say, 800×600, you can take four times as many pictures. Of course, smaller pictures have drawbacks. They may not print well, capture sufficient information, or satisfy your artistic needs.

Use a higher compression scheme. Most cameras support a number of compression schemes. Usually the best-quality pictures are called Fine, the second best are Normal, and the worst are Compact. The terms vary by camera, but the idea is the same. Changing to more compact pictures means you lose picture quality, but it allows more pictures to fit on each card.

Weed your pictures on the fly. When you take a bad picture, throw it out. This keeps your memory card full of lean and mean pictures—only your best.

Unfortunately, all three methods not only reduce your memory usage, but they restrict your results as well. You should use high resolution and low compression to shoot your images using the best possible settings. This allows you to save and use smaller segments of your images. And you'll never say, "I wish I'd shot that using better settings."

The problem with using the third method—tossing photos immediately—is that some "bad" pictures may contain hidden gems. Don't throw away borderline images. Err on the side of keeping bad shots rather than weeding them out. You can never recover a shot already thrown away. Consider the picture in Figure 2.7. It may not look like a keeper. The composition is poor. The subject's moving arm is blurred. A television set intrudes, making the scene too busy. Now examine the image within the black rectangle. From this poor picture, we can extract a great image.

Obviously, if you follow this advice, you will fill your memory cards sooner and more often. In my opinion, rather than try to conserve memory on the fly, most people are better off purchasing more and larger memory cards. Think of the film photographer carrying a lot of extra film. The more memory you bring, the more good pictures you can take.

Pick Your Image Format

Your camera may store your images in any of a number of image formats. These formats range from small, compressed images to large, memory-intensive ones. How your camera stores your pictures will greatly affect how many pictures you can store at any time. The larger the images, the fewer that can be stored. The smaller the images, the more you can fit. Know which formats your particular camera supports and choose the format that best meets your needs.

Common Image Formats

JPEG (pronounced "jay-peg"), which stands for Joint Photographic Experts Group, is the most common image-capture format. It is supported almost universally. You can upload JPEG images to the Web, edit them in all major photo-editing programs, send them by e-mail, and so on. Storing photos using the JPEG standard means easy retrieval and image sharing. JPEG allows you to store your images with a wide range of compression values. This way, you can trade off size and quality.

Another common format is TIFF (Tagged Image File Format). The TIFF format ensures your pictures are stored at the highest possible resolution. This format produces some of the truest pictures, at the cost of image size. TIFF files are huge.

Figure 2.7

Sometimes you can find a gem in an imperfect photo.

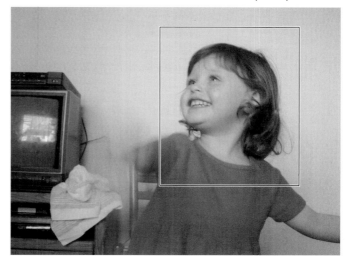

Some cameras produce BMP (Bitmap) images. These images are uncompressed and very large. I highly recommend you convert these pictures to JPEG before attempting to e-mail them.

Proprietary Formats

Along with the more common image formats, you'll find proprietary formats that vary by manufacturer. Fortunately, you can easily find a program that converts these proprietary formats to more widely used and manageable types such as JPEG. For example, a couple of dozen manufacturers—including Nikon, Olympus, and Canon—support CIFF (Camera Image File Format) format. The good news is that these proprietary formats are becoming less common, as more and more manufacturers are switching to JPEG and TIFF.

EXIF (Exchangeable Image File Format) allows your camera to store additional information with your images. Typical information stored includes the date and time the picture was snapped, the resolution, any zoom settings, and so forth. When you use the file browser in Adobe Photoshop Elements (a 30-day trial version is included on the accompanying CD), you can explore the EXIF information associated with your pictures.

JPEG-2000

The big news for digital photography is the introduction of the JPEG-2000 format, which will soon be available (via download) with Adobe Photoshop Elements 2.0 and on several digital camera platforms. This new file type offers tremendous image-quality improvements while providing very small file sizes. JPEG-2000 uses a new technology called *wavelets* to shrink your images to the smallest size possible.

Consider the images shown in Figure 2.8. The right portion of the figure shows the original 1.1MB image. Contrast this with the portion on the left, which shows the same image saved at about 200KB using traditional JPEG compression. Notice the blockiness in the features and the overall loss of fine detail, particularly in the cheek and teeth areas. Next examine the image in the center. In this image, you can see nearly all the fine detail that you do in the original. The surprise is that, unlike the original, it was again saved at 200KB, but using the new JPEG-2000 compression.

Figure 2.8

Save space and pre-serve image quality with JPEG-2000.

200KB JPEG image, with numerous artifacts

200KB JPEG image, with far fewer artifacts

1.1MB original image

Save Your Negatives

The images you capture on your "digital film" really are your "negatives." Store them carefully and make archives of them. You'll be surprised how well you can retrieve images later when they are stored properly.

Storage Media and Format

If possible, you should store your images on CD-Rs. These media are cheap. You can create multiple backups for only a few pennies more. CD-Rs are reliable, have a long shelf life, and are almost universally readable.

Store your "negatives" exactly as they come from the camera. Where possible, use the TIFF format setting, available on many camera models. TIFF compression is lossless. This means that when you decompress a TIFF picture, it will produce an image identical to the original. JPEG images, in contrast, are lossy. This means that they may lose information each time they are compressed or go through the open-and-save cycle. When you set your camera to save in TIFF, you'll retain the highest quality image. If you cannot use TIFF, don't worry. Just save in the best way that your camera lets you.

Photo Folders

Organizing your images will save you a great amount of time when you need to retrieve them. Here's the system that works well for me:

1. Create a directory for each "roll" of digital film. Label this directory with the date the pictures were taken and a description of the event. Use a *YYMMDD* dating scheme.

   This allows you to use Windows' Sort by Name function and keep the dates in chronological order. For example, pictures taken on July 4, 2002, might be labeled 020704 – Independence Day Party.

2. In each directory, keep a log of the pictures. Make a list of the photos that you've stored there and a short description of each shot. This allows you to search for key phrases when you want to find a specific shot.

   I call my logs `zzlog.txt`. Giving the log a name beginning with `zz` makes it appear alphabetically at the end of each directory listing. By naming all of my logs consistently, I can use the Windows or Macintosh Find function to find all the log files on a hard disk or CD. I can then browse or copy them as needed.

3. Create four subdirectories for each "roll":

   Negatives Store your original images in the Negatives directory, just as they are, taken directly from your camera. These photos form your basic picture archive.

   Low-rez Create low-resolution, compressed versions of each picture and store them in a Low-rez directory. This allows you to pull up a version of each image that you can easily e-mail or place on the Web. Don't bother with the hassle of needing to convert photos every time you want to share a few. You don't want to change high-resolution images to low-resolution ones each time you start searching through your archives. Convert them in advance. This way, you can pull up the low-resolution version directly from your CD-R archive. Read more about converting your images in Chapter 8.

Flubs Place any flubbed pictures into the Flubs directory. You can always work on them later.

Processed Store any enhanced images in the Processed directory. Don't confuse images you've fixed up in a photo-editing program with your negatives. Keep them separate so that you'll be able to easily find and use them later.

4. Create a master log on the top level of your CD. Make a list of all the logs in each directory, sorted by date. This allows you to search your entire picture disk from a single file.

Photo-Transfer Hardware

No matter which memory technology your camera employs, eventually you need to transfer your pictures to a computer or another processing device. This section describes the most popular photo-transfer methods.

Cables

These days, almost every camera arrives packaged with one or more cables, typically USB or occasionally FireWire (IEEE-1394, also called iLink) or serial. Using the software packaged with the camera, you transfer your images through the cable to your computer. Simply plug one end of the cable into your computer's port and plug the other end into your digital camera. Start the upload process on your computer and wait for the pictures to transfer. If you're using a serial connection, you'll probably wait and wait and wait. Most people find serial transfer unbearably slow (and they're right). Newer USB and FireWire connections offer high-speed connections that take just a second or two to transfer a picture.

There's only one reason, in my opinion, to use a serial cable to transfer your images: Your camera does not support USB, FireWire, or removable media. Only a few cameras these days truly require you to transfer by serial cable. These include older camera models and what I call "kid-grade" cameras, such as the NickClik and Barbie cameras. With these cameras, you cannot access your pictures without a cable. Fortunately, these older or kid-oriented cameras take smaller pictures, which transfer somewhat faster than those from other types of cameras. It may not seem faster while you're sitting and waiting, but small images make it feasible (if not pleasant) to use serial cable transfer.

USB (Universal Serial Bus) connections have become the new standard. USB, particularly the new USB-2 standard, provides quick and efficient data transfer. Most newer computers provide USB ports, making them an attractive target of opportunity. Most new cameras support USB transfer in place of, or in addition to, the more traditional serial transfer.

> Linux does not actively support USB. Linux users may need to look for alternative serial, parallel, and SCSI compact flash solutions.

FireWire connections, just now arriving, offer even faster connections than USB ones. They provide a huge digital "pipeline" for moving data back and forth between devices and are just picking up speed in the consumer market. A FireWire interface card (requiring Windows 98 Second Edition or later) costs about $50 and can connect to digital cameras, digital video units, and other devices. Most Macintosh computers ship standard with built-in FireWire ports.

> FireWire, which refers to the IEEE 1394 standard, is a brand name, trademarked by Apple, but is used almost universally to refer to this type of high-speed connection. Strictly speaking, PCs use iLink, a brand trademarked by Sony. But like Jell-O and Band-Aid, the FireWire name is moving into common usage. Many people refer to all IEEE-1394 connections as FireWire.

USB Card Readers

For about $25, you can go to your local discount store (such as CompUSA, Wal-Mart, Target, and so forth) and buy a USB card reader. These readers, which appear under various brand names, such as SanDisk (shown in Figure 2.9) and Zio, allow you to connect your solid-state card (such as compact flash or smart media) to your computer. All you need to do is install the driver, connect to your USB port, insert your card, and you're set. Your card will appear on your computer as a readable and writable drive. To recover your images, simply drag your pictures to your hard drive from the card.

Figure 2.9

The SanDisk USB card reader

> Macintosh users must first put away their USB cards (drag them to the trash can) before ejecting them from your computer. If you don't, your computer will complain and ask you to reinsert the card.

FlashPath

If you're a smart media or MMC user with an older, pre-USB computer or laptop, you'll be happy to know that there is an alternative to slow cable transfer to your computer. FlashPath systems transfer data from two to fifteen times faster than serial connections. A FlashPath adapter looks like a 3.5-inch floppy disk and comes with a slot in its side, as shown in Figure 2.10. To use the adapter, just place your media into the slot provided on the disk and stick it into the floppy drive. You're ready to transfer data.

FlashPath adapters work on both Windows and Macintosh systems. A number of vendors—including Toshiba, Olympus, and Fujifilm—produce essentially identical FlashPath devices. Their prices range between $50 and $100.

FlashPath adapters support all smart media and MMC cards. However, they do not work with compact flash cards. Compact flash memory is too thick to fit onto a FlashPath disk.

Here are some things to keep in mind when you're using a FlashPath adapter:

Battery installation and life The first time you use your FlashPath adapter, you must install the included batteries. Just open the battery compartment and place the batteries inside. The FlashPath adapter uses two standard CR2016 lithium batteries to provide power. You can pick up replacements at any RadioShack and many drugstores. Battery life varies with the type of smart media being used. Some smart media use 3.3 volts; others use 5 volts. Additionally, you can prolong the batteries by removing the FlashPath adapter from the floppy disk drive when it isn't in use.

Smart media insertion Always insert the smart media with the electrical contacts down; that is, make sure that the contacts face the bottom of the "floppy." Then place your adapter into your floppy drive.

Figure 2.10

A FlashPath adapter

Driver installation You may need to download a driver from www.smartdisk.com. You can always pick up the latest driver versions—for Windows and Macintosh systems—from this site.

Wireless Transfer Solutions

Some cameras provide wireless data transfer through infrared beaming. Although neat, in a Star Trek sort of way, these ports are unlikely to overwhelm the market. A problem with infrared transfer is that it may not work in warm conditions that interfere with the infrared beam. Also, it's too easy to disturb the connection. When you lose the line of sight, you lose the connection.

Recently, a number of manufacturers announced what they called the first BlueTooth-enabled digital camera platforms (it's hard to say who was actually first). BlueTooth is a radio-based communication standard that allows devices to communicate without cables or physical connections. It may still be a little early to expect BlueTooth on your new digital camera, or it may be too late. Some people argue that the BlueTooth standard needs to be replaced with a more modern and flexible system, such as the Wi-Fi standard. Although radio connections are definitely the next wave of digital image transfer, it's still up in the air which standard will reign supreme.

Your Camera's Optical Components

Take control of the way that your camera "sees" the world. When you focus, zoom, or filter light, you change the way your digital camera captures images. Digital cameras come with built-in optical components. In addition, you can accessorize your unit in a variety of ways.

Zoom Lenses

Everyone loves zoom. We like getting up close and personal. When we buy cameras, zoom capability often influences our purchasing decisions. As you probably know, zoom allows you to magnify parts of a scene and photograph it at a larger scale.

Digital cameras support two types of zoom: optical and digital. Let me tell you right off that digital zoom stinks. Digital zoom works in the following way: It takes a normal picture and then blows up a part of the image, just like you would in a photo-editing program. Then it throws away the rest of your image. You don't really get a larger, more-detailed picture; it just seems like a larger picture. Don't get suckered by digital zoom. Make sure your camera supports real zoom, which is optical zoom—the zoom created by lenses that really do create closer, larger, and more detailed pictures.

That having been said, let's examine the different types of optical zoom you can find on digital cameras.

All optical zoom lenses work in the same way: They change your camera's focal length, magnifying the image passing through the lens to your camera's sensor. If the zoom is built into your camera, it's called a *zoom lens*. If you buy an optional attachment, it's called a *telephoto lens*.

You will find two types of zoom lenses: fixed and adjustable. A *fixed zoom* creates, unsurprisingly, a fixed magnification. Cameras with fixed zoom allow you to swap between normal mode and zoom mode by sliding the zoom lens into place. All telephoto lenses use a fixed zoom. An *adjustable zoom* allows you to select from a range of zoom values by adjusting the optics in stages. These zooms are motorized and can put an extra burden on your camera's batteries. However, they provide finer control over the zoom.

When you're using a zoom, keep in mind that it decreases your camera's depth of field. While your subject will appear in focus, objects in front of or behind your subject may be blurry. Also realize that using zoom magnifies small motions. You may need to use a tripod to steady your camera when using large zoom.

Optical Filters

Optical filters allow you to customize the light entering your camera. You can accessorize your digital camera with optical filters to create a variety of special effects.

Ultraviolet (Skylight) Filters

Ultraviolet (UV) filters help cut through fog and create clearer pictures in misty conditions. Actually, the reason most people use UV filters on their cameras is to provide a surrogate lens cap. They install the filter and leave it on permanently. Most people figure they would rather damage a $10 UV filter than need to replace their digital camera.

UV filters are made from plain glass. They are easier to clean than your camera's lens, less likely to scratch, and more durable. And you never know when you might run across a misty day, right?

Polarizing Filters

You can use polarizing filters in a number of ways. These filters use circular polarization to allow or deny access to certain types of light.

Polarizing filters help cut through glare and minimize reflection. When you're shooting pictures on a beach or at a museum, use your polarizing filter to reduce these artifacts. You can also use your polarizing filter to shoot dramatic sky scenes. These filters produce a greater contrast between the clouds and the sky.

To use your polarizing filter, point either thumb at the sun and extend your forefinger like a make-believe gun. Take note of the line made by your forefinger and extend it (in your imagination) in front and behind you. It's this line that you'll use to set up your picture. Maximum polarization occurs 90 degrees off from the direction of sunlight. Use this technique to create a 90-degree reference to set up your shot. Line up yourself, your camera, and your subject.

Your polarizer works best at midday with the sun directly overhead. As you point your thumb to the sun, you can rotate your finger in almost any direction. At sunset, you'll be able to shoot along only one line.

Next, aim your camera at your subject and manually rotate the polarizing filter. Keep going until you've achieved the maximum effect; you may need to adjust back and forth until you're satisfied with the result. In general, a quarter twist will move between the minimum and maximum effect, as illustrated in Figure 2.11. Remember that all surfaces, no matter how matte-textured, produce some polarized light through reflection. Position and use your polarizer effectively to reduce glare and add depth and richness to your colors.

Eliminating reflections may require a little extra work. When shooting to reduce reflections, position your camera along the 90-degree line, but then shoot your object at an angle of 30 to 45 degrees off that surface, as shown in Figure 2.12. This angle ensures maximum polarization and helps eliminate reflected light. Recall that all reflected light is naturally polarized. It's just the angle that you need to get right for this effect to work.

> If you don't want to purchase a polarizing filter, you can produce almost all of the same effects by using a pair of polarized sunglasses. Just hold the glasses in front of your lens and rotate them to get the effect needed.

Colored Filters

Did you know you could use your digital camera to take terrific black-and-white pictures? Many recent models support black-and-white photography.

When you're taking black-and-white pictures, you can use colored filters to change the color balance and increase contrast within your pictures. In general, red filters enhance blue objects and blue filters enhance red ones. For example, you can snap some superb black-and-white pictures of red flowers by using a blue filter to create a dramatic contrast.

Specialty Filters

Specialty filters produce a wide array of effects. These range from star-shaped highlights to multiple images (produced by prism lenses). My advice as far as digital photography goes is to skip these filters. You can create these same effects in most photo-editing software with less work and for less money. And if you use photo-editing software, you can preserve better-quality images in their original format—an important consideration just in case you hate the way the special effects turn out.

Figure 2.11

Your shooting angle affects the polarization.

Light from the sun

Polarizer is most effective at a 90° angle.

Less polarized light is removed at a 135° angle.

Polarizer is least effective at a 180° angle.

Figure 2.12

**Maximizing polarizer
effectiveness**

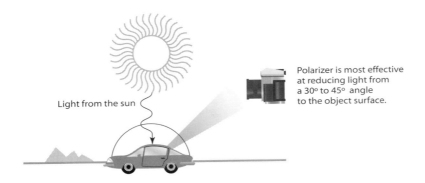

Light from the sun

Polarizer is most effective
at reducing light from
a 30° to 45° angle
to the object surface.

Infrared (IR) Sensitivity and IR Filters

Does your camera see into the infrared? Here's how you can find out: Take out your television remote control, push a button (such as the one to increase the volume), and snap a picture of the remote control's LED (you can usually find it at the tip of your remote control). If your picture shows a bright, glowing light, your camera is sensitive to infrared (IR) light. This can be a good thing, and this can be a bad thing.

The biggest advantage of IR sensitivity is that your camera provides greater sensitivity in low-light conditions. This allows you to take pictures in a wider range of light conditions. There's another advantage, too: You can easily capture infrared-only images. Just purchase an inexpensive IR-pass filter and use it to shoot your pictures. This filter blocks out all light except the infrared and allows you to capture IR images without special film or processing. Digital photography has really opened up IR photography to the masses. With film cameras, shooting IR images is expensive and complicated.

The IR drawback involves capturing image details that your eye would not normally see. This can saturate your camera's sensors and degrade image quality. Many cameras now ship with internal IR-block filters that reduce some of the IR light entering your camera, while allowing regular visible light to pass through. You can also purchase these filters to use with your digital camera. Some photographers use supplemental IR-block filters to ensure truer color capture. On the other hand, most normal digital camera users completely and happily ignore the IR problem entirely.

Accessory Attachments

As you've seen, you can accessorize your camera with a wide range of filters and lenses. In addition to the accessories described in the previous sections, you can purchase fish-eye lenses, neutral-density filters, and many more items for your camera.

Before you buy any accessories, make sure to determine the ring size for your camera and whether it accepts attachments. Many digital camera manufacturers choose odd-sized thread sizes (such as 14mm for my Nikon CoolPix). You may need to purchase a "step-up" or "step-down" ring to convert between your camera's ring size and that of the attachment. For example, if you own a Nikon 950, your 28mm threads will need a step-up ring to attach to, say, a 39mm telephoto lens. When you buy standard filters, you may need to use a step-down adapter so that the components will fit onto your camera. (Although the Nikon-brand filters fit my CoolPix perfectly, they are quite expensive and don't offer the wide variety of the more standard sizes.) You can find these step-down and step-up rings at most camera hobby stores and Web sites.

If your camera does not accept attachments, you can always hold the filter up to your lens and shoot your picture that way. I've snapped photos with a wide variety of filters in this way and had no trouble. Just make sure to hold the filter tight to the lens and keep your fingers out of the picture.

A PHOTO SHOOT PACKING LIST

Going out on a photo shoot? Review the following packing list before you go:

- Bring a lot of batteries and/or a battery pack. Don't run out of power.
- Take along as much memory as you can afford. Don't miss a shot because you're low on digital film.
- Pack a tripod or monopod to steady your camera. Many outdoor sporting stores sell miniature tripods that travel well.
- Consider bringing a device, homemade or purchased, to shade your LCD from direct sunlight.
- Don't forget a lens cap or UV filter to protect your lens from damage.
- A soft lens cloth can keep your lens and LCD clean.
- Bring any filters that you like to use, such as a polarizing filter or neutral-density filter. Make sure to pack these carefully so they don't scratch.
- Gently pack up your extra lenses, such as telephoto and wide-angle attachments. Take good care of these expensive options.
- Don't forget your camera's operations manual. Most are sized to fit into a standard camera bag.
- Consider investing in a large, padded bag to safely hold all of your equipment.

While you're out taking pictures, try to protect your camera from extreme temperatures. Your digital camera is a sensitive beast. Avoid storing your camera and camera equipment in direct sunlight, hot areas of your car, or outside during cold snaps.

Digital Camera Resources

Now that you know all about digital camera equipment, it is time to explore some resources for making the most of your digital camera. You can learn more about your camera from camera manuals, Web sites, and Usenet forums.

Camera Manuals

Read your manual. No matter how vague or poorly translated, it provides the single best resource for determining exactly how your particular camera operates.

If your camera's manual fails to help, you can go buy a better one. Dennis Curtin of Short Courses (www.shortcourses.com) offers how-to manuals for a wide range of cameras. These excellent books run for about $20 to $30, cover all the most recent camera models, and can be purchased online. They're printed on sturdy stock in a handy spiral-bound format.

Camera and Photography Web Sites

Digital cameras seem to breed fan-specific sites. Hop onto your favorite search engine, such as Yahoo! or Infoseek, and hunt down sites that cover your camera model. You might find a few specks of wheat among the great chaff that is the Web.

In addition, you may want to stop by some of my favorite digital camera sites:

- The Digital Camera Resource page (www.dcresource.com) is the best page for up-to-the-minute digital camera news and reviews.

- Steve's Digicam page (www.steves-digicams.com) is a massive digital camera resource site with a wealth of information.

- The Kodak Guide to Better Pictures (www.kodak.com/US/en/consumer/pictureTaking/index.shtml) is not really a digital camera page, but the picture-taking advice is so superb, it's worth a visit or two.

- Digital Photography (For What It's Worth) (www.cliffshade.com/dpfwiw) has a variety of information and tutorials for the digital camera user.

Usenet Groups

Usenet consists of public forums that allow people to share interests and engage in lively discussions. Several Usenet groups are devoted to the topic of digital photography. If you have a question, or just want to stop by and see what people are talking about, these newsgroups may prove to be just the thing for you.

The Rec.photo.digital newsgroup discusses purchasing and using digital cameras. This group always has a high volume of discussion and a lot of newsgroup traffic. A few highly skilled regulars haunt the premises offering assistance. However, new digital camera users account for most of the postings.

`Alt.comp.periphs.dcameras` is another newsgroup devoted to digital cameras, with a more technical slant.

The `Rec.photo.technique.art`, `Rec.photo.technique.misc`, `Rec.photo.technique.nature`, and `Rec.photo.technique.people` newsgroups focus on photographic technique and are open to both traditional and digital camera users.

> Do you want to search through old Usenet discussions? Stop by `http://groups.google.com`. This easy-to-use search engine allows you to look for old discussions directly related to your camera's model.

In This Chapter...

This chapter surveyed the technical components that can fill your digital camera bag of tricks. Here are some tips you'll want to keep in mind:

- Choose a camera with care. Once you pick one, you're likely to live with it for several years at least. Make sure you select a camera that fits your needs and the way you shoot your pictures.

- Always bring a large supply of power and memory wherever you go. Extra batteries can make a huge difference in capturing the moment or losing it forever.

- New digital storage solutions, particularly wallets, allow you to make the most of your solid-state memory. Consider investing in portable storage, particularly if you do a lot of traveling.

- Archive your pictures in their unaltered original state. You can always save additional copies of images with corrected color, contrast, and so forth, but you can never go back to the originals if you overwrite them.

- Learn to use a polarizing filter to help cut glare and reflections. Your pictures will look better and more professional.

- Think before you pack. Bring the equipment you need with you so you're always ready to point and shoot with your digital camera.

CHAPTER 3

An Introduction to PhotoDeluxe

Lucky you! You'll find a free copy of Adobe PhotoDeluxe included on the CD that accompanies this book. This software will help you manipulate, improve, and play with your digital pictures in many ways. Behind its meek and humble interface lies an image-processing tool of surprising power and flexibility. With PhotoDeluxe, you can reproduce many of the same effects and techniques that you would expect to find in a full-fledged image-processing program.

But wait, that's not all. You, too, can learn the secrets of a PhotoDeluxe warrior. You can gain skills that let you slice, dice, and julienne-fry your digital images. And, if you read more now, you'll discover the ultra-secret image-processing recipes that grant you PhotoDeluxe superpowers!

This chapter covers the following topics:

- **A quick tour of PhotoDeluxe**
- **Basic fixes with the Get & Fix Photo activity bar**
- **Advanced PhotoDeluxe skills**
- **Selection tools and techniques**
- **Layers for editing flexibility**

A Quick Tour of PhotoDeluxe

Before you attempt to engage your power-mobile's turbo thrusters and rocket drive, make sure that you're comfortable behind the wheel. Get acquainted with Adobe PhotoDeluxe's most basic mode. Take it for a spin around the block. Kick the tires and get to know your machine. There's plenty of time for supersonic flight after you've mastered the basics.

To begin exploring your new program, start by tooling around the PhotoDeluxe screen. Locate the main features on your handy-dandy road map (see Figure 3.1). Look for these features:

- The activity bar guides you through image-processing activities.
- The photo window displays your current photo.
- The photo window toolbar buttons give you instant access to common image-manipulation tools, such as zoom and text tools.
- The Advanced Menus button opens up the secret world of PhotoDeluxe power.
- The Open Photo bin stores additional open photos while you work in the main photo window.
- The basic menus include File, Edit, and Help.

Figure 3.1

The PhotoDeluxe interface

Open Your Photo in PhotoDeluxe

Take the first step in image processing: Open your photo so you can work on it. These instructions guide you through the task:

1. Click the Get & Fix Photo button to the left of the activity bar at the top of your screen to access the PhotoDeluxe photo-preparation activities.

2. Click Get Photo and select Open File from the list of options. This tells PhotoDeluxe that you wish to open a file from disk.

3. Use the Windows file browser to select your photo. Then click Open to open the file in PhotoDeluxe.

You're now ready to work on your photo. Notice the toolbar buttons that appear just under the title bar in your photo window. These buttons offer a variety of image-control options, including zoom, text insertion, and the all-important undo feature. Figure 3.2 shows the functions of these buttons.

Figure 3.2

These toolbar buttons appear in every PhotoDeluxe image window.

PHOTODELUXE REQUIREMENTS

To run PhotoDeluxe, your system must provide the following features at a minimum:

- Intel Pentium II processor (or 100 percent compatible processor), 233MHz minimum
- Microsoft Windows 95/98/Me or NT 4 with Service Pack 5
- 32MB RAM (64MB RAM for Windows NT)
- 100MB free disk space on your hard drive
- 800 × 600 color monitor with at least 16-bit color (thousands of colors)
- A CD-ROM drive

To install your copy of PhotoDeluxe, insert the CD from this book in your CD-ROM drive and follow the instructions provided on your screen. Once the program is installed, you must keep the CD in the drive while running PhotoDeluxe, because it often needs to load files from the CD to perform functions.

Rotate, Move, and Resize Images

PhotoDeluxe provides a standard interface for rotating, moving, and resizing images. No matter what photo you load or activity you perform, you should know how to manipulate the dots and circles that surround a selection.

By default, when you click anywhere within a photo, you select the entire image (you'll learn about other selection techniques in the "Selection Tools and Techniques" section later in this chapter). As you can see in Figure 3.3, eight dots line the edge of a selected image. These dots appear at every corner and in the middle of each side. In addition, a circle with a rounded arrow is next to each corner. These image-adjustment "handles" allow you to fine-tune your picture.

Here are the basic techniques for manipulating an image:

Resize Drag a corner handle to resize your selection. Drag the handle away from the selection to enlarge the image, or drag the handle into the image to shrink it. The image will resize proportionately—if it starts out a square, it will end up as a square; if it starts out a rectangle, it will end up as a rectangle with similar proportions. You can also resize without preserving the proportions by holding down the Shift key while you drag the handle.

Shrink or stretch The side handles allow you to shrink or stretch your image along one dimension. By dragging a side handle, you can squeeze the image together or stretch it out like Silly Putty. This operation always alters the image proportions.

Rotate When you move your mouse to one of the rotation handles (the circles with rounded arrows), the cursor changes to a curved-line segment. When you see this change happen, you're ready to rotate. Just click and drag the mouse. A rotating outline will follow your mouse and preview your change. Release the mouse to perform the rotation and update the image.

Move To move a selection to a new position, click your mouse within the image and drag it. The selection will move with your dragging motion. When you release the mouse, the image updates to reflect its new location.

Figure 3.3

The PhotoDeluxe interface allows you to rotate, move, and resize your image.

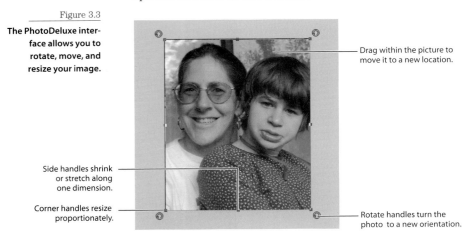

Drag within the picture to move it to a new location.

Side handles shrink or stretch along one dimension.

Corner handles resize proportionately.

Rotate handles turn the photo to a new orientation.

Basic Fixes with the Get & Fix Photo Activity Bar

You can noticeably improve your pictures just by using PhotoDeluxe's basic tools. You should always prepare your photos before you print or share them. Yes, you can use special printers, buy expensive inks and paper, or order high-end photo finishing. These enhance print quality, but they won't overcome poor contrast, poor lighting, or JPEG artifacts. On the other hand, PhotoDeluxe offers some features that can improve your pictures in a few simple steps.

The activity bar at the top of the PhotoDeluxe window has three tabs: Get & Fix Photo, Cards & More, and Share. To prepare your prints, click the Get & Fix Photo button to display that tab. A series of labeled icons replaces the PhotoDeluxe logo, as shown in Figure 3.4. Each icon leads to a set of guided activities that help you process and improve your pictures.

In the instructions for working in PhotoDeluxe, you'll see the → symbol used to indicate chains of selections. For example, "click Get & Fix Photo → Rotate & Size → Rotate Left" means to click the Get & Fix Photo button, then click the Rotate & Size icon, and then click the Rotate Left option in the menu.

Get Photo loads pictures into PhotoDeluxe from disk or the Internet.

Adjust Quality corrects photo quality, such as incorrect contrast and color balance.

Special Effects creates imaginative and artistic picture renderings.

Print creates hard copies of your images.

Rotate & Size adjusts a picture's orientation and dimensions.

Repair Photo retouches flaws in photos.

Save & Send stores pictures on disk.

Figure 3.4

The Get & Fix Photos activity bar

Change Your Photo's Orientation

If you turned your camera to take a portrait picture, your picture will display "on its side" in PhotoDeluxe. You should rotate the portrait back to its correct bearings before you do any work on it, for two reasons. First, looking sideways can strain your neck. Second, our brains are wired to see details more effectively straight on. When photos match our visual orientation, we make better judgment calls about quality.

If your picture is not oriented correctly after you open it in PhotoDeluxe, use the image-rotation tool to turn it. Just click the Get & Fix Photo button to open the activity bar and select Rotate & Size.

The options on this menu offer several techniques for changing the orientation of your photo:

Rotate Left This option rotates your photo in a counter-clockwise direction.

Rotate Right This option rotates your photo in a clockwise rotation direction.

> If you make a mistake and rotate in the wrong direction, simply rotate a few more times until the picture appears in the proper orientation.

Flip Horizontal This option flips your picture across the y-axis, swapping the left and right portions to create a mirror image.

Flip Vertical As with Flip Horizontal, this option helps you create a mirror image. Flip Vertical uses the x-axis to turn your image upside down.

Trim & Size This option offers an interactive solution for cropping your pictures. We'll walk through those steps in the "Resize Your Photo" section later in this chapter.

Use the Instant Fix Tools

PhotoDeluxe delivers a power-punch with a series of Instant Fix tools provided by Extensis. These tools simplify image enhancement by automating most of the correction tasks for you. With just a few clicks, you can fix your pictures instantly.

To access the Instant Fix tools, click Get & Fix Photo → Adjust Quality → Extensis Instant Fix Tools. Take a second or two to note the variety of instant tools you can use to improve your picture.

For instant improvement, select IntelliFix Instant Fix from the menu. This option automatically corrects most image flaws for you.

> We'll explore all of the Extensis Instant Fix tools in Chapter 4, "Digital Photo Editing." If you want to spend a little time experimenting with these tools now, just remember the location of the Undo button (in the photo window toolbar).

Remove Noise from Your Photos

Sometimes tiny parts of your photo appear significantly brighter or dimmer than they should. This is called *noise*. Noise is the gremlin of digital photography in that it shows up in all sorts of digital photos. Noise is caused by small current fluctuations in your camera, and it's generally unavoidable.

You might not even notice the noise in your pictures. Sometimes it can be downright subtle. Still, it affects the quality of your prints. Taking control of noise will produce more attractive prints. Here's how to use PhotoDeluxe to remove some of the noise from your pictures:

1. Click Get & Fix Photo → Repair Photo → Remove Noise. You'll see the steps for the Remove Noise guided activity, as shown in Figure 3.5.

Figure 3.5

The Remove Noise guided activity

2. Click 1 - Graininess → Reduce Graininess. In the dialog box that appears, you can play with the Smoothness setting, or you can accept the default value of 30. Then click the OK button.

At each step, if you're not pleased with the results of the operation, click the Undo button (in the photo window toolbar) or use the Undo shortcut key, Ctrl+Z. Then you can return to the previous step to try again using another setting, or simply proceed to the next step.

3. Click 2 - Moire → Remove Moire. The dialog box that appears allows you to remove diagonal distortions from your picture. You can adjust the Angle setting or accept the default value of 45. Then click the OK button.

4. If your image was not saved in JPEG format, click 4 - Done. If you do have a JPEG picture, click 3 JPEG → Clean Up JPEG. The dialog box that appears lets you remove the colored blocks that sometimes appear when you use JPEG compression. Adjust the Smoothness setting or accept the default value of 10. Click OK. Then click 4 - Done to finish this task.

Resize Your Photo

Are you planning to print this picture at a particular size? Have you already chosen whether you will make a 4 × 6-inch, 5 × 7-inch, or 8 × 10-inch print? PhotoDeluxe can help you prepare your photo to fit almost a dozen standard print sizes. Best of all, this step automatically sets a perfect aspect ratio for the print size you choose. (For more on aspect ratios and print sizes, see Chapter 6, "Digital Photo Printing.") Here's how it works:

1. Click Get & Fix Photo → Rotate & Size → Trim & Size. You'll see the steps for the Trim guided activity, as shown in Figure 3.6.

Figure 3.6

The Trim & Size guided activity

Select a trim size from the drop-down list.

Click the Trim button to create the trim rectangle.

Click OK to perform the trim.

Optionally, click the Undo button to revert to the original picture.

Drag a corner to resize, or drag within the rectangle to move it around your picture.

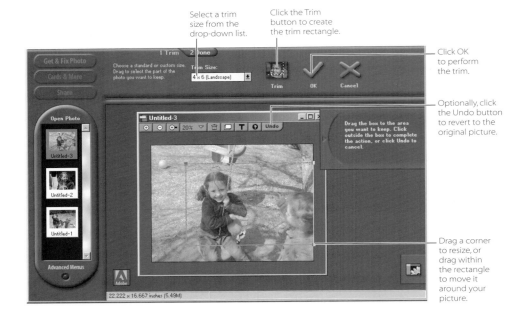

2. Click 1 - Trim, and then click the down arrow on the right side of the box under Trim Size. From the drop-down list, select a print size and orientation. For example, you might click 5 × 7 (Portrait) or 2 × 3 (Wallet-Landscape).

3. Click the Trim icon. A proportionately shaped rectangle will appear on top of your photo. This rectangle provides the correct aspect ratio for the print size and orientation you chose.

4. Drag the corners of this rectangle to resize it and make it fit your picture better. To move the rectangle, drag from inside the corners. Position the rectangle carefully. Everything outside this rectangle will be cropped away in the next step.

5. Click the OK icon. PhotoDeluxe will trim your picture. If you dislike this trimmed image, click Undo. You can return to the previous steps to try another trim size.

6. Click the 2 - Done tab to finish this task.

Save and Export Your Work

Once you've worked on your picture, save it to avoid losing your work. First, you'll need to determine which file format works best for creating your prints. Most online photo finishers require you to save your photos in the JPEG format. However, when you print directly from PhotoDeluxe, you might choose to save your images using its proprietary .pdd Adobe format. This neatly avoids the image-quality losses that sometimes accompany JPEG storage.

When working with JPEG images, avoid the save-load-alter-save cycle. Each time you save a JPEG image and reload it, you can lose image information. JPEG compression is *lossy*, which means that it may not produce identical images after each successive save. Instead, store your photos with another format, such as TIFF or PDD, until you are ready to save the final image.

The following instructions assume that you wish to save your image in JPEG format, perhaps as a prelude to ordering prints from an online finisher (see Chapter 6 for information about using online photo finishers).

1. Click Get & Fix Photo → Save & Send → Export. The Export guided activity steps will appear.

2. Click 1 - Export → Other Export. This tells PhotoDeluxe that you wish to save your file in a non-Adobe format, such as JPEG. (In the Export tab, you can also click the appropriate button to save your photo in GIF, Acrobat, Indexed Color, or Grayscale format.) You'll see the Export dialog box.

3. Enter a name for the file in the File Name text box.

Don't overwrite your original image. Treat your source pictures as your digital "negatives." Save your fixed image to a new file.

4. Select JPEG from the Save As drop-down list, as shown in Figure 3.7.

Figure 3.7

Exporting to other file formats

5. Use the Windows browser to select a folder. PhotoDeluxe will store your image in the folder you choose.

6. Click the Save button. PhotoDeluxe will ask "Continue converting photo to JPEG format?" Click OK.

7. Click the 2 - Done tab to finish.

Advanced PhotoDeluxe Skills

Do you think you can handle the full-leaded, high-test, 16-cylinder PhotoDeluxe roadster? If you're ready, you can unlock the power of PhotoDeluxe and put yourself in control!

Access Advanced Image-Processing Features

PhotoDeluxe's has many hidden image-processing capabilities. Follow these steps to unleash them:

1. Click the Advanced Menus button in the lower-left corner of your screen. Enabling this feature gives you direct access to PhotoDeluxe's full suite of image-processing features through eight additional menus.

2. One of the additional menus is View. Select View → Show Layers. This displays PhotoDeluxe's Layers palette.

3. Select View → Show Selections. This displays PhotoDeluxe's Selections palette.

You now have eight new menus and two palettes on your screen, as shown in Figure 3.8. This is PhotoDeluxe's "advanced mode."

The Layers palette makes it easy to work with layers. Layers allow you to stack photo elements in compartments that float independently. When you change a feature in one layer, it will not affect any features in other layers. For example, in Figure 3.8, the hand, angel, phone, and sun each resides in a separate layer. So, for example, when you move the sun, it does not disturb the hand, angel, or phone.

The Selections palette lets you choose from a variety of selection tools, including Tracing, Object Selection, Circle, SmartSelect, and others. Using the selection tools, you can select portions of images to manipulate.

You'll get some experience using the Layers and Selections palettes later in this chapter. But first, let's check out all of those menus.

Meet the Advanced Menus

PhotoDeluxe's advanced menus offer a wide range of options to greatly expand your image-processing capabilities. The menus allow you to fine-tune your images and access features directly without using guided activities. Try to become familiar with which menu hosts which features. This familiarity will help you operate more effectively in your day-to-day photo processing.

Figure 3.8

PhotoDeluxe's advanced mode reveals many new features

The Selections palette includes tools for choosing and controlling your selections

The Advanced Menu option adds eight new menus.

The Layers palette allows you to add photo elements in free-floating compartments.

File Menu

As you might expect, the File menu offers options for opening, saving, printing, and creating new images. However, the File menu also hosts PhotoDeluxe's preferences. These preferences allow you to control the way PhotoDeluxe looks and operates. For example, you can select different picture background defaults, show or hide the Assistant Drawer, and select cursor sizes.

Edit Menu

The Edit menu offers the same options you will find in most Windows applications. These include Cut, Copy, Paste, Duplicate, and so forth.

Select Menu

The Select menu offers options that allow you to control and manipulate your selections:

Select All and Select None These options allow you to select either all of the image layer or none of it. Interestingly, the keyboard shortcut for Select None is Ctrl+D, a carry-over from Adobe Photoshop (the *D* stands for "Drop" the selection).

Invert This option allows you to invert your selection. If you've selected a circle in the middle of the picture, inverting it will select everything *but* that circle. Invert it again, and you're back to your original selection.

Selection Tools This option opens a submenu that offers nine different selection tools, including shapes, freehand selection, and a special tool called SmartSelect. You can read more about using these tools in the "Selection Tools and Techniques" section later in this chapter.

Send to Back, Send Back One, Bring Forward One, and Bring to Front These options are reordering tools. These allow you to reorder your image layers.

Tools Menu

PhotoDeluxe's Tools menu offers traditional paint tools, such as a brush, a line tool, a text-insertion tool, and an eraser. When you select a tool, a dialog box appears to allow you to choose features associated with the tool. For example, selecting the Text option displays the dialog box shown in Figure 3.9. Here, you enter the text that you want to add to the photo and set the text characteristics.

Orientation Menu

The Orientation menu has options for rotating and flipping images. When you rotate an image, the entire image moves around an imaginary axis. When you flip an image, it mirrors itself either vertically or horizontally.

Size Menu

The Size menu offers several resizing options:

Trim This option crops the entire image to the size of the current selection.

Distort This option lets you "distort" an image by arbitrarily stretching or squashing it, as shown in Figure 3.10. When you select Distort, the selection handles appear (as in Figure 3.10). Drag a corner handle in or out. Each operates independently, so that when you drag one corner, it does not affect the others. You can also drag the side handles to stretch or squeeze your selection. After you specify your distortion, click anywhere but on a handle, and PhotoDeluxe will reshape the picture to your specification.

Perspective This option works like a constrained distortion. While you stretch or squeeze, PhotoDeluxe maintains bilateral symmetry. This allows you to create objects that seem to stretch into the distance or explode into the foreground.

Figure 3.9

The Text tool allows you to add text to your PhotoDeluxe images.

Figure 3.10

The Distort option allows you to arbitrarily stretch your image.

Canvas Size This option allows you to adjust the width and height of your picture without affecting your image. If you run out of space and need to extend your "canvas," you can add more room to your picture. Note that if you make your canvas smaller, some of your image will be cropped.

Photo Size This option lets you specify your image's resolution. Both the image and the canvas are resized to match this resolution.

The Quality Menu

The Quality menu provides fine control over your image's color balance, brightness, and contrast. Of special note is the Variations option, which allows you to carefully tune your picture's colors. This menu also contains the Instant Fix tool, which automatically improves your photo (it's the same as the tool available when you click Get & Fix Photo → Adjust Quality → Extensis Instant Fix Tools).

Photographic floodlights sometimes add too much yellow to your lighting. When this occurs, use Quality → Variations to add blue back into your pictures. Alternatively, you may want to buy blue floodlights, available at your local photo store for about the same price as standard floodlights.

Effects

The Effects menu offers a huge range of image-control features. It rightly deserves a chapter, if not a book, of its own. Features fall into three categories: selection operations, color controls, and artistic filters.

Selection operations include filling a selection with a color or gradient, drawing an outline around your selection, and "feathering." Of these, feathering is the most important. This allows you to soften the edges of your selection so you can gently blend it with other picture elements. You'll get some feathering practice in "the Selection Tools and Techniques" section.

The color controls allow you to transform your colors to black and white. You can also invert your colors to create a "negative" image.

The rest of the Effects menu is a basically a long list of filters associated with Photo-Deluxe. These filters are almost identical to those found in Adobe Photoshop. In addition, you can install your own filters in the PhotoDeluxe Plug-ins directory. Any plug-in that works with Photoshop will generally work with PhotoDeluxe. These filters include everything from turning your pictures into artistic "sketches," to blurring your selections, to adding artificial lighting effects. For example, Figure 3.11 shows some filters applied to the original images shown in Figure 3.8. A number of projects in this book will highlight some individual filters.

> You can experiment with each of the filters available from PhotoDeluxe's Effects menu. For more information, you can pick up a book on the subject. Many, many books have been written on how to use the filters available in the Effects menu. Just find a book on Adobe Photoshop.

Figure 3.11

Effects can stylize all or portions of your PhotoDeluxe images.

Effects → Stylize → Emboss filter was used on the sun.

Effects → Sketch → Chalk & Charcoal filter was used on the hand.

Effects → Noise and Effects → Texture → Crackle was used on the phone.

View Menu

The View menu allows you to see or hide the rulers, the Layers palette, and the Selections palette. It also includes Zoom In and Zoom Out commands.

Selection Tools and Techniques

Much of the work involved in editing digital photos requires a skilled use of selections. Selections allow you to isolate part of an image and then move, copy, or otherwise adjust the area you specify. Once you know how to create selections, you can almost magically transform your digital images.

Use the Selection Tools

You can find the selection tools on both the Selection Tools submenu of the Select menu and on the Selections palette. These tools allow you to select portions of your photo in a variety of ways:

Object Selection tool This tool selects the entire image. This is the default tool, and its use is described in the "Rotate, Move, and Resize Images" section earlier in this chapter.

Polygon tool This tool allows you to select a section point by point. Use this tool to create your selection in a series of "connect-the-dots" steps. It works particularly well when selecting odd-shaped objects that do not require precise edges. Double-click the last point in your polygon to end the selection process.

Trace tool This tool selects an area by precisely tracing its edges. Carefully move the tool around your object's contours. Use this tool to extract fine object detail from your photos.

Rectangle, Oval, Square, and Circle tools These tools work exactly as you might think. Pick any one to select an area by shape. When you drag out one of these tools, it will select a rectangle, an oval, or a circle of the size you specify.

Color Wand tool This tool automatically selects by color similarity. Use this selection tool to select large areas of continuous color such as walls.

> If the Color Wand tool seems to select too much, you can lower the tolerance. If it seems to select too little, you can raise it. Select File → Preferences → Cursors and change the value for the Tolerance setting in the Cursors dialog box.

SmartSelect tool This tool creates a selection that outlines the object you choose. To use it, select the tool, move your mouse to the beginning of your selection, and click. Then trace around the edge of your selection. Don't drag the mouse, but simply move it without pressing either mouse button. You can force the SmartSelect tool to add a point by clicking. When you've reached the end of your selection and you see the text "OK," double-click the mouse.

To practice using the selection tools, work your way through the following examples. They provide a good overview of PhotoDeluxe selection techniques. Master these skills, and you'll find yourself more fully in control of your digital photos.

Feather Edges

When you *feather* a selection, PhotoDeluxe creates a softened outline. The selection edges blur, creating a gradual transition between the background image and the selection on top of it. This allows your images to blend together without obvious sharp edges.

Follow these steps to create a feathered selection:

1. Open your picture in PhotoDeluxe.

2. Select Oval Tool from the drop-down menu on the Selections palette. Drag out an oval to surround your subject, as shown in Figure 3.12.

3. Select Effects → Feather. In the Feather dialog box, enter **10** to feather the edge of the selection 10 pixels, and then click the Delete Background button, as shown in Figure 3.13. Click the OK button to complete the task.

PhotoDeluxe will remove the background, leaving your feathered selection. In the Figure 3.14, notice how this selection blends into the background without any sharp edges.

Oval selection —

Figure 3.12

Use the Oval tool to select part of your image.

Figure 3.13

The Feather dialog box lets you set options for feathering a selection.

Select with SmartSelect

SmartSelect is easily the most powerful selection tool provided by PhotoDeluxe. As you move this tool around your image, PhotoDeluxe automatically looks for edges by comparing color differences. You must move the tool fairly precisely to create a good selection, and this can prove a little difficult. Still, this selection tool grants you a lot of leeway, and you can always backtrack when you make a mistake. When you take things slowly and smoothly, the SmartSelect tool will save you a lot of time and effort in making your selection.

The basic SmartSelect tool creates a simple selection that outlines the object you choose. Sometimes, however, you will want to create "holes" within your selection. As an example, we'll go through the steps for cutting a costume out of a photo:

1. Open your picture in PhotoDeluxe.

2. Select SmartSelect Tool from the Selections palette. Move the mouse to the beginning of the selection and click.

3. Carefully trace the edge of the selection by moving the mouse (don't press a mouse button).

Figure 3.14

A feathered selection (left) blends softly with the background. A regular selection (right) shows hard selection edges.

You can back up your mouse if you've traced a section in error. If you need to back up more than a point (the tool automatically creates these as you trace), press the Backspace key and continue your back tracing. At any time, you can click to add a point. In addition to offering extra control over your selection, this allows you to take a break in the middle of tracing.

4. When you've reached the end of your selection and you see the text "OK," double-click the mouse. The result of using the SmartSelect tool to trace around a costume is shown in Figure 3.15.

5. Remain in SmartSelect tool mode and click Reduce on the Selections palette.

6. Move the mouse to the start of the selection, click, and carefully trace the outline of the area you want to remove. PhotoDeluxe will remove that area from the current outline. In this example, the selection is the face that we want to remove from the costume, as shown in Figure 3.16.

7. Notice that the background remains unselected after both uses of the SmartSelect tool. Now we will remove it. Select Effects → Feather. Enter **5** to feather 5 pixels, click Delete Background, and then click OK. PhotoDeluxe removes all of the image but the costume, as shown in Figure 3.17.

Use this technique to select any sort of object with holes. Here are some ideas:

- Select a pair of eyeglasses and exclude the lenses.

- Copy a door but not its window.

- Cut out a figure of a man with hands on hips and remove the holes between the arms and body.

Once you've created your "holed" selection, you can use it in many different ways. Commonly, such cutouts serve as props. For example, in Figure 3.18, I've placed the cut-out costume on another person. With a little artistic license, I've planted her next to a fellow flower. PhotoDeluxe provides a nice selection of props created in just this manner. To find them, select File → Open Special → Get Sample Photo → Props.

Figure 3.15

Use the SmartSelect tool to create an oddly shaped selection more easily.

Figure 3.16

Use Reduce to remove portions from your selection.

Figure 3.17

Create a "costume" by removing the face and background of the image.

Figure 3.18

Use the costume you created to build interesting collage effects.

Change a Selection

Selection errors occur when you include or exclude areas of your image by mistake. As you saw in the previous section, PhotoDeluxe allows you to adjust your selection by adding or removing regions. This provides you with precise selection control. You can edit your selection until it exactly matches your needs. Below the tool-selection drop-down list on the Selections palette are four buttons that provide more selection options, as shown in Figure 3.19.

Figure 3.19

The Selections palette provides tools for adjusting selections.

You can change your selection as follows:

- Click New to create a fresh selection. When you apply the tool to your image, any previous selection will disappear, and the new selection will take its place.

- Click Add to extend your selection. Apply the selection tool, and it will add new areas to the current selection.

- Click Reduce to remove areas from your selection. When you apply your tool, you take parts away from the current selection.

- Click Move to move your selection around the screen. You can drag to relocate the selected parts of your image.

Let's walk through a selection task so you can see how these operations work. We'll start with the picture of Joanna shown in Figure 3.20. To create this initial selection, I applied the Color Wand tool to the blue-green wall behind Joanna's head. The tool properly selected the wall on the top and left, but it missed a section on the right and incorrectly included a good deal of the shirt.

First, we'll add back the section to the right of Joanna's neck. The tool missed this area because her hair touched the image edge. This blocked the Color Wand from finding this section. Then we'll remove the entire shirt from the selection. Because the shirt's color was too close to that of the wall, quite a lot of it was selected. We'll just shrink the selection by using the Reduce option. Finally, we'll clean up the selection. Here's the procedure:

1. If the Color Wand is not still selected from the initial operation, choose it from the Selections palette and click the Add button. Then click within the new section (in this example, the section to the right of Joanna's neck) to add it to the selection.

2. Choose SmartSelect Tool from the Selections palette, click the Reduce button, and trace the outline of the area that you need to remove from the image (the shirt, in this example).

3. Click the Zoom-in button on the photo window toolbar to enlarge the area you wish to work on.

Figure 3.20

The Color Wand tool in action

Proper wall selection

Missed selection

This shirt area "bled" into the selection.

4. Choose Trace Tool from the Selections palette. This is a freehand tool, which allows you to freely select areas.

5. Carefully use the Add and Reduce functions on your selection. Just trace the edges of the area you wish to change and let PhotoDeluxe do the rest of the work for you. Remember to work a little at a time to prevent mistakes. If you do make a mistake, click Undo to restore your selection to its most recent settings.

SELECTION TECHNIQUES: A QUICK REVIEW

We've covered quite a few important techniques for creating and controlling selections. These techniques are key to working with PhotoDeluxe, and you will use them for many of the neat tricks coming up in this book. Here's a quick review:

Add and Reduce These buttons on the Selections palette allow you to increase a selection or remove parts from one.

Shape selection The Oval, Rectangle, Square, and Circle tools (selected from the Selections palette or by choosing Select → Selection Tools) allow you to create a selection using standard geometric shapes.

Color Wand selection The Color Wand tool (selected from the Selections palette or by choosing Select → Selection Tools) uses color similarity to automatically select picture zones.

SmartSelect selection When you use the SmartSelect tool (selected from the Selections palette or by choosing Select → Selection Tools), you trace the edges of your selection. PhotoDeluxe intelligently performs the fine-detail work for you.

Trace tool and Zoom selection The Trace tool (selected from the Selections palette or by choosing Select → Selection Tools) is a freehand tool you can use to expand or reduce your selection. Get in close by zooming in (click the Zoom-in button on the photo window toolbar), so you can use the Trace tool with very fine control.

Feathering The Feather option on the Effects menu lets you feather your selection. This blends the selection into the picture without sharp edges.

Inverting You can invert your selection (by choosing Select → Invert) to swap back and forth between the subject and the background.

Layers for Editing Flexibility

Moving your selections to PhotoDeluxe layers allows you to work on parts of your image without disturbing the rest of your picture. You can separate individual picture parts into different layers, and if you like, you can merge two or more layers to make them a single layer.

Use layers to isolate your picture elements so you can work on each one individually. Each time you paste a new item into a picture, PhotoDeluxe automatically creates a new layer.

Create Instant Layers

To see how layers work, we'll start with the setup shown in Figure 3.21, which shows three objects, each in its own layer. I created the picture shown in Figure 3.21 by dragging three stock PhotoDeluxe images from the Samples window to a new image window.

> PhotoDeluxe offers many stock photographs. Select File → Open Special → Get Sample Photo and browse through the collection.

Follow these steps to bring the images into separate PhotoDeluxe layers:

1. Select File → Open. Navigate to the PDDEMO folder in your top-level directory. Select `Cherry.jpg` to open the file. Then click the Minimize button to shrink the window into the Open Photo bin.

2. Repeat step 1 to open and minimize the `Pepper.jpg` and `Strawb.jpg` files, located in the PDDEMO folder.

3. Select File → New. Create a new image that is 3.5 × 3.5 inches.

4. Drag the cherry, pepper, and strawberry to your new window. Each time you drag an object to the window, PhotoDeluxe creates a new layer for that object. (If the Layers palette isn't already open, select View → Show Layers.)

5. Resize each object. Click it and use the resizing handles to fit it properly into the window. (See the "Rotate, Move, and Resize Images" section earlier in this chapter for more information about resizing images.)

Figure 3.21

Layers allow you to place image elements in free-floating compartments.

6. Choose each layer and use the SmartSelect tool to select the fruit. On the Selections palette, click the Invert button. Then press the Delete key to remove the background image from your fruit, leaving just the fruit in each layer. (See the "Selection Tools and Techniques" section earlier in this chapter for more information about selecting portions of images.)

In the Layers palette to the left of each layer, you'll see a rectangle. An eye in this rectangle indicates that the layer is visible. When the eye does not appear, the layer is hidden. To change a layer's visibility, simply click in the rectangle. It will toggle that layer from hidden to visible. To activate a layer, click its name. This automatically selects the layer and whatever object appears in it.

You can rename a layer by double-clicking its name. Enter a new name into the Layer Options dialog box, and then click OK.

Work with Layers

Now that you have several layers, you can experiment with manipulating each one. As an example, we'll maneuver the cherry and pepper in the file we created in the previous section.

1. Start by selecting the cherry. Choose Orientation → Flip Horizontal. This mirrors the cherry so the stem points out to the right rather than the left.

2. Move the cherry into place so the stem passes over the pepper's stem loop, as shown in Figure 3.22.

3. With the cherry layer selected, choose the Color Wand selection tool. Click outside the cherry and allow PhotoDeluxe to select everything but the cherry. Click Invert to swap the selection and just select the cherry, as shown in Figure 3.23.

Figure 3.22

The cherry stem passes over the pepper's stem.

Figure 3.23

The cherry is selected.

4. Select the Trace selection tool. Click the icon marked with a minus on the Selections palette.

5. Carefully trace around the cherry to remove it from the selection. Repeat to remove the bits of stem that overlap the yellow portion of the pepper on either side of the pepper's stem. Leave the rough selection near where the pepper overlaps the cherry's stem, as shown in Figure 3.24.

6. In the Layers palette, select the pepper layer. The selection will not visibly change.

7. Choose Edit → Copy, and then choose Edit → Paste. PhotoDeluxe creates a new layer with the copied stem portion, as shown in Figure 3.25.

8. Double-click this new layer and name it **Stem**.

9. In the Layers palette, drag the layer upward until it's above the cherry layer and release the mouse. The layer will reposition, above the cherry, as shown in Figure 3.26.

Voila! The cherry now appears to pierce through the pepper's stem

You can merge multiple layers into one by selecting Merge Layers from the Layers palette drop-down menu. Click the right-pointing arrow that appears to the right of the Text layer to see the drop-down menu. Choosing Merge Layers merges all of the visible layers into a single new layer.

Figure 3.24
Select just the overlap.

Figure 3.25
The stem portion is copied.

Figure 3.26

The pepper stem reappears above the cherry stem.

In This Chapter...

In this chapter, you've learned about how to make the most of PhotoDeluxe. Here are a few critical points that you'll want to keep in mind:

- Many of the jobs you need to do with your photos are covered in the activity bar. Use the activity bar to help you work through your more routine PhotoDeluxe tasks.

- Don't strain your neck. Use the Rotate & Size tools to bring your photos into proper orientation.

- Prepare before you print. When you want to create a 4×6 or 5×7 print, use the Trim & Resize tools to bring your pictures into proper proportion.

- Don't be timid. PhotoDeluxe's advanced menus and tools are there for the taking. Learn how to make the most of these. Most people think you need to step up to professional-level programs like Photoshop to find these high-end features. You don't. They're all there for you in PhotoDeluxe.

- Know your techniques. Learn to select, feather, and use layers. Then practice these techniques.

CHAPTER 4

Digital Photo Editing

Even the best photographers make mistakes. Don't let a little problem ruin your picture. Repair your picture and make the best of it. You'll be surprised how well and how much you can tweak your pictures into their best possible shape. Using the handy tools in Adobe PhotoDeluxe's toolbox, you can perform some major and minor miracles, ranging from adding a bit of contrast to hiding an ugly background. In this chapter, you'll learn the techniques that allow you to make the most of your digital images.

We'll be using Adobe PhotoDeluxe, included on the CD that accompanies this book, to perform the photo fixes covered in this chapter. Before working through this chapter, make sure you've read Chapter 3, "An Introduction to PhotoDeluxe," for details on using PhotoDeluxe.

This chapter covers the following topics:

- **Correct photos automatically**
- **Repair red-eye**
- **Alter photo backgrounds**
- **Fix facial blemishes**
- **Improve focus with a sharpening filter**

Correct Photos Automatically

Wouldn't you like instant and automatic digital photo enhancement? Could you ask for a better friend? Sure, a dog is great, but a quick fix is another matter entirely.

Fortunately for you, PhotoDeluxe arrives with not just one, but five quick-fix tools, courtesy of Extensis. You can use these tools to automatically evaluate your photo, decide what levels and options to use, and perform the fix without any human intervention.

Because the Instant Fix tool is such a boon to digital photographers, I suggested that you use it as part of your basic routine when you first bring a picture into PhotoDeluxe. Just click the Get & Fix Photo button to bring up that activity bar tab, and then select Adjust Quality → Extensis Instant Fix Tools → IntelliFix Instant Fix for miracle picture repair. When you want to be more selective about the instant fixes performed on your photo, you can use one of the other quick-fix tools.

> The photos in this section show "before" and "after" effects in the same picture. In each photo, the left half appears unretouched, and the right half demonstrates the quick-fix tool results. Look carefully to recognize each enhancement. They can be quite subtle.

Snap into Focus: Auto Sharpen

Use the Extensis Auto Sharpen tool to automatically "unblur" your photos. Here's how it works:

1. Launch PhotoDeluxe and open your picture.

2. Select the area you wish to fix. To fix the entire photo, choose Select → All. Otherwise, pick a selection tool from the Selections palette and mark the area you want to change.

3. Click the Get & Fix Photo button next to the activity bar and select Adjust Quality → Extensis Instant Fix Tools → Auto Sharpen.

Figure 4.1

Applying Auto Sharpen

Figure 4.2

Applying Auto Contrast

Figure 4.1 shows what happens after auto-sharpening. You'll notice that there isn't much difference between the original and auto-sharpened areas.

> Of all the Extensis tools provided by PhotoDeluxe, Auto Sharpen ranks as my least favorite. I do not believe it creates particularly good results. Instead, I recommend the sharpening technique covered in the "Improve Focus with a Sharpening Filter" section later in this chapter.

Correct Poor Contrast: Auto Contrast

In contrast (sorry!) to the Extensis Auto Sharpen tool, the Auto Contrast tool works very well indeed. This tool automatically corrects poor contrast caused by any number of lighting problems. Follow these steps to automatically add contrast:

1. Launch PhotoDeluxe and open your picture.

2. Select the area you wish to fix. You can choose Select → All to select the entire photo or use a selection tool to mark an area of the photo.

3. Click the Get & Fix Photo button and select Adjust Quality → Extensis Instant Fix Tools → Auto Contrast.

   In Figure 4.2, you can see that Auto Contrast can improve a photo.

Enhance Light Levels: Auto Brightness

The Extensis Auto Brightness tool enhances ambient light values, although the results are often subtle. It expands your photo's dynamic range so you can see a wide variety of light levels, where, originally, there may have been few. Here are the steps for auto-brightening:

1. Launch PhotoDeluxe and open your picture.

2. Select the area you wish to fix with a selection tool or choose Select → All to select the whole photo.

3. Click the Get & Fix Photo button and select Adjust Quality → Extensis Instant Fix Tools → Auto Brightness.

   You'll need to look very closely at Figure 4.3 to see the effect of using the Auto Brightness tool.

Figure 4.3

Applying Auto Brightness

Remove Fluorescent Light Effects

Fluorescent lights can add unnatural green and yellowish tones to your photos. This makes your subjects look sickly and vampiric. Of course, it's best to turn off fluorescent lights and use natural daylight, photo floodlights, or even your camera's flash where possible. When opportunity does not permit these solutions, you can repair your pictures back at the computer.

PhotoDeluxe provides an Extensis tool designed to automatically readjust your image's flesh tones and restore missing health and vitality. Just apply this tool to improve your photos:

1. Launch PhotoDeluxe and open your picture.

2. Use a selection tool to select the area you wish to fix or choose Select → All to select the entire photo.

3. Click the Get & Fix Photo button and select Adjust Quality → Extensis Instant Fix Tools → Remove Fluorescent Light.

Repair Red-Eye

Do you have red-eye—that demon-look, with those glowing red eyes? How embarrassing— it's almost as bad as halitosis (well, maybe not quite as bad). Whatever can you do?

Red-eye occurs when your subject's eyes dilate too much. Light reflects off the retinas and bounces back to the camera. This creates the signature red glow we hate so much. Sometimes we don't even know that we've caught red-eye. With small LCD screens and obscured visibility, we often do not discover red eyes until we're back at our computer.

Put away those "red-eye marking pens" (otherwise known as expensive magic markers). Shun the black-tipped paintbrush tool. Let PhotoDeluxe leap to your rescue. With just a few quick steps, you can relieve that red-eye condition.

> Instead of trying to repair red-eye, you can sometimes avoid it in the first place. See Chapter 1, " Composition, Lighting, and Posing: Some Tried-and-True Advice," for tips on reducing red-eye when you're shooting pictures.

PhotoDeluxe will walk you through a guided activity that instantly repairs red-eye in your photos. Here are the steps:

1. Open your picture in PhotoDeluxe.

2. Click the Get & Fix Photo button and select Repair Photo → Remove Red Eye.

3. Click 1 - Select → Select Rectangle. Drag a box around the first eye, as shown in Figure 4.4.

> Keep your box small and do not attempt to correct both eyes at once. PhotoDeluxe sometimes creates weird side effects when you attempt to remove red-eye with a large selection.

4. Click 2 - Remove → Remove Red Eye. PhotoDeluxe automatically corrects the eye for you.

5. Repeat steps 3 and 4 to correct the second eye, as shown in Figure 4.5.

6. You can repeat this process for each eye in your photo. (No, I'm not suggesting your subject has more than two eyes—I'm suggesting that your picture may have more than one subject!)

7. Click 3 - Done to finish.

Remove and Replace Unwanted Elements

At times, unwanted but subtle details seem to creep into our pictures. We never even notice them until long after we've shot our photo. Often, we're back at the computer, sorting through the "rolls," and up crops a marvelous picture with one or two minor flaws.

Take charge of your pictures. Don't "learn to live with it." You can fix these flaws and bring your photos to their full potential. The secret is *cloning*. When you clone a part of a picture, you replace the flaws you don't want with other, more desirable, features. The big advantage is that these features share the same general lighting and texture as the rest of the picture. You hide flaws with authentic picture parts.

Use PhotoDeluxe's Clone Tool

PhotoDeluxe provides an easy-to-use Clone tool. With this tool, you set a bulls-eye at your replacement source. Then you brush this texture over the area you want to hide. The tool replaces the flaw with the copied texture and blends it into your picture.

Figure 4.4

Select the first eye.

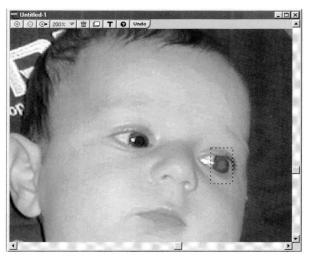

Figure 4.5

Select the second eye.

Figure 4.6

**The original,
flawed image**

This protruding hand calls
unwanted attention to itself.

Suppose that you took the picture in Figure 4.6. It would be a great shot, if only you could get rid of the hand and the book it's holding in the background behind the subject's back. This is where the Clone tool saves the day (or more precisely, the photo). Using it, you can replace the hand and book with additional fiberboard. This works because it will paint over the intrusion with a nice, mottled texture that should blend into the rest of the background.

"Clone-away" your picture problem areas with just a few steps. Follow these instructions to clean up your photos:

1. Launch PhotoDeluxe, set up power mode (click the Advanced Menus button if the advanced menus are not already displayed and show the Layers and Selection palettes), and open your picture.

2. Choose SmartSelect Tool from the Selections palette. Draw an outline around the features you wish to remove.

3. Select Tools → Clone. Drag the bulls-eye to an area that has the texture you want to use to replace the features you're removing, as shown in Figure 4.7.

4. Paint your selection with this texture. Your picture is now rid of its flaws, as shown in Figure 4.8.

Photo Cloning Tips and Tricks

Here are a few tips to help you make the most of your cloning:

Tune your selection area. Select precisely when a flaw rests next to your subject, but select loosely when it's adjacent to a common texture. You're trying to balance two issues here.

Figure 4.7

**Select the texture for
replacement.**

The bulls-eye sets the center
of the area to be cloned.

Select the area you
wish to replace.

First, you don't want to remove any part of your subject. A careful selection ensures that your subject will remain entirely intact. On the other hand, you want to avoid "ghost" edges. These may form at the edges of your selections when you select too closely. When you need to replace a feature with a texture, you'll want to make sure you completely cover it.

Place your bulls-eye carefully. Set your bulls-eye in the middle of a texture rather than at an edge. This affords you the greatest latitude in sweeping your brush back and forth. After all, you don't want to go beyond the edge of your texture and start cloning actual features like hands, houses, and trees.

Use small strokes for small areas. When your texture area is small, make many small brush strokes. The clone "resets" after each repetition. By keeping your strokes small, you ensure that you do not stray from your desired texture.

Stick to backgrounds. Do not attempt to hide a flaw by cloning a "feature." The whole point of this repair exercise is that the noise and randomness inherent in your texture will blend in well. When you attempt to cover a wall-socket with a chair, you'll invariably produce a lot of edge effects (artificial transitions between the original and the added image elements) that will not blend well.

Figure 4.8

The corrected image.

Alter Photo Backgrounds

Sometimes a lovely picture happens against an ugly background. Figure 4.9 shows a typical nice foreground/awful background image. In this picture, the subject poses in front of construction site. Behind her, you can see plywood, protective plastic sheeting, and part of a warning sign. Fortunately, this problem is easy to fix. When you de-emphasize the background, the focus switches to your subject. The key is to camouflage any feature that might draw away the viewer's eye. You can do this through filters.

PhotoDeluxe filters allow you to alter image quality in a variety of ways. Many filters produce blurred and distorted versions of an image. When you apply these effects exclusively to the background of your image, you bring your subject into sharp relief.

> To fix an ugly background, you'll need to use PhotoDeluxe layers and selection tools. Chapter 3 provides information about using these features.

You can use any of a number of filters to produce the effect you need. However, no matter which filter you choose, the method you follow to create the distorted background remains the same. These instructions will show you how to isolate the foreground of your image and apply a filter to the rest:

1. Launch PhotoDeluxe, set up power mode (click the Advanced Menus button if the advanced menus are not already displayed and show the Layers and Selection palettes), and open your picture.

2. In the Layers palette, pull Layer 0 (your picture) down to the paper icon and release it. This will create Layer 0 copy, a copy of your original image.

3. Click Layer 0 copy. Choose SmartSelect Tool from the Selections palette and outline your subject.

4. Select Effects → Feather. Specify a nice, wide feathering, such as 6. Click Delete Background, and then click OK. This will remove the background from Layer 0 copy, but create a smooth transition between your subject and the background.

5. In the Layers palette, click Layer 0 and choose Select → All.

6. Apply your filter of choice by selecting it from the Effects menu.

Now that you know the general method for applying a filter to a background, let's take a look at what each of these filters can do.

Create a Mosaic of Dots with the Pointillize Filter

The Pointillize filter transforms your background into a mosaic of tiny dots. In an attempt to emulate French Pointillism, it produces dreamy, unrealistic pastels that contrast sharply with the vibrant colors of your subject.

To apply the Pointillize filter, select Effects → Pixelate → Pointillize. This filter obscures many of the background details to the point that they cannot be identified by those unfamiliar with the original, as you can see in Figure 4.10. This, too, helps move the image focal point to your subject.

Figure 4.9

Posed in front of an ugly background

Figure 4.10

A "pointillized" background

Remove Background Color

By removing all color from your background, you create an eerie blend of reality and fantasy. Your subject becomes a splash of color in an otherwise colorless world. When you remove background color, it seems to also remove emotional contact at some level. We relate more fully and emotionally to full-color images than to black-and-white ones.

The Black/White effect draws the eye, particularly because many people do not realize for a few seconds what is "wrong" with the background. This effect can produce some truly eye-catching results. To apply this effect, select Effects → Color to Black/White.

Distort with the Ripple Filter

When you apply the Ripple filter, your background appears as if you were looking at it through a pane of rippled glass, as shown in Figure 4.11. This filter produces a blurry, not-quite-real overlay, while leaving major background features undisturbed.

To apply the Ripple filter, select Effects → Distort → Ripple, choose a very high ripple amount, such as 999, and click OK. After you apply the filter, click the Undo button a few times. Look closely as you move back and forth between the original image and the filtered one. You'll be surprised at how little the actual features change, yet they distort just enough to push away the eye and force attention on your subject.

Roughen with the Crackle Filter

The Crackle filter makes the background appear as if it were painted on stucco. Small cracks and crevices appear in the image, and the shadows that fill these add noise and texture to the photo.

Because of the added shadows, the Crackle filter will also tend to darken the background somewhat. As the background grain and roughness increase, the subject is left to provide a smooth refuge for your eye, as shown in Figure 4.12. To apply the Crackle filter, select Effects → Texture → Crackle.

Add Texture with the Emboss Filter

Embossing your background turns it into a gray, textured backdrop, reminiscent of a fabric. Details remain, but at a very subdued level, as shown in Figure 4.13. Although you could create a similar effect by filling the background with a simple color, this filter retains many textural details that provide lingering visual interest without strong detail. To apply this filter, select Effects → Stylize → Emboss.

Figure 4.11

A rippled background

Figure 4.12

A crackled background

Figure 4.13

An embossed background.

Fix Facial Blemishes

Facial blemishes happen to the best of us. When you set out to create precious heirlooms, why not take the time to digitally clean up your loved one's face and create a more flattering portrait? As you can see in the "before" image in Figure 4.14, even the sweetest baby occasionally suffers imperfections. With just a little work, as in the "after" image, you can eradicate some obvious flaws and produce a more timeless keepsake.

Use PhotoDeluxe's Smudge tool (Tools → Smudge) to nudge away any blemishes. Select a medium to small brush and pull color in from just above, below, or to the side of a flaw. Here are some tips for a smooth cover-up:

Use small strokes. These will give you more control over the smudging effect.

Avoid pulling in color from too far away. This will just magnify the existing problems. Our eyes are very sensitive to sudden changes in color. Bypass this neurological quirk by using nearby colors instead.

Blend smudges. After you've smudged away your flaw, you may want to blend it a little. Use a selection tool, like the Trace tool or the Circle tool, to select a small area around the former blemish. Then choose Effects → Blur → Blur More to even out the changes you've made.

Figure 4.14

Fixing flaws

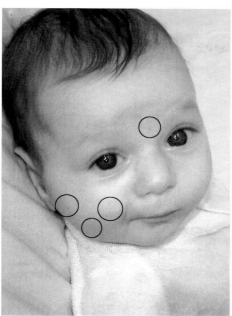

Before touchup (the circled areas are the "problem spots")

After touchup

Do not give in to the temptation to use the Clone tool to clean up blemishes. Although it might seem like an ideal solution (copy smooth skin areas to the problem spot), you'll create more problems than you solve. The skin patch you copy will not naturally blend into the new spot. Human skin of every flavor, color, and gender is not highly textured. It displays smooth gradations from one point to another. You just cannot expect to match this gradual color change with a relocated patch.

Improve Focus with a Sharpening Filter

You snap a picture, and the focus is off. Your image turns out soft and a bit blurry. What can you do?

I offer three alternatives to dealing with those fuzzy pictures. Ponder them carefully and choose the option that best suits your needs.

First, you can throw up your hands, indulge in a well-deserved hissy fit, and throw away the picture (and, optionally, the camera). Scream out loud. "These pictures are an insult to me as an artist! I refuse to acknowledge them. They are the spawn of evil technology. I shall now return to painting outlines of my hands on cave walls. That will show them!" (Whoever "they" are.) In technical jargon, this is known as "walking away from the problem."

Second, you can adjust your way of thinking. Or, as they say in biz-speak, "create a paradigm shift." Instead of bemoaning your lost photo opportunity, learn to "celebrate" your mistakes. Point out how soft focus enhances the beauty and romance of your image. After all, they used soft focus in the Star Trek classics all the time. Every time the camera angle changed from Captain Kirk to the pretty girl, the focus would go out of whack. Explain to others that you are paying homage to the 1960's retro-tradition of soft-focus photography. Rather than admit that you (or the camera) messed up the focus, state firmly that you were aiming for the "indeterminate transition effect expressed as a rejection of overstructured object independence."

Finally, you can fire up PhotoDeluxe and attempt to sharpen your picture with an image filter. The results won't be great, I assure you, but you can often add a little optical clarity to a fuzzy situation. This may not offer the emotional release of the prior two methods, but it does allow you to create pictures with some small visual improvement. To apply a sharpening filter, open your picture in PhotoDeluxe and choose Edit → Select All. Then select Effects → Sharpen → Sharpen *or* Effects → Sharpen → Sharpen More. Repeat as desired.

Applying a sharpening filter is more an art than a science. You must control each iteration and decide when the picture has reached its peak. These tips should help you when sharpening:

Use a copy. Copy the image to a new layer and experiment with the copy. This allows you to test different approaches without altering your original picture. To copy a layer, drag it to the paper icon on the bottom-left side of the Layers palette. (Don't forget to turn off the display of the original image by clicking the eye icon.)

Use the Undo function liberally. After you test a sharpening effect, revert it with Undo to swap between the new and the old. This allows you to compare the results and decide whether you like the new effect or not.

Zoom in. View your picture with at least a 100% zoom. A picture will naturally look better when shrunk down. A larger view allows you to see image flaws more clearly.

Balance too much and too little. You must decide how much sharpening your image requires. Sharpen too little, and you won't see much difference between your original and the new. Sharpen too much, and you'll introduce noise, darkness, and unflattering edge effects.

Blur a little. If the results between one sharpening and the next introduce too much noise, you can add a light blur or "unsharp" effect. This reduces the high-frequency edge effects. Select Effects → Blur → Soften and adjust the radius until the noise just barely disappears.

Watch an eye. Although you can pick any feature to compare before and after, eyes offer a great combination of lines and texture. Watch the eye as you sharpen your image and see how image quality improves.

As I noted earlier, a sharpening filter cannot turn a blurry picture into an in-focus one. However, using the techniques described here, you can usually improve your photo to some degree.

In This Chapter...

This chapter described how to conquer those visual flaws that stand between you and a great picture. Keep these tips in mind:

- PhotoDeluxe's Instant Fix tools are an absolute treasure. With a single click, you can bring your pictures into perfect contrast and color.

- Use the individual auto-fix tools to provide finer control over the picture-correction process.

- Don't live with red-eye; remove it!

- Don't be afraid to edit your pictures. The Clone tool can help hide details that take away from the main subject of your image.

- If your backgrounds are simply unredeemable, replace them! Use one of the techniques discussed in this chapter to hide the background entirely.

- Even the most beautiful among us will display the occasional blemish in pictures. Use PhotoDeluxe's tools to remove unsightly features and restore your subject to the best possible look.

CHAPTER 5

New Viewpoints: Postprocessing Your Images

Many people get caught up in what I call a 4-by-6 mentality. By this, I mean that they think the beginning and end of digital photography lies in snapping and producing photographs that can be placed in family photo albums. You can do so much more with your digital images.

In this chapter, you'll learn how to postprocess your digital images with your computer to enhance them and look at them in novel ways. By using special software, you can create panoramic views, murals, 3D models, and entire 3D scenes. You can even blow up your digital images to poster size or larger. Let your computer's processing power calculate new viewpoints for your digital snapshots.

This chapter covers the following topics:

- **Create panoramas**
- **Create 3D images**
- **Blow up your images**

Create Panoramas

Does your vision exceed your viewfinder? Does your resolution fall short of your landscape? Sometimes we come across scenes so big, detailed, or geometrically complex, we cannot hope to photograph them in their entirety—or at least with just one picture.

Panoramas can capture a greater whole. With panoramas, you can stitch together a series of images to produce a composite image of arbitrary size. Panoramas create a wider reality than any single image can hope to show. For example, a panorama can present the entire arc of a rainbow, as shown in Figure 5.1.

You may run across two basic varieties of panoramas:

Vista The more common row-type is generally referred to as a *vista*. To produce a simple vista, you stitch together a linear series of pictures.

Quilt A two-dimensional version is called a *quilt*. Quilts are made up of photos snapped in two dimensions, both rows and columns. Stitched together, side by side and up and down, these form a full mosaic.

When you create a panorama, you can either work by hand or with a special-purpose program that stitches your image for you. Each has its advantages. Working by hand is essentially free. It can be done quickly in almost any image-processing program. It also allows you to stitch quilts, a capability that many stitching programs lack.

In contrast, a stitching program creates much better results without the obvious edges you'll find in homemade panoramas. It automatically handles image rotation and warping caused by camera angle, unsteady hands, and varying lens properties. Stitching programs range from freeware to quite costly commercial products. They generally produce superb results, but you may need to wait a while for your panorama to process.

Panoramas with PhotoDeluxe

You can create your own panorama using Adobe PhotoDeluxe. (See Chapter 3, "An Introduction to PhotoDeluxe," for information about setting up PhotoDeluxe power mode and using other PhotoDeluxe features.)

Figure 5.1

A series of shots creates this panorama of a rainbow.

Take out your digital camera and snap a few pictures along some natural line. After you've taken your panoramic shots, follow these steps:

1. Fire up PhotoDeluxe and set up in power mode (display the advanced menus, Layers palette, and Selections palette).

2. Create a new, large, blank image in PhotoDeluxe. Select an image size larger than you think you'll ever need space for. You can always crop it later.

3. One by one, copy your images into separate layers. Open each image, copy it, and paste it into the panorama image. PhotoDeluxe will create a layer for each pasted copy.

4. Use PhotoDeluxe's move and rotate features to arrange your images. Make sure that common features align correctly. If you need to see both layers at once, double-click the upper layer and reduce the layer transparency to 50%. Align the layer, and then make it opaque again.

5. Merge the image layers. Click the right-pointing arrow below the Close button on the Layers palette (to the right of the Text layer) and select Merge Layers. This will collapse your image into a single layer.

6. Click the Get & Fix Photo button next to the activity bar and select Rotate & Size → Trim & Size.

7. Click 1 - Trim → Trim. Outline the final image, omitting the uneven edges. Then click OK.

8. Click 2 - Done to complete the task.

This method provides a simple way to create a panorama. However, it almost always produces natural flaws. Take a look at the image shown in Figure 5.2. The rectangles highlight the obvious stitching errors: the clouds that moved between the shots, slight rotation errors where the tree does not line up with itself, and the lighting gradient between the right and left edges of each image.

Figure 5.2

Hand-stitching almost always produces flawed panoramas.

Panoramas with PhotoVista

Compare the results of creating a panorama in PhotoDeluxe (the rainbow in Figure 5.1) with the panorama shown in Figure 5.3, which was created with Roxio/MGI's Photovista software. The features of Photovista Virtual Tour and more can also be found in the PhotoSuite package from Roxio/MGI. Information about PhotoSuite can be found at `http://www.roxio.com/en/products/photosuite/index.jhtml`. This software produces an almost flawless image, displaying none of the imaging errors inherent in a hand-stitching attempt.

Figure 5.3

Roxio/MGI's PhotoVista creates a flawless panorama.

Roxio/MGI Photovista Virtual Tour (www.mgisoft.com/roxio_index.asp) provides excellent panoramic vista creation and interaction software. This software allows you to stitch panoramas into immersible views. If you like, you can upload a special interactive version to your favorite Internet hosting site. On-site, you and your online friends can dive into your vistas. A special-purpose Java applet lets you zoom around your panorama. With just a few steps, you can create a "virtual reality" of your own.

Generate Your Panorama

Photovista stitches your photos together automatically. To create a panorama, install the Photovista software, and then follow these steps:

1. Select File → Open Source Images.

2. Select the images you wish to add and drag them to the Source Files box on the right side of the window. Then click OK.

3. If you snapped your pictures in portrait mode, click the rotation icon (the bent arrow) until your photos return to their upright and locked position.

4. If needed, drag each image into its correct position.

5. Click the camera icon, select your camera, and click OK. Your pictures are ready to stitch, as in the example shown in Figure 5.4.

6. Click the stitch panorama icon, located on the bottom-right side of the screen (it looks like a series of upright rectangles), to bring up the Stitch Options dialog box. If you're stitching a circular panorama, make sure to check the Full 360 Degree Panorama option. You can either preview the stitch or simply click Full Stitch to create your vista.

Figure 5.4

In Virtual Tour, you begin by laying out your pictures in the correct order before you stitch them together.

Other stitching options allow you to disable the warping and blending functions and to crop nonimage areas from your results.

7. Wait for the stitching to finish. In the case of a full stitch, this may take several minutes.

8. Enjoy and explore your new panorama. You can move between the stitched image and the panoramic viewer by selecting from the Panorama menu. You can also print your panorama by choosing File → Print View.

9. When you're satisfied with your creation, you can save it as a picture file. Select File → Save As, choose JPEG or Bitmap, navigate to any location on the disk, name the file, and click Save.

Upload Your Panorama

After saving your picture as a flat image, you may now want to explore Photovista's 3D fly-around capabilities. To continue, you must keep the Stitched Result window open.

1. Select Panorama → Save As and choose the Flashpix file type in the Save Panorama dialog box, as shown in Figure 5.5. Select For Java from the Export to HTML drop-down list, navigate to where you wish to save your file, name it, and click Save.

Figure 5.5

Save your panorama to Java format to enable fly-around capabilities.

2. Choose an image quality level and click OK. The better the quality, the bigger the file size.

3. In the directory you specified, you will find four files. In the example I used in Figure 5.5, Photovista created `my_export.jpg`, `my_export.ivr`, `my_export.htm`, and `panoapplet.jar`. The names of the first three depend on the filename you specified. The last is always named `panoapplet.jar`. Upload these four files to your favorite Web hosting site, or open the `my_export.htm` file locally in your Web browser. The interactive applet will appear, as shown in Figure 5.6.

You can explore the panoramic view by panning through it and zooming in and out, as follows:

- Drag your mouse along the image, and the panorama will move in that direction. (It's a little counterintuitive, but it works.)

- Keep the mouse button depressed to continue panning. You don't need to move the mouse once the pan starts.

- As you move the mouse farther from the image center, the pan speed increases.

- Tap the A key to zoom in and the Z key to zoom out.

Figure 5.6

View your interactive, Java-based panorama in your favorite Web browser.

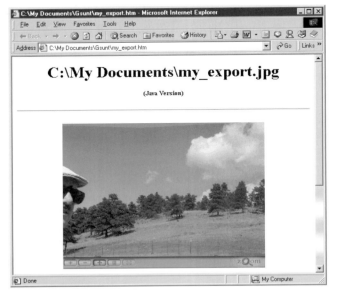

Compare Panorama Software

Photovista's excellent rendering and superior output offer the most important reasons to use this software. Compare the image output shown in Figure 5.7 from Photovista, Ulead Cool 360, and Adobe Photoshop Elements. Notice the difference in quality along the blends, particularly among the buffalo on the right side of the panorama. Only Photovista gets each buffalo right, without a telltale stitching shadow.

In addition, the Roxio/MGI package offers 3D object creation and virtual tours. By photographing an object from multiple angles, you can create a "fly-around" that allows people to see the object from all sides. This can prove especially useful for those who want to buy or sell on an auction site, such as eBay. Potential buyers can see an object from many angles. The virtual tours add hotspots to your interactive panoramas so your viewers can "click through" to associated Web pages. For example, clicking a restaurant in an image of a city street might link the user to that restaurant's menu. This feature takes panoramas into a whole new dimension, adding meaning and function to mere fly-around capabilities.

Low-Tech Panoramas

Are you looking for the truly low-tech approach to creating a composite image? Try this one: Snap a whole bunch of overlapping pictures that cover a small area, print them, and tape them together by hand. You cannot get any more primitive than that. This method allows you to create life-size or near-life-size collages. A lot of detail is the result of minimal computer work.

Take a look at the baby (Sofia) next to her mural in Figure 5.8. Of course, the fine details in this image might have worked better had she stayed asleep during the photo session. (Sometimes, it's hard to combine good lighting and no flash with a sleeping baby.) To assure uniform image distance, I laid a yardstick over the rails of her crib and used it to steady my digital camera. It's important that you don't vary the distance. When elements scale differently, they cannot be matched between photos.

I printed each image on large-sized, stiff paper, and then reassembled her on the wall. With some scotch tape, a little scissors work, and patience, I was able to create a special and unique montage.

Figure 5.7

Panorama software offers various levels of quality.

Roxio/MGI PhotoVista

Ulead Cool 360

Adobe Photoshop Elements

Panorama Tips

Digital cameras easily capture panoramas. Just fit pictures together with your favorite image program or stitch them in a special-purpose application. Shoot as many images as you can—the more, the better—and overlap, overlap, overlap! Here are some tips for creating panoramas:

Take a lot of pictures. With digital cameras, you never know which picture will turn out to be the best. Image quality varies, as do color, contrast, and focus. Don't try to be efficient when snapping your pictures. Trying to match image edges is a surefire way to lose important pieces of your picture. Instead, overlap and take extra shots where possible. You'll be surprised as many unimportant details become fascinating or merely helpful when you compile the collage. Take many pictures to maximize your keepers. Remember that there's no film to waste in digital cameras.

Keep your camera steady. Tripods hold your digital camera steady. Admittedly, they are cumbersome and cannot be carried in your pocket the way you carry a digital camera. If you don't have a traditional tripod with you, use a makeshift object to level your camera—a flat fence top, a friend's shoulder, or even an upright stick.

Maintain a uniform distance. Scaling occurs when pictures are taken at different distances from a relatively close object (a building, say, rather than distant mountains). Try to maintain a uniform distance from your subject when you get close up.

Rotate your camera for distant panoramas. For faraway panoramas, rotate your camera to take pictures of rainbows, mountains, or city skylines. Because they are far away, the scenery does not change significantly when you move left and right. Instead, swing your camera around a fixed point to capture a distant panorama.

Move your camera along straight lines for nearby panoramas. For nearby panoramas of murals, houses, family groups, and so forth, be careful how you move your camera. Odd angles may distort nearby objects, so you should set up your tripod parallel to the desired scene and move your camera strictly left and right, up and down, to shoot your pictures.

Figure 5.8

Sofia, just beside herself

Cool Panorama Ideas

Panoramic vistas give us a view of the world that we normally wouldn't see. Panoramas can take place outside or inside, with multiple subjects or just a few, and very close in or very far away.

You'll be surprised at the varying ways you can use panoramas in your everyday life. Here are some ideas:

Home selling If you're selling your house, use a panorama to let people "walk" around your rooms and get a better feel for the property. Create a 360-degree panorama to allow people to visualize space from any angle. Since panoramas work both inside and outside, you can just as easily create a panorama of your living room as your backyard.

Gardens When you're visiting a garden, panoramas let you get very close to a bed of flowers or a vine-laced trellis. Stitch together the small "detail" pictures, and you'll get to see all the little facets and textures that make up the planting. Detail panoramas also allow you to photograph a favorite painting or tapestry.

Crowds Perhaps you need to take a picture of a large group of people, such as a graduating class or the crowd at a football game. Stitch together your images, and you've created a complete picture that offers greater image detail and a wider scope than you could possibly capture in a single snapshot.

Nature Head up to the mountains to create a panorama. Panoramas easily capture the magnificence of nature. Photograph the wide vistas as they completely surround you. Nothing works better for feeling immersed in a scene than a photo that extends beyond your natural limits of view. Whether you're on a plateau or in a valley, a panorama can capture that special feeling of "being there."

Decoration If you're decorating a room, you can use a your panoramas to create a wall border or a special art piece. Let your imagination go wild!

Create 3D Images

Let's put aside the camera and the software for a moment and work with our hands. Hold your thumb out at arm's length and look at it first with one eye and then the other. Notice how it seems to move a little? Now move your thumb about 6 inches away from your eye and repeat. Your thumb will seem to jump even more as you switch eyes. Put down your arm and look at some object far across the room. When you switch between your left and right eyes, it will hardly appear to move at all. This magical property is called *parallax* or *stereopsis*, and it's how we humans see three dimensions. When our eyes record slightly different positions for objects in our view, our brains go to work and figure out how far away each object lies.

"How quaint," you might be thinking as you glance surreptitiously at your watch. Don't be so blasé! This wonderful expression of optical science allows you to create your own 3D photos. With just your digital camera and a little careful alignment, you can tame parallax.

The 3D Key

The key to creating 3D photos is to begin with two photos that approximate the location of our eyes. You need a left image and a right image taken at exactly the same height and orientation, but offset horizontally by about 2.5 inches. You can do this the easy way or the precise way.

Here's the easy way: Hold your camera's viewfinder up to your left eye and snap, and then transfer the viewfinder to your right eye and snap again. You need to stay very still between the two images, and you must keep the camera absolutely level. This cheap and fast method gives decent results for very little effort. It's the one that I use most of the time, particularly when I'm on vacation. For reasons that I don't begin to understand, this technique is called the "Cha Cha" or "Rock and Roll" method.

> By changing the spacing between the images, you will change the way we see 3D. Use a larger spacing, such as 6 or 8 inches, to make your subjects appear smaller, as if seen from a "giant's eye" viewpoint. A smaller spacing enlarges your subjects, as viewed from an "ant's eye" viewpoint.

The precise way to create 3D pictures requires only a tripod and a yardstick. Tape the yardstick to the ground perpendicular to your subject. Set up your tripod with two legs facing forward, each touching the yardstick. After snapping your first image, slide your tripod along the yardstick to ensure that you maintain absolute horizontal integrity. The yardstick will also help you measure the absolute change of 2.5 inches.

Whichever way you decide to snap your pictures, make sure to remember which image is right and which image is left. You'll need this information when you return to your computer and prepare your 3D stereo pair.

> If you have the time, the money, and the will, you can purchase a special-purpose dual-CCD digital camera that takes stereo images with a single click. These cameras tend to be bought by 3D hobbyists with a lot of money. You can see one at www.stereoscopy.com/3d-images/camera.html.

Use your macro lens to get in close to a flower, butterfly, or stone. Then step back and allow your wide-angle lens to take in the entire vast splendor of nature in the grander scheme of things.

Never forget that your digital camera is supposed to be fun. Use your camera and Adobe Photo-Deluxe to add spice, interest, and above all, enjoyment to your life. These images use feathering, color variations, and filters to match the original artwork.

Don't settle for the stiff and formal when transforming your subjects into digital works of art. Allow real and lively expression to bring character and interest to your work.

▲Don't feel you must always photograph your subjects face-on. A simple image of unconscious grace makes a lovely picture.

▼Simple shapes, like triangles, resonate with your viewer's eye. You might be surprised where you'll find natural patterns: ripples across the sand, the bend in the road, a row of glass doors in an office building.

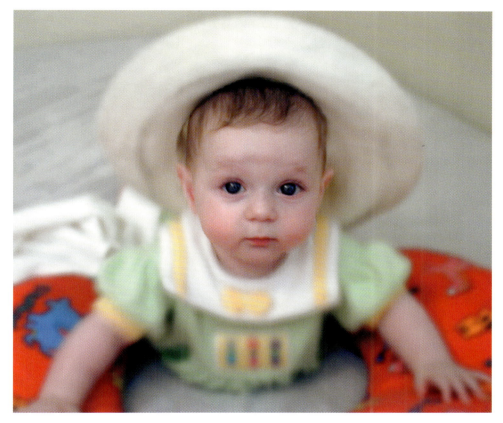

▲This image of a double rainbow was created by snapping a series of exposures. Then the exposures were assembled by hand in an image-processing program. By overlapping the images, an image "quilt" was created.

▼A subject in focus surrounded by a fuzzy background produces a particularly artistic image. You can achieve this effect by adjusting your camera settings when you take the shot or by editing the photo in an image-editing program. This image was captured using maximum zoom, which produced a very shallow depth of field.

Let your subjects guide you, but open yourself to experimentation. Sometimes a subdued pose best flatters an outgoing personality or vice versa. Take risks, and you will often find rewards in your portraits.

You never know when the right pose will come along. The more pictures you take, the more likely you'll capture the perfect shot when it arrives. This proves especially important when shooting pictures with multiple subjects. Keep snapping and don't miss that perfect shot!

Backlighting can destroy a beautiful moment. The best way to avoid backlight is to turn your subjects around. Have them face the light. Move yourself and the camera to make the most of natural illumination. When this is simply not possible, turn on your camera's flash to fill in a backlit picture and reveal your subject.

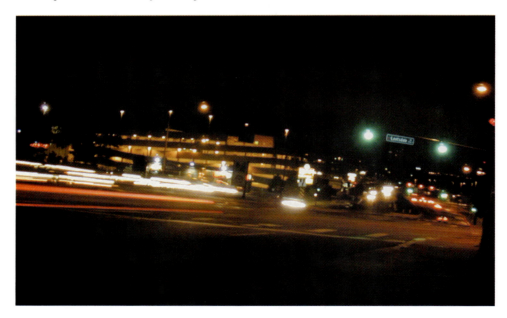

Long exposures taken at night can produce eerily beautiful images. With proper timing, you just might capture a ghost! Make sure to use a tripod to steady your camera and start your shot early. This exposes your subject for the longest time possible and produces the best results.

Poster project

iMorph project

▲Adobe PhotoDeluxe provides the tools you need to create fun and exciting picture projects, including detailed poster work.

►ArcSoft's PhotoIsland Web site offers unusual photo-manipulation projects. iMorph allows you to stretch and bend any photograph.

▼Indulge yourself in a little freehand fun. Play with your photos and see where they take you.

Freehand project

Without a
polarizing filter

With a polarizing filter

A polarizing filter on your camera cuts glare and enriches color. The cloud-filled sky in this photo was given a more dramatic contrast with a polarizing filter.

Without a
polarizing filter

With a polarizing filter

All reflected light—such as from a mirror, the glass in a picture frame, or a pond—produces polarized light. Use a polarizing filter to remove some of these reflections.

About 40 degrees (the reflections are nearly gone)

About 15 degrees

About 60 degrees

You'll find the most polarized light between 30 and 45 degrees from any surface. Shoot within these angles to remove reflections and glare.

Some polarizing effect (1/8 twist)

No polarizing effect

Complete polarizing effect (1/4 twist)

Twist your polarizing filter until the reflections are nearly gone. A quarter-twist is usually all you need.

Original picture

After Instant Fix

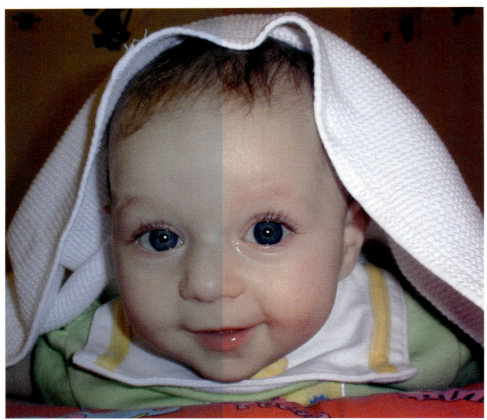

Before (left half) and after (right half) Instant Fix

Adobe PhotoDeluxe's Instant Fix tool (provided by Extensis) will automatically improve your image's brightness, contrast, color balance, and sharpness in one step. Use this tool to produce better pictures instantly.

Original image, with hand holding book in backgroun

Using the Clone tool

Fixed image

Don't let a small flaw ruin a great picture. Use Adobe PhotoDeluxe's Clone tool to remove an unwanted feature from your photo. In this example, the intruding hand was removed from behind the subject's back. Then the hand was selected and the particleboard was cloned from the upper-left portion of the photo. This covers the hand and repairs the image.

Original image

Posterize filter

Accented Edges filter

Pond Ripple filter

Spherize filter

Wind filter

Emboss filter

Patchwork filter

Bas Relief filter

Lighting Effects filter

Pointillize filter

Mezzotint filter

Negative effect

Black and White effect

Page Curl filter

Glowing Edges filter

Adobe PhotoDeluxe offers many built-in filters and special effects. They can produce artistic and dramatic results. Select one from the Effects menu and try it on your picture. This sampler displays only a fraction of the available effects.

▲A splash of natural color lends particular beauty to your digital photos. Zoos, aquariums, and botanical gardens provide fruitful sources for rich and varied color.

▼Use natural frames wherever you find them. They add important artistry to your pictures. Look for doors, windows, overhanging branches, sculptures, planters, and trellises. Keep your depth of field in mind. Both your "frame" and your image should remain in focus at the same time.

Side by Side

It's easy to create a stereo pair, like the sample shown in Figure 5.9. You just print the left image next to the right one. However, getting them both on the same page, aligned, and the right sizes may take a few steps. You can use PhotoDeluxe's sizing tools to match up your images.

You'll want to end up with a small, sharp print. The following steps set a final print width of 6 inches, a stereo-image standard. You can choose other widths as desired. You may also opt for resolutions other than 300 pixels per inch, although this resolution provides high pixel density while shrinking the print size.

1. Start PhotoDeluxe and open your "right" image. Select Size → Photo Size. Change the resolution to 300 pixels per inch and the width to 3 inches. Notice that the height resizes automatically. Click OK. Minimize the window.

2. Repeat step 1 for the "left" image. This time, leave the window open and displayed.

3. Select Size → Canvas Size. Change the width to 6 inches and click OK.

4. Drag the left image all the way to the left of the canvas.

5. Open the right image and drag a copy of it onto the right side of the canvas. Adjust the alignment as needed.

6. Save your image and print it.

Congratulations! You've just created your first stereo image pair.

Figure 5.9

To create a stereo pair, align the sized images.

Stereo Viewing

When I was in school, we learned to cross our eyes to see stereo pairs. The cross-eye method works by teaching you to focus your eyes at infinity rather than on a particular object. Do you see the two circles below? If you can relax your eyes until you see three circles rather than two, you can learn to view stereograms without a special viewer.

On the other hand, if this headache-inducing method is not for you, I offer two alternatives: You can use a commercial viewing product, or you can create your own stereo-viewing box.

Use a Lorgnette

Lorgnettes are a type of glasses with a short handle. You hold the handle and look through the lenses.

Berezin Stereo Photography Products offers a 3D viewing lorgnette for just a few dollars. (To order or get more information about the Berezin lorgnette, visit `www.berezin.com/3d/cardview.htm`.) This lorgnette, shown in Figure 5.10, allows you to view stereo pairs without effort. The special optics do all of the work for you. Just hold the lorgnette in front of your eyes (or eyeglasses) and move your stereo picture until it "pops" into 3D. The effect is spectacular.

Figure 5.10

Look through the Berezin lorgnette to view stereo pictures.

The lorgnette arrives flat in a standard envelope. Remove it and fold down the spacer bar at the top of the unit. Hold the lorgnette by the handle and place the spacer bar at the top of your nose. With your other hand, hold the stereo image pair at arm's distance. Slowly move it back and forth until the two pictures merge into a single 3D view—that's all there is to it. With a lorgnette, viewing stereo pairs is a snap!

Build Your Own Viewer

Are you ready to build your own stereo viewer? All you need is a shoebox, a manila file folder, tape, and scissors. This box approximates the stereo-optiscopes that were all the rage in the nineteenth century. You can still find 3D stereo pictures at most antique stores and auctions. In fact, there are entire books devoted to stereo images from the U.S. Civil War.

Here are step-by-step instructions for this project:

1. Cut two holes on one of the short sides of the shoebox, as illustrated in Figure 5.11. You will look through these holes to see the pictures. Make them about three-quarters inch across and spaced comfortably to look through. You may also add a space to accommodate your nose so it will not press against the box.

2. Place the folder, with the bent side down, along the side of the box. Fold the folder top over the side, as shown in Figure 5.12.

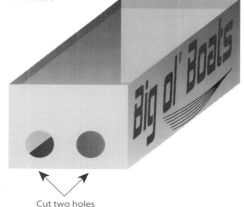

Figure 5.11

To create your viewer, begin by adding viewing holes.

Cut two holes

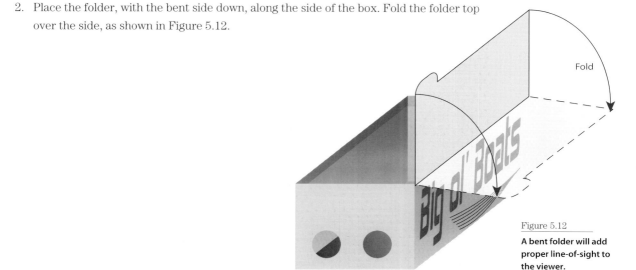

Fold

Figure 5.12

A bent folder will add proper line-of-sight to the viewer.

3. Staple or tape the bottom of the folder to keep it together. Open the top to make a T-shape along the crease you just made, as shown in Figure 5.13.

4. Tape the folder to the exact center of the box with the top of the T-shape resting on the top of the shoebox. When you look through the holes, you should now see only one side or the other of the folder. Make sure to leave some space at the end of the box to insert your pictures and to allow light in, as shown in Figure 5.14.

5. Place your picture opposite and facing the eyeholes. Look through the eyeholes—you should be seeing in 3D. It's not exactly a View-Master, but it works.

Figure 5.13

By transforming the folder into a T-shape, you create two visual paths.

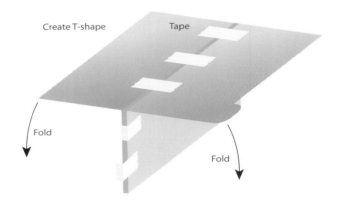

Figure 5.14

The finished viewer

Fisher Price offers a service where you can order your own custom View-Master 3D discs. Unfortunately, the minimum order is 1000 units ($1.08 per disc, $350 setup fee). It may sound a little pricey, but these are great for promotions, fund raising, marketing, real estate sales, and so forth. Submit your digital images on a CD using full color, at 2424 × 2048 pixels. Visit www.customviewmaster.com or call 716-687-3899 for more details.

Stereo Prints

When you read the instructions for sizing your image pairs, you may have wondered why you needed 3 inches per stereo view. There are two reasons for this sizing. First, many historical 3D viewers used 3-inch prints. Second, 6 inches just happens to be the width of the most common photo print, the 4 × 6–inch print.

If you've created two 3 × 3–inch stereo pictures, you can easily order prints. Just use one of the many online photo-finishing services. Combine your prints with a pair of viewing lorgnettes, and you're ready to roll out an entire stereo world of your own.

Make sure to avoid the Zoom to Fit or Zoom and Crop options when ordering your prints. You may want to fit your pictures in a black-filled 4 × 6–inch frame before uploading them.

Are you looking for a larger solution? Several online finishing sites, most notably Wolf Camera (www.wolfcamera.com), provide "panorama-sized" finishes, which are approximately 4 × 10 inches. These prints cost under a dollar and allow you to print larger-format stereo pairs.

You can read more about using online photo-finishing services in Chapter 6, "Digital Photo Printing." Also, see the "Field Guide to Online Photo Finishing and Album Sites" appendix at the back of this book.

Lenticular Prints

Have you ever seen a display at an airport, train station, or other major venue that seemed to change depending on your viewing angle? For example, a picture might show a tiger when viewed from one direction and a corporate logo when viewed from another angle. These displays are called *lenticular images* and were actually invented back in the 1960s.

The lenticular process works with image stripes and lenses. At the back of the picture lies an image made up of hundreds of thin stripes. Each stripe is from any one of a group of pictures. Most displays use two, three, or four pictures, but you can find lenticular pictures that use more source images. (In Japan, they've recently produced displays that contain no fewer than 18 images.) The authoring process mixes the sets of stripes from each picture with the stripes from the others, forming a unified but incoherent underlay. The key to viewing each picture lies in seeing only those stripes that belong to one picture at any time. Lenses make that happen.

Each lenticular display is overlaid with a special plastic sheet that covers the stripy picture underneath. The sheet, which is made of hundreds or thousands of tiny lenses, focuses light in such a way that you can see just one set of stripes. This way, each angle of view shows one picture at a time. Change your viewing angle, and the lenses change the picture that you see. There's no magic—just optics, lenses, and math.

Until recently, lenticular pictures lay solely in the domain of businessmen and artists willing to blow a few thousand dollars on a cool display technique. Fortunately, that limitation has now changed. In the fall of 2002, Orasee (`www.orasee.com`) will introduce a consumer product called SOHO (at a price of approximately $50) that allows you to print lenticular images on your home ink-jet printer. Select the images you want to use, and the software will slice them up and form the striped underlay image. (This is called *interlacing* the images). You can then print the underlay on your home printer using a special lenticular sheet (there will be ten sheets per package). Voilà, instant lenticular prints!

> While I was writing this book, I had a chance to use the beta SOHO software and print several lenticular prints. The process really is as easy as promised. The software allowed me to create prints from individual images and from video clips. The printing worked well using my ink-jet printer, but the lenticular sheet melted in my laser printer.

Lenticular prints come in two styles, depending on the pictures you use to create them. The first, called *3D*, uses stereoscopic images to produce the three-dimensional viewing effect seen earlier in this section. The second is called *flip* and lets you flip back and forth between two unrelated images.

Blow Up Your Images

Figure 5.15

Choose GF PrintPro to save your file using fractals.

You can always recognize 35mm snobs. They pin you to a wall at parties, talk about how wonderful traditional optics are, and lecture on how digital photography will never catch up. In particular, they mention how they can enlarge their photos "to the limits of the silver-halide molecules," a feat that you can never hope to accomplish with your new-fangled (and doomed-to-obscurity) digital camera. This may have been true once, but it isn't any more.

With Genuine Fractals PrintPro, a LizardTech (formerly Altamira) product, your digital images can decorate the side of a barn. Go ahead and snicker at the poor 35mm camera snobs holding tight to their miserable and costly poster-sized enlargements. With Genuine Fractals, the power is digital, and it's only going to get better.

Here's how it works: The Genuine Fractals PrintPro product converts your image into a highly accurate, scalable, mathematical representation of your original image. The best part is that this representation is resolution-independent. With fractals, you don't deal with pixels; you deal with scalable textures. And you can scale these textures arbitrarily. The mathematical model allows you to open your pictures at any virtual resolution. You can create images ten times as large as the original or bigger.

> Genuine Fractals PrintPro uses a special technology called *wavelets* to encode your image. Unlike other wavelet products (such as JPEG 2000), Genuine Fractals places emphasis on image scaling rather than file compression, although a certain degree of image compression occurs as a side effect.

Install the Plug-in

A demo version of Genuine Fractals PrintPro is included on the CD that accompanies this book. You'll need to install the demo plug-in so that you can try it out. After you run the CD's installation program for your trial software, follow these steps to add the plug-in:

1. Open the PrintPro folder on your hard drive. You'll find it at `C:\Program Files\Lizard Tech\Genuine Fractals PrintPro Trial`. Locate the plug-in and drag a copy to your Desktop.

2. Open the PhotoDeluxe folder on your hard drive. Locate the PhotoDeluxe plug-ins folder, which can usually be found at `C:\Program Files\Adobe\PhotoDeluxe Home Edition 4.1\Plugins\`.

3. Drag the plug-in from your Desktop into this `Plugins` folder.

Put a Picture in Genuine Fractals Format

Once you've installed the Genuine Fractals PrintPro demo, you're ready to try it out. First, fire up PhotoDeluxe, load a picture, and save it in the Genuine Fractals format. Then you can reopen your picture and scale it, as described in the next section.

Here are the steps for putting a picture in Genuine Fractals format:

1. Open your image in PhotoDeluxe and select File → Export → File Format.

2. Choose GF PrintPro from the Save As drop-down list, as shown in Figure 5.15.

3. Name your image with the `.stn` extension and click Save to save it to disk.

4. The LizardTech demo screen appears, as shown in Figure 5.16. This screen tells you how many demo uses you have left before your demo license expires. In all, the demo allows you to open or save files 20 times. Click this screen to continue.

Figure 5.16

The LizardTech opening screen shows the number of remaining trial uses.

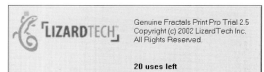

Genuine Fractals Print Pro Trial 2.5
Copyright (c) 2002 LizardTech Inc.
All Rights Reserved.

20 uses left

5. Choose an encoding scheme. As shown in Figure 5.17, your choices are Lossless or Visually Lossless. Lossless takes more space but preserves image quality exactly. Visually Lossless provides more disk-efficient encoding at the price of small changes in your image. Click OK to save your file in Genuine Fractals format.

Figure 5.17

Choose between perfect (lossless) or near perfect (visually lossless) image reproduction.

Enlarge Your Photo

When you save your image using Genuine Fractals PrintPro, it converts your photos into a fractal representation and writes it out to disk. To enlarge your photo, you need to read the

image back from disk. Because Genuine Fractal images are saved without pixels, each time you open a fractal file, you must re-create an image.

Here's how you can open and resize your Genuine Fractal file:

1. From PhotoDeluxe, select File → Open File and double-click the Genuine Fractals file (with an `.stn` extension) that you wish to open.

2. The LizardTech demo screen appears. Click this screen to continue.

Figure 5.18

The options dialog box allows you to set how your new image will be created from the fractal representation. You may use near-arbitrary scaling.

3. The Genuine Fractals PrintPro options dialog box opens, as shown in Figure 5.18. This dialog box allows you to specify the size of the window you wish to open. For this example, in the Scale section at the bottom of the dialog box, set the Width option to 300 percent. The Height scale will automatically update.

4. Click OK. Your image will open in PhotoDeluxe. The new photo will be nine times larger than your original (both the height and width are scaled by a factor of three). As with other PhotoDeluxe operations, a progress bar will appear at the bottom of the window. Watch this bar to estimate the amount of time left to reconstruct your photo. The larger the original photo and the larger the magnification, the more time it will take your computer to create the new image.

5. Save, print, and enjoy your enlarged image.

Figure 5.19

An original photo and the Genuine Fractals PrintPro enlargement

As an example of the results, Figure 5.19 shows an original photo superimposed on the enlargement. Compare the sizes of the images and the excellent quality of the blown-up image. Keep in mind that the original is 700 × 800 pixels.

Enlarging images to excess can adversely affect your computer. Always keep your PC's memory limitations in mind. Ideally, when working with digital images, you should have as much RAM, speed, and hard disk space as you can afford. What makes up the ideal computer darkroom? It's hard to say. However, working with the image shown above regularly crashed my 96MB, 366MHz PC.

Figure 5.20 shows detail from the left eyes of both images above. The original image, zoomed, is on the left. The Genuine Fractal version sits to its right. I've used PhotoDeluxe's built-in resizing to expand the original to the same dimensions as the Genuine Fractals image.

Figure 5.20

Compare the detail between the interpolated original image (left) and the fractal enlargement (right).

When using Genuine Fractals PrintPro, keep in mind that it needs a fairly large picture to start with. When it creates fractals, more data means better enlargements. I've gotten terrific results with my Nikon CoolPix 800, a 1200 × 1600 pixel camera. However, I've also gotten decent enlargements from my Ricoh-2e, with only 768 × 512 pixels. Most people use Genuine Fractals with scanned pictures and negatives, but it works extremely well with digital camera shots, too.

PhotoDeluxe, like many other image-editing programs, uses bicubic interpolation to guess intermediate values between pixels. The fractal results don't need to guess. They build texture from underlying patterns and lack that blocky, zoomed-in look you usually get when enlarging photos.

In This Chapter...

This chapter covered new ways to view digital photos, made possible by postprocessing your images with your computer. Here are some points to remember:

- Panoramas are a great way to see more of the world in expansive and intricate ways. Whether you choose to produce a machine- or hand-stitched version, you'll be delighted by the results.

- People's minds are *wired* for three-dimensional images. The 3D approach makes pictures appear to be more real, interactive, and fleshed out.

- If you have trouble crossing your eyes to see three-dimensional images, consider picking up an inexpensive lorgnette. The little plastic device does all the work for you.

- Lenticular prints offer an innovative way to interact with your digital pictures. It's fun to move your head around and see different viewpoints. They also make great marketing products.

- You don't need to use Genuine Fractals just to create poster-sized versions of your pictures (although, of course, you can). The software works just as well blowing up 4 × 6 or 5 × 7 images to 8 × 10 or 10 × 12 sizes. These larger sizes work well for pictures you want to frame and hang on the wall.

CHAPTER 6

Digital Photo Printing

Your mother was right—you should share. Your digital camera captures great memories. Shouldn't you share them with friends and family? Sure, you could e-mail the digital versions, but a print is something tangible that doesn't require a computer to access. You can frame a print and hang it on a wall, place a print in an album, stick it on a refrigerator, and so forth.

It's easy to turn your digital photos into prints, either at home on your own printer or by using a finishing service. Today's printers offer a range of printing solutions, and many of them offer high-quality output. With only a few steps, you can make memories that really will last a lifetime or beyond.

This chapter covers the following topics:

- **Know your printer**
- **Know your paper**
- **Print your photos**
- **Send your photos to a photo finisher**

Know Your Printer

These days, you can create good-quality prints using your home printer. A home-based printer excels when you want to print just a few pictures at a time and you need rapid turn-around. The prints may not match the quality and durability of those from a photo finisher, but often you don't need those features. You may want to produce a birthday card, a poster, a business proposal, or a school assignment. For these projects, you can save time and energy by using your printer.

Ink-jet printers are the most common for home use, but there are several other types that can handle photo printing. This section provides a quick summary of the main printer styles.

Ink-Jet Printers

Ink-jet printers are today's belles of the ball. These printers provide affordable and convenient printing solutions. You can pick up a high-quality ink-jet system for a very reasonable price. Many stores even bundle an ink-jet printer with a computer purchase. These printers produce good resolution and high-quality colors, and they are easy to use. Over the past few years, ink-jet quality has continued to climb higher. If you were put off by ink-jet quality in the past, look again. Today's printers are much improved.

Ink-jet printers work by squirting colored dyes onto paper. The paper absorbs these quick-drying inks to create your output. Ink-jet printers work well with both black and colored inks. This allows you to mix pictures and text on a single page. You can buy special-quality ink-jet photo paper, which works with your printer's dyes to produce professional-looking, glossy images. By picking the right paper (see the "Know Your Paper" section later in this chapter), you can create masterpieces without ever leaving your home.

On the downside, ink-jet printers have some disadvantages:

- They can be fussy. You must regularly clean their ink nozzles.

- If you print a lot of color pictures, you will need to refill your ink, and refills can be expensive. Ink-jet cartridges often cost as much as $40 each.

- Ink-jets are notoriously slow, although more recent models can zip along nicely.

- Sometimes the paper-advance mechanism creates white lines within your picture.

- When you print a goof, you're stuck with it. You've lost the ink, paper, and the time it took to create that goof.

- Even the best quality output from a "photo-printer" ink-jet will not match the clarity and quality of traditional silver-halide prints—the kind you get when you develop and print film.

You may not want to use an ink-jet printer to create special keepsakes. For all other print jobs, it usually produces satisfactory prints.

Sometimes after running your ink cartridges through a self-clean cycle, they may still seem clogged. You can use cotton swabs to clean the nozzles. Dip the swabs in rubbing alcohol and dab lightly at the nozzles to loosen and clear the ink. Avoid dripping the alcohol, and use care when dabbing.

Dye-Sublimation Printers

Dye-sublimation (dye-sub for short) printers are just starting to infiltrate the consumer market. Although expensive, these printers produce outstanding quality prints. Looking at a photo printed on a dye-sub printer, you might compare it favorably to a picture you see in a magazine.

Many manufacturers have begun to offer consumer-grade dye sub units. For example, Olympus has introduced the P-330 printer, which costs about $500 and produces high-quality 3×5–inch prints. A 60-page replacement kit (paper and ribbon) costs about $50, so you can expect to pay about a dollar a print beyond the initial cost of the printer.

Dye-sub printers work by heating ribbons of colored inks. The melted inks bond with the paper. The higher the heat, the more ink transferred and the more intense the color produced.

Dye-sub printers may produce great quality, but they do have their drawbacks:

- Along with the high cost for the printer itself comes the high cost for its supplies. Keeping your printer in ink can strain the wallet.

- They do not fare well at printing text. You cannot replace your general-function printer with a dye-sub unit. At best, you can use it as a special-purpose second printer.

- Only the most expensive models (over $800) can create full-size (8×10–inch) output. Many dye-sub printers can create only small images.

I own a dye-sublimation printer that is a few years old. It creates 0.75×1.5–inch prints! Of course, today's dye-sub printers work with more standard output sizes, creating 4×6–inch and 8×10–inch prints among other standard sizes.

Laser Printers

You can produce decent black-and-white prints using a laser printer. You probably won't want to frame these prints, but they work very well in school reports and business proposals when you don't need true color.

Laser printers approximate tone by using a technique called *dithering*. Darker areas print using more dots. Lighter areas use fewer dots.

Of course, if you really have the bucks to spend, you can pick up a color laser printer. These cost only a few thousand dollars.

Know Your Paper

Many people think, "paper is paper." They are wrong, at least when it comes to the paper for photo prints. Paper quality affects print quality. Often, the paper you print on can enhance or detract from your images. Today, you can purchase a vast range of paper types.

Plain Paper

Printing on "plain paper" offers both advantages and drawbacks. Paper cost is low; you can pick up a ream for a few dollars. On the other hand, the fibrous nature of the paper means that ink will spread to some degree before drying. The fibers wick the dyes as they are applied. Because of this, you can expect pictures printed on untreated paper to look a little fuzzier than those printed on special, photo-quality paper.

You can improve your plain-paper prints by purchasing bright, heavy stock. When shopping, look for key advertising phrases: Bright White, Brighter White, Heavy Weight, and Premium Grade. Brighter paper improves color quality and trueness. Heavier paper produces stiffer, more durable prints, with fewer curling problems. Avoid cheap, low-weight paper, because eventually the loose fibers can clog your printer.

There's one more tip for plain-paper printing: Purchase high-quality ink-jet paper from the same manufacturer that made your ink-jet printer. Each manufacturer fine-tunes its printer in different ways. You can be sure that each printer is tuned to produce the best results on its companion product.

Glossy Photo Paper

You can pick up ink-jet photographic-quality paper at almost any office supply store. This paper is very stiff (photo weight) and very bright. It is designed to avoid spreading ink and to produce a glossy finish after printing. Prices have dropped significantly over the last year or so, and you can now pick up a hundred sheets for about $10 to $20.

Here are few tips to keep in mind when using photo paper with your ink-jet printer:

Print on the correct side. Print on the slightly rough/slightly glossy side. Although the way that you load paper varies by printer, you can always determine which side receives the ink. Orient the paper so that the photo will be printed on the rougher, glossier side.

Avoid handling the paper. Keep fingerprints off the page, both before and after printing.

Keep your paper dry and cool. Moisture and high temperatures can destroy both your prints and your paper.

Don't mix paper types. I recommend that you insert only one sheet of photo paper in your printer at a time. This avoids some jamming issues and ensures that you print your picture on the correct stock.

Specify your paper Carefully adjust your printing dialog box settings. Make sure to specify a photo-grade paper and the best print quality before printing.

Air-dry your prints. Let your prints air dry, image side up, for about an hour after printing. During that time, avoid touching or breathing on your paper. This allows your colors to set. (Ambient humidity and ink quality will affect drying time.)

Use care when stacking prints. You may stack your dried prints, but insert plain paper between each print. If any ink "bleeds," it will affect the inserts rather than the next print.

Match brands. As with plain paper, you should try to match your photo paper brand to your printer. You can be sure each manufacturer has fine-tuned its printer to work best with its own brand of photo paper.

Avoid sunlight. Photo paper is sensitive to ultraviolet (UV) light. When displaying your pictures, be sure to keep your photo out of direct sunlight and, if possible, use UV-blocking glass for the picture frame.

Special-Purpose Paper

Today, you can purchase an almost unlimited variety of specialty papers. These range from heavy-bond sheets to glossy print-to-the-edge cards. Check the paper section in your local office supply store or craft shop to get an idea of the range of product offerings.

Each package of specialty paper should contain instructions. Read these directions and follow them. They will help you to produce the best results with each paper type.

> If you're printing greeting cards, you can save a lot of money by buying bulk card stock rather than the pre-folded variety. Recently, I visited Wal-Mart and purchased a pack of 10 half-fold card stock (with envelopes) for about $8. At the same visit, I bought a pack of 150 (yes, that's right, 150, but without envelopes) unfolded card stock for $4. I consider 15 times the stock at half the cost to be a nice deal.

Print Your Photos

If you want to print some pictures on your new, expensive specialty paper (or even your cheap, plain paper), but find it's a pain to get the prints to look just right, you can let someone else do the hard work for you. Adobe PhotoDeluxe provides a variety of print styles and layouts. (See Chapter 3, "An Introduction to PhotoDeluxe," for information about using Adobe PhotoDeluxe.) These help you conserve paper while printing one or more images at a time.

Before you begin, here's a tip to help you minimize your risk and conserve your specialty paper: Test print on plain paper before committing to your specialty stock. Sure, this consumes extra ink, but glossy or photo-weight stock usually costs a lot more per print than the ink.

Print One Photo

Okay, we're not talking rocket science here. We're just going to print one copy of a picture on one page. Can it get any simpler?

1. Launch PhotoDeluxe and open your picture.

2. Click the Get & Fix Photo button next to the activity bar. Then click Print → Print Preview. This step allows you to preview how your picture will print before committing it to your printer. You will print everything within the large rectangle. When you finish examining the preview, click OK. You're now ready to print.

Figure 6.1

Make sure to specify the print quality that matches your paper.

3. Click Print → Print. The Print dialog box will appear, as shown in Figure 6.1.

4. Select an output quality for your PhotoDeluxe image. Choose between Draft, Good, Better, and Best. When using specialty print stock, always select Best.

5. Click the Setup button to set your paper type, select between black-and-white and color output, and choose the orientation. Click OK to return to the Print dialog box.

6. Make sure your print options and output quality are set correctly, and then click OK to begin printing.

Make sure to set the correct orientation. Both PhotoDeluxe and your system's Print dialog box will let you choose between landscape or portrait prints. In the Print dialog box, simply click Setup and choose the correct orientation. In PhotoDeluxe, choose File → Page Setup or Get & Fix Photo → Print → Page Setup. Don't waste paper by forgetting this step.

Print Many Photos

PhotoDeluxe allows you to print several copies of a photo on a single page. This both increases your printing efficiency (less wasted paper) and allows you to print on special-purpose stock. Your stock options (okay, forgive me, but it was an obvious pun) include such choices as sheets of labels, business cards, or stickers.

Here's how to print multiple copies on a single page:

1. Launch PhotoDeluxe and open your picture.

2. Click the Get & Fix Photo button next to the activity bar. Then click Print → Print Multiple on a Page. The Print Multiple dialog box will appear. As shown in Figure 6.2, this dialog box presents a preview of your print job, showing the maximum number of images that will fit on your page.

PhotoDeluxe does not resize your images. If you want to fit more items on your page than shown in the Print Multiple dialog box, you'll need to resize the picture to make it smaller first, and then choose Print Multiple on a Page.

Figure 6.2

The Print Multiple dialog box allows you to create many copies of an image on a single page.

3. If you want to print fewer copies than the maximum, reduce the number of copies in either the Copies Across or Copies Down box.

4. PhotoDeluxe assumes you'll print on plain 8.5 × 11-inch paper. To print on another stock size, click the Change button, select your correct paper brand and type, and then click OK.

5. Click the Print button to continue. The Print dialog box will appear. As when you're printing a single copy (described in the previous section), set the options for your print job. Then click OK to begin printing.

After you've printed multiple photo copies on a page, you'll want to cut out the separate prints. See the "Cut Out Your Individual Prints" section for some cutting tips.

Print Standard Sizes

When you print pictures using standard sizes, you can fit them into standard picture frames and photo album pockets. Unlike when you use the Print Multiple on a Page option, PhotoDeluxe's Print Standard Sizes option does not try to use every inch of the page. Instead, you select from a variety of print sheet layouts. These include two 4 × 6-inch prints or a 5 × 7-inch photo surrounded by a bunch of wallet-sized photos. If you've ever ordered pictures from a photo studio, these sheets will look familiar. You also have the option of printing different photos on the same page.

Figure 6.3

With the Print Standard Sizes option, you can print several pictures that are guaranteed to fit into standard frame sizes.

Here's how to print standard sizes:

1. Launch PhotoDeluxe. Click the Get & Fix Photo button next to the activity bar and select Print → Print Standard Sizes. The activity bar will display the steps in the Print Standard Sizes guided activity.

2. Click 1 - Style → Different Photos. (Choose this option even if you decide to use only one photo.)

3. Click 2 - Layout → Choose Layout. Double-click one of the page templates.

4. Click 3 - Add → Open File. Select your first image using the file browser. Click Open to confirm your selection. PhotoDeluxe will add your photo to the first standard print, automatically sizing it. Continue to find and open the file for each print on the page. Your page will look something like the one shown in Figure 6.3.

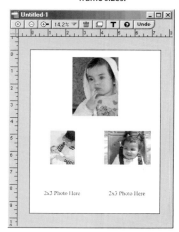

5. Click 4 - Print ➔ Print. The Print dialog box will appear. As when you're printing one or multiple copies, set the options for your print job. Then click OK.

6. Click 5 - Done.

Now you can cut out your standard prints, as described in the next section.

Cut Out Your Individual Prints

Some paper stock arrives perforated, but most doesn't. When you print multiple images on an unperforated page, you'll need to cut it to detach the individual prints. Here are some tips to keep in mind for the best results:

Avoid scissors. Most people cannot cut clean lines using hand-held scissors.

Use a rotary paper cutter. When possible, use a rotary paper cutter. This style of paper cutter creates more uniform and controlled cuts. The other, guillotine-style, paper cutter may rotate a page during cutting and unintentionally cut into your photos.

Delay scrapbook tooling. Use scrapbook tools (such as circular cutters, crimping shears, and so forth) *after* separating the photos. This protects your other pictures from any tool-based errors such as slips and overcuts.

Make full-page cuts first. Determine which cut lines completely bisect your page and perform these cuts before any others. Do not attempt a "halfway" cut. This usually results in overcutting into a picture or torn areas where cuts do not intersect.

Send Your Photos to a Photo Finisher

Did you know that you can make real photos from your digital pictures? Over the past years, many photo finishers have added digital imaging to their product lines. These photos will last as long as "normal" photos, with the same durability, feel, and archival quality. In fact, they really are normal photos.

The photo finishers print your photos on real photo paper (traditional photo-quality silver-halide) and produce pictures that look nearly as good as (or, with sufficient pixels, as good as) 35mm prints. The difference is that instead of printing from negatives, they print using digital projection. Typically, a set of three high-resolution colored lasers draw on photo paper using complementary colors. Then the finisher develops the photo paper using a standard "wet" process.

Choose Your Finisher

You can find any number of digital photo finishers on the Internet. These sites offer many of the most exciting and innovative digital-imaging solutions around. They allow you to upload your pictures and order prints in a wide variety of styles and sizes, but that's not all. Most allow you to arrange your photos, annotate them, store them in albums, and share them with friends as well. Some sites support guest books; others offer slide shows.

Choosing between finishers can be hard. So many offer such wonderful deals and service that you may end up, like me, creating accounts on a dozen or more. Don't be put off by that. With a few exceptions, these sites provide free membership, generous storage allocations, and almost unlimited storage time. Recently, large stores like Wal-Mart have entered the photo-finishing arena. The advantage here is that since these megastores are so ubiquitous, you can just drive over and pick up your order at their store, saving you a bundle on shipping and handling fees.

Expect to pay somewhere between 15 and 75 cents for most 3 × 5-inch and 4 × 6-inch prints. On top of that, add a dollar or two or three for shipping and handling. Always check for specials before submitting your order. Some processors offer bulk discounts, especially when you order multiple prints of the same photo.

The following sections describe the basic types of photo finishers. See the "Field Guide to Online Photo Finishing and Album Sites" appendix for descriptions and contact information for many online photo finishers.

> Print kiosks are a common sight at many convenience stores and drugstores. Some of these kiosks, which operate under many brand names (including Kodak, Fuji, and so on), allow you to print from your digital storage—but at a price. A single print can cost about $7 or more. Contrast this with the 20 to 30 cents you pay for a print from standard labs. You may want to skip the kiosk in favor of online developers or walk-in labs.

Web Finishers

Some former startup companies, such as Ofoto (www.ofoto.com), Shutterfly (www.shutterfly .com) and PhotoAccess (www.photoaccess.com), started their lives on the World Wide Web rather than migrating from existing corporations. They allow you to upload photos and order prints at very competitive pricing. These finishers survived through the great tech-bubble die-off because they provided a necessary service with good pricing and low overhead. In other words, they turned a profit. The best of these companies made their money by providing one main service—digital photo printing—and doing it well. Many of these companies have since been bought out by larger corporate entities. For example, Ofoto is now a subsidiary of Kodak.

Large Development Labs

Some of the most famous 35mm development labs—such as Mystic Color Lab (www. mysticcolorlab.com), MotoPhoto (www.motophoto.com), and Wolf Camera (www.wolfcamera.com)— expanded their services from traditional film to digital in the past few years. These labs uniformly offer excellent print quality, but usually at fairly high prices. They may offer the same sort of services (such as calibration prints for your monitor) as the finishers who were designed from the start as digital labs.

Small Businesses

Some small family businesses, such as ez prints (`www.ezprints.com`), made the leap from traditional printing to digital, from store-based to Web-based. Like Ofoto and Shutterfly, some of these businesses have grown extremely large. For example, until about a year or so ago, you could call ez prints and reach a friendly owner on the other end. Now you must navigate through the corporate halls of voicemail. Still, ez prints remains the geek developer of choice.

Discount Developers

Who would have dreamt a few years ago that Wal-Mart (`www.walmart.com`) and Costco (`www.costco.com`) would provide insanely cheap, good-quality photo prints—sometimes in less than an hour?

You can load your CD-R with a roll of pictures, pop over to Wal-Mart's 1-hour walk-in photo service, and drop off the disc. An hour later, for under 30 cents a print, you'll walk away with excellent silver-halide prints. Wal-Mart stores use state-of-the-art Fuji printing equipment. If you want to, you can save about 7 cents a print by uploading your pictures to `www.walmart.com`. You can choose to pick up your prints at one of the Wal-Mart stores or, for a small charge, have your prints delivered to your door.

Costco offers similar service (partnered with Kodak). I recently printed a few large family photos with Costco and was very satisfied with the results.

Overseas Labs

Some excellent and affordable prints are to be had from labs located overseas. Color Mailer, in particular, is a favorite of many European customers.

Understand Resolution and Aspect Ratio

When you plan to use a photo-finishing service, you must keep two key things in mind: resolution and aspect ratio. The greater your camera's resolution, the better your prints will look and the bigger the prints you can order. The aspect ratio determines how your pictures work with standard print sizes. Before you order your prints, take the time to learn more about resolution and aspect ratio.

Resolution

Your camera's resolution determines how you can choose a proper print size. Often, people order large prints from small images. This is a big mistake. These pictures will look rotten. Small images simply do not contain enough information to create a large print. The print will look blocky and fuzzy. Instead, use Table 6.1 to determine the minimum print size for your images.

As explained in Chapter 2, "Digital Camera Equipment," megapixel cameras capture more than a million picture elements, or pixels, at once. As the pixel count increases, so does the quality of your images and (not coincidentally) the camera price. Inexpensive cameras may capture images as small as 320×240 pixels. Other, very expensive, models might take pictures containing multiple millions of pixels.

This means that if you own a 640×480 camera, you should try to stick to $3.5 \times$ 5-inch prints. If you own a 1280×960 camera, you might order prints in any size up to 8×10 inches. The 8×10-inch print may not look spectacular, but it should hold up to reasonable scrutiny.

In general, you can always select a smaller print size than your image resolution might suggest. In fact, print quality improves as you print smaller, because image density increases. You can see this phenomenon in a 35mm print. Use a magnifying glass to look closely at the print. The closer you look, the more details you see, because 35mm prints have very high image density. It works the same way with digital prints—the higher the image density, the finer the detail and sharpness in your print.

PRINT SIZE (IN INCHES)	MINIMUM SIZE (IN PIXELS)	GOOD SIZE (IN PIXELS)
3.5×5	640×480	800×600
4×6	800×600	1024×768
5×7	1024×768	1280×960
8×10	1280×960	1600×1200
11×14	1600×1200	1712×1368
12×18	1712×1368	2400×3600
16×24	1600×2400	3200×4800
24×36	2400×3600	4800×7200

Table 6.1

Print Size-to-Pixel Resolution Chart

I've recently developed what I like to call "Erica's Photo Print Rule of 100's." When ordering prints, include at least 100 pixels per linear inch of height and width. When printing a 5×7, aim for at least 500×700 pixels. For an 8×10 print, nothing smaller than 800×1000 pixels will print particularly well. Of course, 200 or more pixels per linear inch will produce even better results. Most finishers consider 300 ppi to produce "best" quality prints. Keep in mind that this rule applies primarily to digital photos, rather than scanned images. Always use higher resolutions for scanned sources because of the quality loss introduced by the scanning process.

Aspect Ratios

An aspect ratio is defined by the ratio between your image's width and height. Table 6.2 shows print sizes and their aspect ratios.

PRINT SIZE	ASPECT RATIO	IMAGE SIZE	ASPECT RATIO
3.5 × 5	1:1.43	320 × 240	1:1.33
4 × 6	1:1.50	640 × 480	1:1.33
5 × 7	1:1.40	768 × 512	1:1.50
8 × 10	1:1.25	1024 × 768	1:1.33
11 × 14	1:1.27	1600 × 1200	1:1.33

Sometimes the aspect ratio of a digital image does not exactly match the aspect ratio of a print. When this happens, your picture's proportions will not precisely match those of the printed version. In this case, the photo finisher must choose between two approaches, which are illustrated in Figure 6.4.

First, the finisher can retain the image's aspect ratio by leaving white space on one or both sides of the print. This allows you to cut off the excess paper and return your print to your original aspect ratio. Unfortunately, if you do so, your image may not fit in a standard size frame or photo album insert. Also, be aware that although the excess white space usually appears as a white color, some finishers digitally fill your picture with a black background, so the excess space may appear black. Results will vary by finisher.

Figure 6.4

When aspect ratios do not match, you must choose between adding white space or cropping your picture before developing.

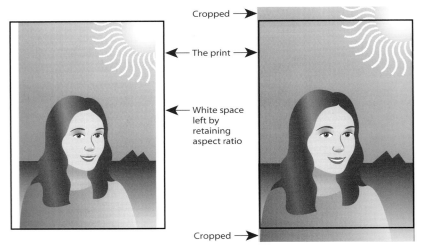

Choice 1: Leaving extra white space

Choice 2: Cropping to match aspect ratio

Second, the finisher can adjust the image's aspect ratio by cropping the top, bottom, or both. This usually works great and produces a pleasing, standard-size picture. Unfortunately, sometimes things can go wrong—photos may arrive with missing heads or feet (or missing ears, when the "top" of a photo in portrait orientation is cropped). Also, by taking this chop-to-fit approach, the finisher changes the underlying composition. Although this method generally produces the most successful prints, sometimes it can create the biggest goofs.

So what can you do? Many photo finishers now allow *you* to choose which method you want to use for your images. By allowing the decision to rest with the customer, they increase satisfaction while limiting unpleasant surprises. If your finisher does not allow you to choose, make sure to determine in advance which method will be used. If you don't like their method, find another finisher.

Another way to avoid problems is to adjust your pictures in advance. PhotoDeluxe allows you to trim your photos to a standard size. With this feature, you control exactly how your pictures will turn out. Say you want to create a 5 × 7-inch print. You can create an image with a 1:1.4 aspect ratio before submitting it to the photo finisher. In this way, you can ensure that the print you order will visually match the image you upload. To size your images, follow the instructions in the "Print Standard Sizes" section earlier in this chapter.

Order Your Prints

The ease and convenience of today's online photo finishing cannot be matched. When you're ready to order your high-quality prints from a photo finisher, just follow these steps:

1. Prepare your photos in PhotoDeluxe (see Chapter 3 for details).

2. Select an online finisher (see the "Field Guide to Online Photo Finishing and Album Sites" appendix for a list of finishers). Determine that the finisher's pricing and delivery methods are satisfactory.

3. Upload your images to the finishing site (upload options are discussed after these steps). Several finishers now offer a variety of finish styles, including matte, glossy, and satin. Before you order, you may want to check if you can request a particular finish.

4. Place your order and wait. Your photos should be delivered within a week.

Did you know you could order your pictures as gift items as well as prints? Most finishers offer photo gift items or have partnered with sites that do. You can order photos on items as diverse as mouse pads, tote bags, T-shirts, license plates, boxer briefs, and ceramic tiles. Be sure to check out the offerings on each finishing site to get some great gift ideas.

Each photo-finishing site provides one or more upload solutions, which vary by finisher. Make sure to determine which works best for you and with your computer. These include the following solutions:

Web page uploads Nearly every site offers a Web page that allows you to upload one or more images at once. Although this provides the most universal solution, this method has many drawbacks. Uploads proceed slowly and without any feedback. You must individually select each image for upload. You cannot use drag and drop. Often, you cannot upload more than five or ten images at once. Sometimes, you cannot determine if your computer is merely busy uploading or has crashed.

Stand-alone applications Most sites now provide Windows-compatible (and, occasionally, Macintosh-compatible) programs that allow you to upload many pictures at once. These programs can run unattended, allowing you to send a large number of pictures without human intervention. Also, many of them allow you to select an upload folder so you don't need to add each photo individually.

Plug-ins Some sites offer Netscape or Microsoft Internet Explorer plug-ins. These expand the capabilities of your Web browser, allowing you to upload one or more images using drag-and-drop techniques. These plug-ins are becoming more and more rare over time.

E-mail upload A few finishing sites allow you to attach your images to e-mail. Just write a letter to the site, attach an image, and send the message. This method is tremendously convenient and avoids problems associated with software compatibility and browser types. In fact, this method opens up photo finishing to WebTV users who might not own a personal computer.

FTP sites Some sites have started to provide upload access through FTP (File Transfer Protocol). While this procedure targets more computer-proficient customers, it offers a number of advantages. You probably won't need to install yet another piece of software on your machine; an FTP program is already built into many operating systems and works with any site that supports FTP transfer. You can use FTP to transfer a large number of pictures at once, with a minimum of interaction. Most FTP programs work happily in the background as you turn your attention to other tasks. Also, this procedure allows Linux users (and users of other nonstandard operating systems) to access sites and purchase prints from finishers who might otherwise not be able to accept their business.

Disks by mail and walk-in Some finishers allow you to stop by a storefront and drop off a disk or send a CD-R or floppy disk by regular mail. Floppy disk acceptance, however, is dropping by the wayside. Some finishers that used to accept floppy disks (containing a Zip or Stuff-It archive of your images) now reject them because better cameras produce larger pictures that, even when zipped, don't fit well or at all on a floppy disk. In contrast, CD acceptance continues to grow. To submit a CD, simply create a CD-R containing your images.

Unless instructed to do otherwise, don't put your pictures into folders or subdirectories. Check ahead and see what image formats are supported by your finisher. Do not submit any pictures or files that your finisher cannot print.

> When submitting your digital photos on a CD, try to keep things simple. Remember that the person receiving and processing your CD is, more likely than not, a part-time high-school student earning minimum wage.

In This Chapter...

This chapter introduced many of the key issues surrounding creating prints from your digital photos. When you're thinking about printing solutions, here are a few issues to keep in mind:

- When you're looking for long-lasting photos for yourself or to share with others, you would be hard-pressed to do better than ordering silver-halide prints. The quality of prints you create at home will never match that of real photos, the way that the commercial prints can. At a cost of a quarter or so a print, you may actually end up saving money.

- Special-purpose paper costs more than ordinary copy paper. Make the most of your investment by printing more than one picture on a page.

- Invest in a rotary cutter. A bad trim wastes paper, ruins a lot of hard work, and can make the photographer cranky. Don't ruin your prints with scissors or swing-blade paper cutters. Rotary cutters are inexpensive and can come in handy for other projects.

- Plan your pictures before you print them. On a regular basis, use PhotoDeluxe (or your favorite image-editing software) to correct the colors and brightness in your image before you print. Use the cropping tools to make sure you print just the right portion of your pictures and that your pictures will match the paper they're printed on, both in size and resolution.

CHAPTER 7

Photos on CDs and DVDs

Storing your pictures on CDs or DVDs can prove advantageous in several ways. It allows you to archive, organize, and share your images in a convenient fashion. CDs and DVDs are lightweight, durable, and portable. A single disc can easily hold hundreds of pictures. But don't let the obvious archival use limit your mindset to creating permanent records. You can do more than simply burn an archive onto a CD-R. Today's technology allows you to create interactive slide shows that you can play back on computers and commercial players.

The most well-known example of commercial offerings, the Kodak Picture CD, provides just a hint of the interactive and archival capabilities now available. New Video on CD (VCD) and DVD-R solutions offer many of the same features as the commercial Kodak product, but with a bonus of easy consumer authoring.

In this chapter, you'll learn how to create computer-based interactive slide shows, picture VCDs, and home-authored DVDs. You'll find step-by-step instructions that explain how to take advantage of the software and technology available for putting your pictures on disc.

This chapter covers the following topics:

- **Create an interactive CD photo album**
- **Create a VCD slide show**
- **Create a DVD-based slide show**

Create an Interactive CD Photo Album

CD-based slide shows allow you to share your pictures with anyone who owns a compatible computer with a built-in CD player. All you need is the proper software, a CD burner, and a collection of great images to share.

PhotoDex's CompuPic Pro (www.photodex.com) offers a picture CD creation tool that allows you to author CD-based photo albums, complete with playback software. Just add your pictures and let CompuPic Pro do the rest. You'll end up with a fully interactive photo CD. You'll find a time-limited demo version of CompuPic Pro on the CD that accompanies this book.

Registered users can freely distribute these photo CDs to friends, family members, and colleagues. This process also creates an Internet-ready set of Web pages that you can upload to your favorite hosting site.

> CompuPic supports only a limited number of burners. Stop by www.photodex.com/support/ faqs/pro_cdr.html to find a list of supported hardware. If your hardware is not supported, skip to the "Create a Picture CD with Unsupported Hardware" section for further instructions.

Create a Picture CD with CompuPic Pro

Creating a CD-based photo album is simple. After installing CompuPic Pro, just follow these steps:

1. Select the files you want to include on the CD, using the file browser on the top-left side of the CompuPic Pro screen. You can use standard Windows selection methods (Ctrl+click and Shift+click) to choose your picture files.

2. After selecting your files, choose Tools → Picture CD → Write Picture CD. This will open the Create Picture CD dialog box, shown in Figure 7.1.

3. For the CD Writer Selection option, CompuPic Pro will show the CD writer it found on your system. (As you can see in Figure 7.1, CompuPic Pro correctly found my sole Sony CD-RW drive.) If you have multiple recording drives, the drop-down list allows you to specify which one you want to use.

Figure 7.1

The Create Picture CD dialog box allows you to set CD-burning options.

4. Specify a CD title in the CD Volume Name (Title) text box. You can leave the default title Photodex_CD or replace it with another title.

5. If desired, change the template directory and image location settings. The template directory points to a picture CD master, with all the autorun and readme files that CompuPic Pro will place on your CD. The image location is used to create a temporary CD image file before burning. I strongly recommend that you leave the defaults for these settings.

6. In the Picture CD Format Options section, check the formatting you want to use for your picture CD:

- Joliet File System (when unchecked, you use the default ISO-9660 standard instead)

- Use Mode 2 (an extended architecture that allows error correction)

- Support Long Filenames (longer than eight characters with a three-character extension)

- No Filename Version Numbers (for ISO-9660 compatibility)

- Close Session (to prevent multiple writes and allow more CD-ROM drives to read your disc)

- Eject When Complete (a convenience option that opens your drive bay after writing your disc)

- Test CD Writer (a feature that tests your disc without writing)

7. After choosing your options, click Create Picture CD. CompuPic Pro will burn your CD, storing your pictures, a photo-viewer program, and an autorun file. This autorun file launches your album when you start your computer with the CD inserted or, when CD notification is turned on, you load your CD into its drive.

After following these steps, you'll have created an interactive picture CD, ready to run on any Windows PC.

Those looking for a more professional playback interface might want to investigate FlipAlbum (www.flipalbum.com). This software allows you to create great-looking interactive albums. The software isn't easy to use, but the results are very good.

Create a Picture CD with Unsupported Hardware

If CompuPic Pro doesn't support your CD burner, you can still use it to prepare your picture CD. Then you can use your own CD-burning software to burn the CD manually.

1. Create a new folder to store your work. I usually create a folder named PictureCD Work within the My Documents folder.

2. Create a subfolder named Pictures. Inside the Pictures folder, create two more folders called THUMB and WEB. This structure mimics exactly how CompuPic Pro creates the folders during its picture CD creation process.

3. Navigate to the CompuPic Pro folder on your disk, typically C:\Program

Figure 7.2

The cdmaster folder contains all the software you need to set up a picture CD.

autorun text file

view16 executable

`Files\CompuPic Pro`. Here, you'll find a cdmaster folder. Open this folder, as shown in Figure 7.2.

4. Copy the autorun text file and view16 executable file to your work folder. Rename the view16 program to **autorun**. (Because the text file and executable are different file types, they have different filename extensions, so you will end up with `autorun.exe` and `autorun.txt`.)

5. Copy your photos to your Pictures folder.

6. Launch CompuPic Pro and use the file browser on the top-left side of the screen to move to your folder. A list of your pictures, complete with thumbnails, will appear in the main window.

7. Scroll through your pictures and make sure they are the ones you want. You can delete pictures or move them to another directory if they don't fit. (Alternatively, you can leave them in place and not select them in step 9.)

   - To move a picture to another directory, drag a picture from the right window to its new location in the file browser (on the top-left side of the screen).

   - To delete a picture from your hard disk, right-click it and select Delete from the pop-up menu.

8. Check the orientation of your pictures. If a picture is oriented incorrectly, either on its side or upside down, select Tools → Lossless Image Modification and choose from the rotation options. You can rotate +90 degrees (a clockwise rotation), –90 degrees (a counter-clockwise rotation), or 180 degrees (to turn an image around). These commands will change your actual files, but they will do so in a lossless way, so your images don't lose any resolution.

9. Shift+click to select all your pictures.

10. Select Internet → Web Page Generator → Create Thumbnail Web Pages. The Create Thumbnail Web Pages dialog box appears.

11. CompuPic Pro creates Web pages at the same time it produces your thumbnails and other files needed for your Picture CD. If you plan to upload these generated Web pages to the Internet, you may pick themes for your thumbnail and main image pages from the drop-down lists on the right side of the dialog box. When you select a theme, CompuPic Pro will preview it for you in the left portion of the dialog box.

12. Select Output options from the drop-down list in the upper-right corner of the dialog box. You need to set the folder locations for the four output types. For each, click the Browse button on the right, navigate to the correct folder, as shown in Figure 7.3, and click Select.

Figure 7.3

Choose a folder to output your images.

- For the thumbnail pages, select your Pictures folder.

- For the thumbnail images, select your THUMB folder.

- For both the image pages and files, select your WEB directory.

13. Deselect the Launch Web Browser When Complete option and click the Create button.

14. Exit CompuPic Pro and test your setup. Double-click the orange Autorun icon and determine if everything has worked correctly.

15. Launch your favorite CD-burning program and start a new data disc. Copy the files from your work folder and burn them onto your CD, as shown in Figure 7.4.

Figure 7.4

Burn your picture CD using your CD-burning program.

Run Your Picture CD Software

After burning your picture CD, you're ready to share it with others or enjoy it yourself. Insert your new CD into your computer's CD drive, and take some time to survey the surprising power of this handy utility that you burned on the CD along with your pictures. Figure 7.5 shows the PhotoDex Photo Viewer that serves as your picture CD interface.

To view the pictures on your CD as a slide show, just click the Slide Show option on the left side of the orange menu bar at the top of the screen. Once the show begins, this menu changes. You can click Slower or Faster to change the playback rate. Choose Stop Slide Show to return to the main menu.

If you want to see a particular picture on the CD, scroll through the image thumbnails on the right side of the main window until you find that picture. Then click it to load it into the main viewing area.

The orange menu bar near the top of the screen allows you to choose from a number of options. Select Print to create a hard copy of your currently selected image. Use the Copy option to copy your selected image to the system clipboard. The Save option allows you to copy the selected image to your hard drive.

The controls on the left side of the Photo Viewer screen allow you to adjust the currently selected picture. Use these to change the brightness, contrast, orientation, and zoom of the image. You can save this adjusted picture to disc by clicking the Save option on the menu bar.

Figure 7.5

The PhotoDex picture CD interface

Upload Your Web Pages to the Internet

As mentioned earlier, CompuPic Pro creates fully functional Web pages when you make your picture CD. You can send these pages to any Internet site. Simply upload the contents of your Pictures folder. Use `index.html`, found in the Pictures folder, as your main page.

> Many other image-cataloging programs, most notably Cerious ThumbsPlus (`www.cerious.com`), offer Web-page-generation capabilities.

Create a VCD Slide Show

Video CDs (VCDs) offer a novel way for you to share and present your digital images. VCDs store pictures and video data on standard CDs that play back in many DVD players. VCDs are small, lightweight, and easy to copy and distribute. By burning your photo albums on VCDs, you can share your images on a television rather than on a computer.

The VCD standard was created by JVC, Philips, Sony, and Matsushita (Panasonic) in 1993 as a way to store MPEG-1 video on CDs. In 1995, the 2.0 (White Book) standard introduced slide show support. While this may seem like ancient history, it's only now that commercial DVD players have made inroads into the United States consumer market, with players now providing VCD playback support.

> VCDs are new to the United States, but not to the world at large. VCDs are extremely popular in southeast Asia, where you can even buy stand-alone VCD players. In fact, VCDs have almost entirely replaced the videotape for movie rentals and sales in some countries.

Check Your DVD Player's VCD Support

VCD compatibility with any DVD unit is determined by two factors: format and media type. Of these two, format is the easiest to predict. It's on the box. If it says "VCD support," your player probably has it. Media type is another story. That's often a matter for trial, error, and a lot of experimentation. Some players accept CD-R blanks. Most accept CD-RWs (recordable and rewritable CDs). Stop by the informative VCD Help site (`www.vcdhelp.com`) to look up your player and see which formats and media types it supports.

If you can, start with CD-RW blanks. CD-RW blanks play back on more DVD players and you can experiment more, without throwing out discs, until you perfect your VCD-burning technique. I found it took quite a few tries before I got my VCD slide shows to work just right. By using CD-RWs, I saved some grief and minimized environmental impact from my discards.

DVD players use red 635- or 650-nanometer (nm) lasers to play back DVD movies. CD-Rs and CD-RWs weren't designed for lasers of these frequencies. CD drives on your computer use a 780nm infrared laser. The organic CD-R dyes and CD-RW compounds, designed to reflect 780nm light, might not reflect sufficient 635nm or 650nm light to create a clear signal. To fix this, some DVD players use two lasers to support VCD.

Prepare Your Pictures for VCD Burning

VCD playback works best with properly sized images. Where possible, batch size your images in advance and do not rely on your DVD player to do the work for you. Table 7.1 shows the ideal size, in pixels, for your images. You'll find frame sizes for both standard VCD and super VCD (SVCD). Many image cataloging and conversion programs, such as CompuPic Pro (www.photodex.com), Graphic Converter (www.lemkesoft.com), and ThumbsPlus (www.cerious.com) offer batch-resizing functions.

Table 7.1

Image Size for VCD Playback

VCD	NORMAL QUALITY (PIXELS)	HIGH QUALITY (PIXELS)
NTSC	352 × 240	704 × 480
PAL	352 × 288	704 × 576
SVCD		
NTSC	480 × 480	704 × 480
PAL	480 × 576	704 × 576

In my experience, smaller works better than larger. My 1600 × 1200-pixel images crashed zmy DVD player. Although they were less than ideal, 320 × 240-pixel images worked fine. I achieved the highest (subjective) image quality when using 704 × 480-pixel pictures.

The Usenet group rec.video.desktop offers the latest and most informative discussions about all sorts of video editing and VCD burning topics. You can search this group by using Google's Usenet search engine (http://groups.google.com).

Use Nero 5.5 to Create a Slide Show

Nero 5.5 (www.nero.com) offers one of the most powerful and flexible CD-burning packages available on the market today. Among its other functions, it allows you to quickly and easily create a photo VCD that can play back on many DVD players. Most important, the VCD playback is reliable. The VCDs created by Nero have proven more consistent in conforming to the White Book standard than VCDs created by any other general-purpose CD-burning software. Stop by the Nero Web site to download a 30-day demo version.

Follow these steps to create and burn your own VCD slide show with Nero.

1. Launch Nero 5.5 and wait for the Nero Wizard to appear. Select Compile a New CD and click Next. Choose Other CD Formats and click Next. Select Video CD and click Next. Then click Finish.

2. Use the file browser on the right side of the Nero window to navigate to your images. Drag your images onto the left portion of the screen and add them to your slide show.

3. By default, Nero adds an infinite pause after each image. This means that your slide show cannot advance until you press the Next Chapter button on your remote control. You can change this, if you wish, to allow the slide show to advance on its own. To do so, select one or all of the images and then double-click a selected image. The video properties window will appear. Select Seconds from the Pause drop-down list and enter a number, such as 15, into the text field. Click OK to continue. Figure 7.6 shows a Nero VCD slide show, ready to be burned to disc. (Notice the precalculated image sizes that correspond to the sizes suggested above.)

4. Select File → Compilation Info. This will bring up the Info dialog box, where you can perform some fine-tuning.

5. Click the Video CD tab. Make sure the encoding resolution is set correctly. My version always defaults to PAL. I live in the United States, so I change this to NTSC.

6. Click the Menu tab. You can add a menu to your VCD to show thumbnails of the first 99 items in your slide show. (You may add more than 99 items to the show itself, but you cannot create a more detailed menu.) To add a menu, select the Enable Menu check box. Choose a layout from the Layout drop-down list. (The layouts represent various ways you can structure your interactive menus; I like the 9 and 12 thumbnail layouts in particular.) If desired, add a background picture and titles for the header and footer.

7. Click the ISO tab. I find that my discs work best when I select ISO level 1, with the DOS character set. I deselect Joliet and the two path options.

8. Click the Label tab. Enter any volume name you desire. Since I use these discs in my DVD player rather than a PC, I usually stick to the default name.

9. Click the Burn tab. When I burn my VCDs, I choose the Simulation and Write options from the top set. Because I own an older burner, I keep my writing speed slow, to prevent buffer underruns.

10. Click OK to save your options and close the dialog box.

11. Click the "burning disk" icon to open the Nero Wizard Burn CD dialog box, as shown in Figure 7.7. Choose either Test and Burn or Burn, and then click the Burn button to create your VCD.

Figure 7.6

A Nero VCD slide show ready for burning. All the images have been added in order and the image pauses set.

Figure 7.7

The Nero Wizard lets you set write speed and other options when you're ready to burn.

If you wish to burn additional copies of your CD at a later time, you can save either a compilation file, which contains all the filenames and settings, or an image file, which is a binary image of the CD contents.

Create a DVD-based Slide Show

Ulead DVD PictureShow (www.ulead.com) is an inexpensive utility whose job is to create interactive slide shows. Because this program focuses on one job, it does it thoroughly and well. With the PictureShow software, you can design your slide show and then burn it to either a CD (for VCD) or, if you own a DVD recordable drive, to a DVD-R. You'll find a demo version of DVD PictureShow on the CD that accompanies this book.

Burn a Slide Show with DVD PictureShow

DVD PictureShow uses a wizard-based approach to design. A series of interactive windows allows you to instruct the program how you wish to organize and present your images. Unlike when you're creating your slide show with Nero, you do not need to preprocess your images for PictureShow in any way. The software knows how to resize your pictures for you.

Follow these steps to build either a DVD or VCD slide show:

1. Install Ulead DVD PictureShow on your Windows computer and then launch the program.

2. The opening screen asks you to choose between VCD 2.0 format and DVD. Select either option and click Next. In the screenshots for this example, I'm actually creating a VCD because I do not own a PC DVD burner. If you're building a DVD, there's no difference in method. The following steps are identical for DVD and VCD creation. The only difference occurs when you're ready to burn your disc.

3. Choose Images from File from the image source drop-down list in the upper-left corner of the Create Slideshow window. If you've never used the program before, this is the default option. It allows you to select a new collection of pictures from your computer.

4. Click Add Slideshow. PictureShow launches a new Create Slideshow window, as shown in Figure 7.8.

5. Use the file browser on the top left to navigate to the folder where your pictures are stored. Select the images you wish to add (use Shift+click or Ctrl+click to add more than one image at a time) and click the Add Image button. Alternatively, click the Add All button to add the entire image contents of the folder at once. The images you've added appear in the strip at the bottom of the Create Slideshow window.

6. If necessary, adjust picture ordering and orientation.

- To reorder your slides inline, drag them to a new position on the image strip. Alternatively, click the Arrange button to bring up the Change Order window.

- If your images are incorrectly oriented, click one of the rotate buttons (90 degrees left or 90 degrees right) on the top right above the image strip.

- To remove a slide, select it and click the remove image button (the one with an X) on the top right above the image strip.

7. Set a delay time, in seconds, in the Delay Time text box. This sets the number of seconds that occurs between each slide presentation. The default is 5 seconds, but you may wish to increase this for more viewing time or decrease it for a faster show.

8. Click the Slideshow Title button and enter a title for your show. To add new lines, press Ctrl+Enter. (Just pressing Enter is the same as finishing and clicking OK). After you've entered your title, click OK.

9. If desired, click the Background Music button and choose to select music for this slide show. Navigate to your favorite MP3 or WAV file, select it, and click Open. (MP3 and WAV files automatically loop during playback.)

10. After setting all your options, click the play button (with the right-pointing arrow) on the top right above the image strip to preview your slide show. Click the stop button (same position) to stop the playback.

Figure 7.8

The Create Slideshow window allows you to build a slide show from pictures on your computer.

The Navigation pane

Picture selection area

Slideshow controls (title, music, and delay)

Image strip

11. Make any further changes needed to perfect your slide show, and then click Done. DVD PictureShow returns to the original window, adding your slide show to the list of already created shows. Repeat steps 4 through 10 to add more shows to your disk. With this software, you can add up to 99 shows (each holding 99 pictures). Figure 7.9 shows how the window might look after adding two slide shows.

12. After adding all your slide shows, click Next.

13. The next stage of creating your slide show involves selecting a menu template. Choose one of the project templates from the Project Template list on the right side of the screen, as shown in Figure 7.10. A drop-down list at the top of this section allows you to choose themes from the Business, Classic, Cool, Cute, and Romance collections.

14. If desired, add music to the background of this menu page by clicking the Background Music button, just as you did for your slide shown in step 9. When you've finished choosing a background theme and music, click Next.

15. Ulead shows you a full preview of your interactive slide show, as shown in Figure 7.11. Use the remote control to navigate through your menus and shows. To finish, click Next.

Figure 7.9

DVD PictureShow with two slide shows added

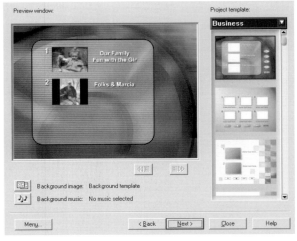

Figure 7.10

DVD PictureShow allows you to select from a large collection of menu themes.

16. An output and burn settings window appears, as shown in Figure 7.12 (with options for my Sony CD-RW burner). The options will vary depending on your burner. Set the burn speed and other options as desired. Then click Next.

17. Click Create DVD (or Create VCD if you're burning a VCD) and wait for DVD Picture-Show to burn your disc. This may take several minutes, depending on the amount of information to write and the burn speed you selected in the previous step.

18. After burning, DVD PictureShow reports that the operation was successfully completed. Click OK to dismiss the report, and then click Close to close the project.

After following these steps, you will have created a DVD or VCD slide show that you can play back and enjoy for years.

Show Your Slide Show in Your DVD Player

Play back your new DVD as you normally would. To play a VCD, insert it in your DVD player, just as you would a DVD. In general, unlike DVDs, VCDs will not automatically start play-back. You'll probably need to press the play button to begin. You can stop playback at any time, using your DVD player's stop button.

After your first picture loads, you can manage playback using your remote control. If you've entered a delay for each image, you won't need to use the remote control once play-back begins. After the number of seconds that you specified when you created the slide show, it will automatically progress to the next image.

Figure 7.11

Navigate through the slide show preview with the virtual remote control.

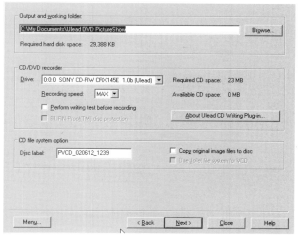

Figure 7.12

Set options for your burn.

In This Chapter...

This chapter discussed how you can use a variety of pictures-on-disc solutions to organize and share your images. Here are a few key points to keep in mind:

- When deciding whether to share your pictures on normal CDs or on VCDs or DVDs, consider the equipment limitations of your prospective viewer. More people own Windows-based computers with CD drives than own DVD-set top players.

- Make sure to stop by `www.vcdhelp.com` to determine if your DVD player can play back VCDs and DVD-Rs.

- Authoring VCDs and CD-based slide shows these days is incredibly cheap. CD-R blanks often sell for just pennies.

- No matter which medium you use to share your images, make sure to correct the image orientation before you burn your CD or DVD. Nothing is more annoying than finding a picture on its side or upside down in the middle of a slide show.

- Don't be afraid to make mistakes. CD-RWs are made for reburning. Although they cost a little more, they allow you to feel more environmentally aware and responsible as you reuse them. Many DVD burners now support DVD-R and DVD-RW formats, which allow you to reuse your discs, just as with CD-RW technology.

CHAPTER 8

Share Your Pictures

It has been well-documented: Today's global society isolates too many of us. Do you sometimes miss your friends and family? Do you wish you could share your pictures with them, even when you're hundreds or thousands of miles apart? Well, there are a lot of new and exciting ways to do so. VHS tapes are just the beginning.

The Internet adds new alternatives to picture sharing. With e-mail, Web pages, and innovative solutions like the Internet-ready Ceiva frame, friends, family, and colleagues from all over the world can experience your digital photographs. The new Internet technologies have done an amazing thing: They allow people to share words and experiences, regardless of their location or time zone.

This chapter covers the following topics:

- **Use your camera's video-out port**
- **Use your computer's TV-out port for screen mirroring**
- **E-mail your pictures**
- **Create streaming video**
- **Protect your pictures**
- **Use Ceiva picture frames to share with the PC-less**

Use Your Camera's Video-Out Port

If your camera offers a video-out port, you can use it in two very interesting ways. First, you can hook it up to a VCR. This allows you to become a moviemaker, recording your playback on tape and creating a video record of your pictures. (If your camera doesn't have a video-out port but your computer has a TV-out port, you can make videos as described in the "Use Your Computer's TV-Out Port" section later in this chapter.) Second, if you're a WebTV owner, you can use your camera's video-out port to take advantage of WebTV's photo e-mail capabilities.

Create Videos

Digital cameras can make terrific videos. Just hook up your digital camera to your VCR and record your images on videotape. You can send this tape to anyone who has access to a VCR (no need for a computer), and they'll be able to watch it. Many people can watch the video at once for that "whole family" experience.

When you make your video, you can easily mix live action with your digital camera still shots. You might also want to add music to enhance the image-montage effect.

When I make a video, I just hook up the digital camera to the video-in port and connect a nice album to the audio-in port. Then, with the camera captions turned off and VCR recording turned on, I present a slide show paced to the music. When I'm finished, I pop out the tape, and it's ready to send to the grandparents.

> Recently, out-of-town guests visited for a long weekend, during which I snapped a fair number of shots on my digital camera. The last night of their visit, I pulled out the camera, hooked it up to the VCR, and played back a slide show (with music) for our departing friends. Unknown to them, I simultaneously recorded this on the VCR. When they left, they happily took a copy of the tape as a lasting souvenir of our time together.

Follow these steps to make a video:

1. Load your images into your camera via card (such as compact flash or smart media) or cable (such as serial or USB).

2. Place a fresh tape in your VCR and set the VCR to Short Play (SP). This setting provides high-quality recording and playback for up to two hours, usually. I recommend that you select Short Play for all your image slide shows.

3. Connect your camera's video-out port to your VCR's video-in port, usually a yellow-colored RCA jack. You may use any cables supported by both your VCR and camera. The connection type varies by model.

4. Connect your sound device, such as cassette player or CD player, to your VCR's audio-in port or ports. Newer VCRs provide stereo recording, but older VCRs do not. Check the back of the VCR, looking for a pair of RCA jacks with red and white coloring. When in doubt, use the white RCA cord to connect for mono recordings.

5. Turn the volume up on your sound device. A higher volume works better because it provides a clearer audio track and allows your viewers to adjust down the playback volume on their television sets. (Do not, however, turn up the volume so loud that it distorts the audio.)

6. Before proceeding, test your playback. Make sure the camera is connected correctly and you can see your images on a television connected to your VCR. Power on your sound source and make sure you can hear it through the television.

7. Set your camera to the first picture in your slide show.

8. Turn off captions on your camera. This function varies by manufacturer, but usually involves a "display" option in a menu or a special button. For instance, I press the "monitor" button once on my Nikon 800 to turn captions off.

9. Begin playback of your audio source.

10. Press Record on the VCR.

11. Slowly cycle through your camera's images. You may wish to use the second hand on a watch or count the seconds to yourself to time the playback for each image.

12. Optionally, when the slide show finishes, turn down the volume on your sound system to provide an audio fade-out effect.

13. Press the Stop button on your VCR, or if you plan to add to the videotape, press the Pause button.

See Chapter 9, "Digital Camera Versatility," for details about creating business presentations and using slides with your digital camera.

Here are some additional tips for making good videos:

Go slow. People want time to really look at each picture before the next one appears. Display each shot for 10 to 20 seconds.

Follow the music. Let the rhythm tell you when to advance your image playback. The closer you match your pictures to the beat, the more professional the video will seem to the audience.

Get rid of bad pictures before you tape. Omit obvious flubs such as shots with closed eyes, embarrassingly bad poses, and so forth.

Keep as many "in between" shots as you can. These include views of people's backs, faces turning away, people getting ready to pose, or a group breaking up after the formal pose. These types of shots provide great transition material between posed shots and add to the total story.

Send Photos Via WebTV E-mail

If your digital camera provides a video-out port, you can send your photos by WebTV e-mail. Here's how:

1. Connect your camera to WebTV's digital video-in port. (You must be using WebTV Plus; WebTV Classic does not support this feature.)
2. Compose a new e-mail message by selecting Write from your Mail List screen.
3. While writing your message, move the yellow box to Photo and press Return.

Make sure to turn off your captions and photo numbering before sending your pictures by e-mail. Otherwise, these features will overlay your images and detract from them.

4. Select Video from the TV/Video toggle on the lower-left side of the video-capture screen. Move the yellow box to Video and press Return.
5. Make sure your camera is on and connected correctly. Your photo should display on your WebTV unit. If your unit says, "No video signal," check both your power and connections.
6. Select the Freeze button. Move the yellow box to the button and press Return.
7. Add your image to your e-mail. Move the yellow box to Add to Message and press Return.
8. Send your message as you normally would.

Use Your Computer's TV-Out Port for Screen Mirroring

Many newer computer video cards include TV-out ports. These cards allow you to use a television as your monitor or hook up a VCR and record your screen. This way, you can create a computer-based slide show and record it directly to a VCR. Your video card will create the television signal, making adjustments for screen size as needed. This provides an excellent way to create a video slide show when your camera does not offer a video-out port.

Video cards with TV-out ports cost about $30 or more. Stop by About.com's peripherals list (http://peripherals.about.com/cs/vidcaptvvendor/index.htm?once=true&) for a fairly complete list of video-card vendors.

To create your video, you will need an image program that handles slide shows. There are many available, but my favorites include CompuPic Pro (www.photodex.com) for the PC, which is included on the CD that accompanies this book, and Graphic Converter (www.lemkesoft.com) for the Macintosh.

Follow these steps to use a TV-out port to record your slide show:

1. Connect your VCR to your TV-out port. You can use any cables supported by both your VCR and video card—coaxial cable, RCA plugs, or S-Video. The connection type varies by model.

2. Place a fresh tape in your VCR and set the VCR to Short Play (SP). This setting provides high-quality recording and playback for up to two hours. I recommend that you select Short Play for all your image slide shows.

3. Load your pictures into your slide show software.

4. Before proceeding, test your playback. Make sure you know how to start the full-screen slide show feature of your software.

> Be careful when you're recording. You may accidentally record computer artifacts, such as menus and your cursor. When you record too early, you'll capture screen shots before the playback. Instead, start recording just as full-screen slide show begins.

5. Press Record on the VCR.

6. Begin playback (preferably full screen) on your computer.

7. Wait for your slide show to play out, as the VCR records.

8. When the slide show finishes, press the Stop button on your VCR, or if you plan to add more to the videotape, press the Pause button.

SCREEN MIRRORING WITHOUT A TV-OUT PORT

In theory, you can mirror to a television by hooking up a low-cost USB-based video-out device to your computer. These devices are, however, notoriously slow and not recommended. A normal USB cable (pre-USB 2) cannot transmit sufficient bandwidth to create good-quality video. One unit I tested tended to hang for a second in the middle of every other slide. This caused an odd and unpleasant presentation, with half of the new slide on top and half the old slide on the bottom.

If you really want to mirror your entire television and do not own a TV-out port, use a scan converter instead. Scan converters transform the signal that normally gets sent to a monitor into a television signal instead. They run about $100 and are available at most computer retailers.

E-mail Your Pictures

Sharing images by e-mail offers the best and most immediate way to enjoy pictures over long distance. Most people are quite adept at the mechanics of attaching a digital photo to an e-mail missive. However, one essential point to keep in mind is that pictures (and all other types of attachments, for that matter) occupy precious space. Most people have a limited amount of space available to them in their mailbox. Additionally, many people still access the Internet without broadband connections. It's not courteous to send large files over your friend's slow phone line. Here, we'll look at some ways to keep your pictures compact, as well as an efficient method for preparing your images for e-mailing.

Reduce Image Size

When size is everything, method counts. My dad recently bought a 1-megapixel camera that snaps photos using the uncompressed BMP standard. Every now and then, a huge 2MB picture (the image uses more than one byte per pixel) arrives in my mailbox. This is not a big problem for me, but it could be a very large problem for people with limited bandwidth and mailbox space. Here are some tips that will help you better compress your images and reduce the overall size of your attachments:

Downsize the pixels. Avoid sending large images by e-mail. I personally never share images larger than 640 × 480 pixels. There are many programs that allow you to resize your pictures to a maximum size that you specify. Use these utilities to create small-sized, e-mailable photos that won't overwhelm your viewer's screen. The next section discusses some programs that convert images in batches.

Pick a good format. When sending e-mail, avoid BMP and TIFF images in favor of a compressed format like JPEG. JPEG is nearly universally readable and offers excellent compression options.

Archive your image. When you cannot avoid sending a BMP or uncompressed TIFF image, compress your image with an archive program such as WinZip or StuffIt. This allows you to shrink your images considerably without losing quality on the other end.

Compress without fear. Do not hesitate to compress your images. I typically compress my JPEG pictures down to 40 percent quality before e-mailing them. This can reduce their total size by as much as 80 or 90 percent. In my JPEG compression program, 40 percent corresponds to medium-quality images, which are fine for e-mailing. I don't expect my friends, colleagues, and relatives to blow up these images to look for fine detail. Because of that, I can get away with high compression without losing viewability.

Preview your images. Inspect your images before you e-mail them. Make sure that the compression does not make your images unviewable. Many programs allow you to preview the image as you choose the compression, so this usually does not require an extra step.

Keep final size in mind. Your friends and colleagues with dial-up Internet service will not thank you for sending 1MB pictures to their mailbox. Try to limit your images to 100KB to 200KB for high-quality pictures.

Batch Convert Images for E-mail

I find that the best way to prepare my images for e-mail is to batch-convert them, an entire "roll" at a time. As discussed in Chapter 2, "Digital Camera Equipment," I archive a low-resolution version of my rolls on the same CD as my untouched originals. This allows me instant access to the versions of my images that are optimized for e-mail. Batch conversion provides a quick (and brainless) approach to having e-mailable images readily available.

There are many programs, some inexpensive or even free, that allow you perform these automated conversions. Here is just a sampling of what's available:

JPEG Optimizer xat.com's JPEG Optimizer (www.xat.com) allows you to prepare JPEG images for e-mail or for the Web. If you're interested in a more professional version, consider xat.com's Image Optimizer software, which offers advanced features with greater control over your compression.

JPEG Wizard Offered by Pegasus Imaging (www.jpegwizard.com), JPEG Wizard comes in both normal and batchable versions. JPEG Wizard takes advantage of Pegasus's proprietary JPEG technology, including regional compression and more.

JPEG Compress Dreamscape Software (www.dreamscapesoftware.com) offers a free utility that now provides batch conversion in addition to its existing compression technology.

JPEG Cruncher Spinwave (www.spinwave.com) offers JPEG Cruncher, a convenient tool that provides batch processing. JPEG Cruncher handles cropping, resizing, and optimization, among other helpful features.

PictureTray PictureTray (www.picturetray.com) allows you to resize multiple pictures at once, and this program is free. Just drag your images into the In tray and set the output size. PictureTray automatically converts your pictures into perfect e-mail–sized versions.

Graphic Converter Macintosh users shouldn't feel left out of the batch converter arena. Lemke-Soft's Graphic Converter (www.lemkesoft.com) does perfect batch conversions and much, much more. This is one of the best shareware products I've ever bought, and I highly recommend it.

E-mailing Tips

Along with keeping your photo attachments as small as possible, here are few other tips for good picture-sending etiquette:

Faces matter. When sending pictures, keep them focused on your main subject. Use Photo-Deluxe or your favorite image editor to crop your images down to just the main subject. In photos, as in writing, conciseness matters. Send only the portion of the image that is of interest to your recipients.

Avoid redundancy. Most photographers snap several shots at a time of a single event. However, people don't gain much from seeing several versions of a single scene. Instead, pick the shot that best communicates the moment and send just that one.

Correct orientation errors. Don't send images that are not correctly oriented. Nothing is more frustrating than viewing an image on its side. Use PhotoDeluxe to fix the orientation before you send your pictures.

Check with the intended recipient before you send. When you're sending images by e-mail to a person you've never sent large attachments to before, it's polite to ask first. Always make sure that your recipient can accept and view images before you send them.

Create Streaming Video

As more and more households hook up to the Internet with high-speed broadband connections, the possibility of sending video over the Internet has become real. With streaming media, you can broadcast your movies to friends, family, customers, and business partners around the world.

Create a Narrated Slide Show with Ulead VideoStudio

If you happen to own a copy of Ulead VideoStudio (www.ulead.com), you can quickly and easily create a streaming slide show with narration. While other video editors offer slide show capabilities, VideoStudio stands apart with its ability to integrate narration over slides as they play back. Figure 8.1 shows VideoStudio's main window.

Figure 8.1

Ulead VideoStudio's main window

Follow these steps to create your narrated slide show with Ulead VideoStudio:

1. Launch VideoStudio and click the New Project icon in the upper-left corner of the window (shown in Figure 8.2).

2. Navigate to where you wish to save your work and enter a name for your project, such as **SlideShow**. You may also add a subject and a description. Select AVI 720× 480 DV NTSC from the Available Project Templates drop-down list and click OK.

3. Select the Storyboard step.

4. Click the Insert Media Files button in the lower-left portion of the window (shown in Figure 8.3) and choose Add Image from the pop-up menu that appears.

5. Choose your slide duration and enter it in the fields at the bottom of the Add Image dialog box. This value defaults to 3 seconds. I prefer longer delays of 5, 10, or even 15 seconds for narrated slide shows.

6. Navigate to the folder where you've stored your images. Select all your images at once and click Open. VideoStudio will load your images and add them in order to your movie.

7. Choose the Voice step. Make sure you've attached a microphone to the mic-in port of your computer.

8. Move the video playhead to the very start of your slide show, all the way to the left. The playhead is the green-colored downward arrow found among the time codes, just above the storyboard timeline.

9. Look at the Controls panel. Just under the Record button, you'll find an option called Record with Preview (shown in Figure 8.4). Make sure this option is checked.

10. Click the Record button at the very top of the Controls panel (shown in Figure 8.5).

11. In the Adjust Volume dialog box that appears, use the level meter to make any necessary volume adjustments, as shown in Figure 8.6. Then click the Start button.

12. Start speaking, narrating your pictures. The secret here is to watch the video playback window as you narrate. Discuss what's happening and try to keep an informal, interesting tone. After finishing your narration, click the Record button again to stop recording.

13. If desired, click the Music step and add a music track to your video. (Check your VideoStudio manual for specific instructions on how to do this.) If you plan to exhibit this video to an audience outside your immediate family or on the Internet, make sure to use royalty-free tracks.

14. Select the Finish step and Click the Make a Movie icon in the upper-left corner of the window (shown in Figure 8.7).

Figure 8.2

The New Project icon looks like a folded sheet of paper.

Figure 8.3

The Insert Media Files button looks like a small file folder.

Figure 8.4

The Record with Preview option appears in the Controls panel for the Voice step.

Figure 8.5

Click the Record button to begin recording your voice.

Figure 8.6

The Adjust Volume dialog box sets your recording volume.

15. Select from any of the following four options: High Quality RealVideo, Low Quality RealVideo, High Quality Windows Media, and Low Quality Windows Media. Navigate to where you wish to save your streaming video and click Save.

Share Your Streaming Media over the Internet

Figure 8.7

The Make a Movie icon looks like a reel of film.

For just a few dollars a month, several sites, like PlayStream (`www.playstream.com`) and SpotLife (`www.spotlife.com`), allow you to store and share your streaming video over the Internet. These and other sites provide video hosting for RealVideo, QuickTime, and Windows Media clips.

Each streaming video site varies in its offerings and pricing. Some offer great sign-up deals, so check around before you put your money on the line. Look for a site with generous storage space and *transfer*, which refers to total bandwidth use and is what allows people to view your video. The more people watch it, the more transfer you use. Pick a site that best matches your needs. Most providers allow you to switch between plans if your needs grow beyond the introductory limits.

If you own VideoStudio 5 or newer with the DVD plug-in, you can burn your narrated slideshow to VCD or DVD. See Chapter 7, "Photos on CDs and DVDs," to learn more about VCD and DVD technologies.

Protect Your Pictures

Any picture you snap with your digital camera belongs to you. It's your creation and your expression of how you see the world around you. By default, you own the copyright to your own work and thus have the exclusive right to produce, exhibit, and reproduce that material in print or on the Internet. Only you have the right to change your photos and create what's called a "derivative work" from those photos. All of these rights automatically belong to you and cannot be taken away or forced from you unless you decide to assign those rights to others.

Here, we'll look at some ways that you can protect your pictures. These include marking them with watermarks and using software that prevents reproduction of your images. We'll also discuss a way to protect yourself when you want to publish your pictures: collecting waivers signed by your subjects.

Add Watermarks

It used to be that you could hold up most good-quality paper to the light and reveal faint marks, lettering, and patterns. These elements were known as *watermarks*, and were invented by Italian papermakers around the twelfth or thirteenth century. To create the marks, the papermakers pressed designs over wet pulp. As the paper dried, the marks "disappeared," except when held up to light. These hallmarks worked in much the same way as those you find on silver, porcelain, or other handcrafted products: They identified the maker.

Over time, watermarks have become a crucial part of document security, particularly in the creation of currency. Today, an electronic form of watermarks helps identify ownership and copyright of digital images. You can also add visible watermarks to protect your images.

Electronic Watermarks

Digimarc Corporation (`www.digimarc.com`) offers today's premiere digital watermarking product. Using proprietary technology, a marked image offers instant identification of the true creator. The information is stored directly in the pixels of the image. Most important, it doesn't degrade the quality of your picture. The watermarks are designed to withstand standard image edits, compression, and resizing. Even if someone copies and modifies your image, the watermark should remain to declare the true owner.

To use Digimarc's technology, you sign up for one of three services offered: ImageBridge, ImageBridge Plus, or ImageBridge Pro. Fees vary by the number of images you watermark and the level of service you choose.

After signing up, you'll be assigned a creator identification code to use when watermarking your pictures. This identifier links to an identifying Web page. From there, anyone can view the copyright information associated with an image.

The basic service offers a free trial version that lets you watermark up to 99 pictures per year. The ImageBridge Plus service offers greater Web page customization, allowing you to add more information about yourself and your organization. The ImageBridge Pro service provides full Web customization and greater tracking information. You'll be able to monitor individual transactions and provide image-specific links for information and ordering.

To embed a watermark, you must use a plug-in built into many image-processing and cataloging products. These products include Adobe Photoshop, Cerious ThumbsPlus, Corel PhotoPaint, Extensis Portfolio, Jasc Paintshop Pro, and Ulead PhotoImpact. (Stop by the Digimarc site for a full list.) The embedding function works much the same in each program. The following are instructions for embedding a watermark in Adobe Photoshop. The only difference between these steps and the steps for other programs is the menu where you find the embedding and detection functions.

1. With your image open, select Filter → Digimarc → Embed Watermark.

2. The Embed Watermark dialog box appears, as shown in Figure 8.8. Notice how it's customized to my Digimarc ID (799051). When you register for your service, you'll be assigned a Digimarc ID.

3. Enter the year for the copyright, select the watermark durability, and click OK. Your watermark will be automatically added to your picture.

> The Image Attribute options offer additional communication to people who view your watermark. These options do not change the watermark or make it any more or less robust. Instead, they establish your intention for how the image should be used. Restricted means that you declare a copyright—the image is not in the public domain. Do Not Copy and Adult Content mean exactly what they suggest.

4. Save your picture.

After saving your picture, you may now detect the watermark you created. Just load your picture in Photoshop (or whatever program you used to embed the watermark) and select Filter → Digimarc → Read Watermark to open the Watermark Information dialog box, shown in Figure 8.9.

Click OK if you simply wish to see the creator ID. Otherwise, click Web Lookup to connect to Digimarc's locator service. The copyright and contact information will appear in your Web browser, looking something like Figure 8.10.

Figure 8.8

Photoshop's Embed Watermark dialog box

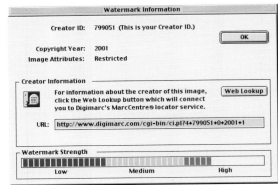

Figure 8.9

Photoshop's Watermark Information dialog box

For an additional fee, Digimarc offers the MarcSpider image-tracking service. This program automatically searches the Web to locate watermarked images. You'll receive regular service reports that indicate the Web sites on which your images were found and provide information about the images, including when they were last modified.

Contact Information
Digimarc ID: 799051 -- Erica Sadun Technical Writing
©2001

Figure 8.10

Digimarc allows you to track down the copyright owner of a marked picture.

Visible Watermarks

Another way to use watermarks involves overlaying your image with a translucent pattern. Photographers who wish to display their work yet protect their originals use this method. You'll find these watermarks on many sites that sell publishing rights, such as news photo services. Users see the picture they wish to use. Then they pay a fee and are given access to the original (without watermarks) for their magazine, newspaper, or other publication.

You can easily create a watermark like this in Photoshop, Photoshop Elements, and other higher-end image-processing programs. Just add a patterned layer over your image and adjust the transparency down to about 25 percent. Your original image will show through clearly, yet it's quite difficult to remove the markings that result. Figure 8.11 shows an example of a watermark added with Photoshop.

Prevent Replication

Alchemedia (`www.alchemedia.com`) offers an innovative way to protect your images. Mirage (formerly called Clever Content) thwarts unauthorized use of digital images by preventing copying, printing, and taking screenshots. This enables you to post your digital pictures on the Web, knowing they're nearly impossible to duplicate. To view a Mirage image, you need a special viewer, which is freely available for download for both PC and Macintosh platforms (`www.alchemedia.com/products/install.html`). Without this viewer, people cannot see your image at all.

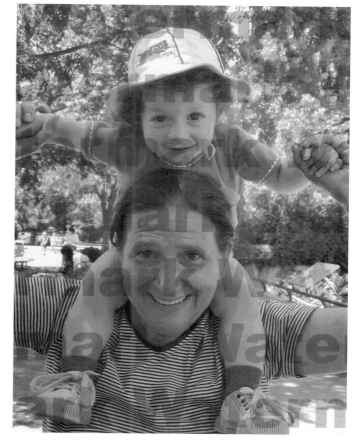

Figure 8.11

Translucent layers allow you to create your own watermarks.

Figure 8.12

When you try to capture a protected Mirage picture, you'll end up with an image that looks like this actual screenshot.

With Mirage, your image automatically hides itself. When someone attempts to duplicate your image, they will copy a logo screen instead, as shown in Figure 8.12. This is an actual screenshot, taken of a screen that contained a normal-looking photograph. When the viewer detects the screenshot function, it covers the image with this pattern until the capture has finished. Then it redisplays the original picture.

Mirage protection is not limited to digital photographs. It can protect text and Adobe PDF files as well.

Obtain Subject Waivers

In general, when you want to publish your pictures in any way, including on the Internet, your subjects should sign a waiver. This allows you to use their image and name, and protects you from lawsuits. Whenever I go out to shoot pictures, I carry a number of blank waivers with me. Subject waiver forms don't need to be complex; in fact, all you really need are the following elements:

Granting the right to use an image and name   The subject gives the photographer (and his or her licensees, successors in interest, legal representatives, and heirs) the irrevocable right to use his or her name and picture.

Approving alterations   The subject must acknowledge that the picture may be altered for any lawful purpose. He or she waives any right to inspect or approve the alterations.

Holding harmless   The subject promises to hold the photographer harmless (except where malice occurs).

Acknowledging copyright   The subject acknowledges that copyright belongs to the photographer. He or she waives any claims based on how the photographer uses or sells the pictures (as long as they're not used for defamation or associated with pornography or other prurient interests).

Binding agreement   The agreement must be binding under a state or the District of Columbia.

Consent for minors   If the subject is a minor, the parent or guardian must sign the release.

Signature   The subject must sign and date the release and provide basic contact information.

COPYRIGHT LAW RESOURCES

While only a lawyer can give you specific details regarding issues pertaining to copyright law, there are a number of important Web sites that you might want to investigate. These include the following:

United States Copyright Home Page The main Library of Congress site (http://lcweb.loc.gov/copyright/).

Copyright Office's Recording and Deposit System From here, you can download forms to fill out, but as of this writing, you cannot submit them electronically (http://lcweb.loc.gov/copyright/cords).

1971 Bern Convention Cornell's coverage of the 1971 Berne Convention treaty to provide international protection to intellectual property (www.law.cornell.edu/treaties/berne/overview.html).

Use Ceiva Picture Frames to Share with the PC-Less

Every now and then, a gadget comes along that makes your heart run fast, your palms sweat, and thoughts of the Tenth Commandment run through your head. The Ceiva Internet-connected picture frame is one of them. With a Ceiva frame, you can share your digital photos with people who don't even own a PC!

You can pick up your own Ceiva for just $99 after a $100 rebate. A one-year service subscription starts at $79. Stop by www.ceiva.com for more information.

The Ceiva looks more or less like any picture frame, as you can see in Figure 8.13, except that it arrives with an A/C adapter and a phone cord. Plug your frame into the appropriate wall jack, and it springs to life, displaying your digital image. You can show just one picture continuously, or present a slide show of up to 20 images. Once a day, the Ceiva dials into a special account and checks for new pictures. When it finds them waiting, it automatically downloads them to your frame and displays them. With a Ceiva, not only can you display your digital images on grandma's nightstand, you can update them from day to day or week to week.

Figure 8.13

The Ceiva picture frame allows you to share and display digital pictures without a computer.

The first night your Ceiva unit is plugged in, it makes a call to a special toll-free number. This helps your frame determine your location and download a local access number that it will use for all further nightly calls. If you travel or change locations frequently, you can use a national, toll-free 800 access number for a monthly fee.

Each Ceiva system actually consists of two parts: a special Web site and the picture frame receiver. The Ceiva Web site stores incoming pictures and allows you to upload new ones. The receiver connects to this site, downloads pictures, and displays them.

The Ceiva unit receives new pictures by "calling home" once a day. It picks an off hour, usually near midnight, and connects to the Ceiva Web site via the phone line. This connection occurs without sound and should not disturb anyone in the house. (If the line is busy, it will try again later.) The unit scans the Web-based inbox. When it finds new pictures waiting, it downloads up to 20 of them. These pictures displace any images already on the unit, transferring them to your "recently removed" outbox. At the same time, your Ceiva also downloads any new settings. Each call lasts approximately 5 to 10 minutes. After the download process concludes, the Ceiva will begin to display the new pictures.

Ceivas make great presents for people who don't own a PC. When you send friends or family a receiver, you can transmit your latest and greatest pictures directly to them. (But remember, you'll be managing their Ceiva Web account yourself.)

Prepare Your Pictures

With a few exceptions, prepare your pictures according to the instructions in Chapter 3, "Introduction to PhotoDeluxe." Here are some tips for getting your pictures ready for the Ceiva frame:

High-contrast images work best. Make sure to select pictures with good contrast. The picture quality on early Ceiva models can best be described as "iffy." The better the contrast, the better your images will appear.

Don't pick large images. Keep in mind that your images should not exceed 640 × 480 pixels. Typically, this works out to about 64KB per image. In no case should you upload any image larger than 3MB.

Use a proper format. Save your images in BMP, JPEG, PICT, PSD, TIFF, or GIF format.

Set Up Your Account

Although Ceiva sets up your account automatically when you establish service, you can bypass the default settings. To accomplish this, use the online Web-based Settings page. For example, this can prove particularly useful when you commute between two homes. My parents live part-time in Florida and part-time in New York. By using the Settings page, they can easily update their location every six months.

I recommend that you set up both the frame and Web site before commencing regular use. I learned this lesson the hard way. My Ceiva arrived configured for California, across the country from my location. (The nice folks at Ceiva set up the account for my publisher, who was located in California.) For the first two weeks, my Ceiva unit made daily long-distance calls. Had I first set it up correctly, I could have avoided a few dollars in long-distance charges. Although I strongly doubt this will happen to you, a few moments of preparation can almost always prevent an unpleasant surprise.

To set up preferences for your Ceiva account, follow these steps:

1. Point your browser at `www.ceiva.com` and log in according to the instructions in your Welcome letter that arrives with your frame.

2. Click Frame Settings. The Settings page will appear.

3. For the Slide Show Interval option, specify the duration between showing each image. You can select from 5 seconds to 1 minute.

4. You can set the Picture Off option to turn off the picture to save energy and keep the room dark. Picture Off times run from 6 P.M. to 2 A.M.. You can also choose Never, to leave the picture on at all times.

5. If you specified a time to turn the picture off, set a Picture On time to specify when to turn the picture back on. You may select from 4 A.M. to 11 A.M..

6. In the Your Phone Number field, make sure you enter your phone number correctly. Your area code will determine the local access number.

7. In the Dialing Prefix field, enter any prefix needed to dial out.

8. Click Update to complete the account setup process.

Post Your Pictures

Your Ceiva frame can hold up to 20 pictures at any time and arrives with 20 "factory-wrapped" images onboard. Most of us have a least one family member who will insist on knowing who "those strange people" are. Side-step the whole issue by preloading 20 pictures of your own.

Here's how to add your pictures to the Ceiva frame:

1. Visit your Ceiva home page at `www.ceiva.com` by logging in to your account. Locate the Send Pictures section and click Send Multiple. (I use this page, which I have bookmarked, to perform all my Ceiva uploads, rather than using the single Send a Picture page.)

2. Choose your Ceiva from the list and click the next (right-arrow) button.

3. Click Browse and select an image from your computer. You can upload just one image or as many as ten at a time.

4. Click Upload My Selections, and then go get a cup of coffee. Uploading images can take a lot of time.

This process adds pictures to your Ceiva inbox. The next time your unit connects, it will download your images from your inbox to your frame.

Manage Your Ceiva

If you're lucky enough to own a Ceiva, you'll find that it offers a lot of extra features for your picture display. You can switch between a slide show and single picture, update pictures at any time, lock your favorite pictures, and more.

Set the Slide Show in Motion

Your Ceiva unit can display either a single picture or a slide show of multiple photos. You can move between these two modes at any time. When you wish to activate the slide show, press and hold the white button for about 5 seconds. Release the white button when you see the message "Let go now to start the slide show."

Update Your Pictures

You never need to wait until tomorrow when you want to see new pictures today. At any time, you can press and hold the white button to tell your frame to check for new pictures. Hold the button for about 10 seconds, until your unit says, "You can let go now, I'm connecting." A progress bar will appear at the bottom of the screen to show how the call proceeds.

Manually Select a Picture

To select a specific picture, tap the white button. At each tap, your Ceiva will advance to the next image. When you select a picture in this manner, you exit the slide show mode.

Adjust Brightness

To adjust the brightness, tap the black button. This button will cycle through the eight levels of brightness supported by your Ceiva. If you push once too often, don't worry—just push another six times, and you're set.

Lock a Picture

Do you have a picture that you absolutely love? You can "lock" it. This allows it to remain on your unit after your Ceiva downloads the next set of images. Here's how you can lock a picture:

1. Point your browser at www.ceiva.com and log in to your Ceiva account.
2. Click Now Showing (under the My Frame section). You'll see a page similar to the one shown in Figure 8.14. From this page, you can lock and unlock photos, send pictures, and remove pictures.
3. Click the arrow buttons to navigate to the picture that you wish to lock.
4. Click the picture you wish to lock, and then click Un/lock to toggle the locking mode.
5. Click Done to complete the process.

Pick an Orientation

You can use your Ceiva in portrait mode as well as landscape mode. Just flip your unit on its side. Of course, you must make sure you rotate your images correctly. Use counter-clockwise rotation, or the frame won't stand up correctly. In PhotoDeluxe, rotate your portraits to the left (see Chapter 3 for information about rotating pictures with PhotoDeluxe). The first time I tried this, I chose the wrong option. My children ended up on their heads.

Whether you decide to upload landscape or (rotated) portrait pictures, be consistent. Once you decide on one or the other, make sure that every picture on your Ceiva has the same orientation, especially when you use the slide show mode.

Figure 8.14

Manage your current pictures with Ceiva's Now Showing Web page.

Use the Buddy System

Did you know that other people could send pictures to your Ceiva? Just add their username to your buddy list. When a buddy sends a picture to your Ceiva, it enters your inbox, just like any other image.

To add a buddy, click Buddy List from your Ceiva home page. Enter your new buddy's Ceiva site username and click Add. Then click Done. If you need to remove a buddy, just select your ex-pal from the buddy list, click Remove, and then click Done.

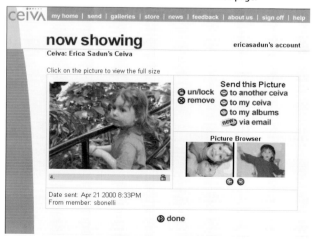

Cool Ceiva Ideas

Although your Ceiva shines at sharing family photos, you can use it in other ways, too. Consider the following ideas:

Greeting cards Send a birthday card to a friend's Ceiva or a Mother's Day card to your mom's Ceiva. Your buddies will feel special when they wake up to see your greeting card on their Ceiva.

Clues Send a series of visual "clues" to your special buddy to hint at a special gift or get-together. Don't forget to label them as "clues."

Invitations Send an invitation for a special night out. In fact, why not send a picture of a dozen roses, too?

Jokes Send a good joke. Combine a picture of yourself laughing with a great pun and upload it to your buddy's inbox.

Reminders Is your buddy forgetful? Why not send a helpful reminder or a grocery list?

Animations Try "animating" your Ceiva. Use your digital camera to take a series of pictures moving closer and closer to your subject. Don't forget to upload the photos in the correct order!

Ceiva Business Uses

You can also use your Ceiva in your business. For under $100 plus service fees, you can place a unit at your point of sale or in your store window. These ideas only begin to suggest how you can showcase your special offerings or services:

- Set up your Ceiva at the front of your restaurant and upload pictures of today's specials.
- Place a Ceiva on your hotel's reception desk and have it cycle through today's weather report, activity schedule, welcome for convention members, and so forth.
- Place a Ceiva in a locker room to demonstrate the stretch-of-the-day and remind your clients to stay hydrated.
- Set up a Ceiva to show off the latest fashions that have just arrived at your store.
- Place a Ceiva at your teller windows and sell "advertising" space to local businesses.

Upcoming Ceiva Features

Ceiva continues to develop and introduce creative sharing solutions. Over the next year or so, look for the following products to debut:

PDAs Soon, you'll be able to share your Ceiva pictures on PDAs, such as the Palm Pilot, as well as electronic frames.

Integrated printing Ceiva is working to integrate your frame with a number of printing solutions. Soon, the company will offer wireless printing to connect with your Ceiva frame. In addition, they've partnered with online photo finishers to create silver-halide prints from your Ceiva images.

Ceiva 2 Watch for the next generation of Ceiva picture frames, offering expanded memory and better picture resolution, to debut sometime in late 2002 or early 2003.

In This Chapter...

This chapter covered many topics related to sharing your pictures with others. Here are some key points to keep in mind:

- When you share your pictures, you allow others to experience part of your life. Pictures do more than just provide visual records. They create a sense of attachment between people who care about each other.

- Whether you use your camera's video-out or your computer's TV-out port, putting your pictures on videotape lets you share them in a way that allows group viewing in a comfortable environment. Gathering around a television to watch a video of family pictures is a wonderful way to enjoy digital images.

- Narrated slide shows offer a terrific medium to showcase your products or business, as well as to create a personal presentation.

- Be courteous when e-mailing pictures. Don't overload mailboxes or modem connections. Use good sense and good compression to lighten the burden of enjoying shared pictures.

- If your business involves digital imagery, make sure you protect your rights and your pictures. Learn more about copyright laws and watermarking to make sure your images are safeguarded.

- Ceiva frames are one of the best Mother's Day or Father's Day presents available. Don't let distance isolate you from relatives. With Ceiva, you create an immediate connection that doesn't require parents or grandparents to turn on a computer to enjoy the family.

CHAPTER 9

Digital Camera Versatility

Who ever said that digital cameras were just for taking pretty pictures? You can use digital cameras for purposes you might never have imagined.

In this chapter, you'll learn to think about your digital camera as a personal extension of yourself. You'll discover ways to bring the camera into your everyday operations. You'll see that you can simply do *more* with your digital camera near you.

The applications suggested in this chapter range from using your camera as a visual aid, to creating business presentations, to protecting yourself against fraud and monetary loss. The examples presented here should give you an idea of just how useful your digital camera can be.

This chapter covers the following topics:

- **See the unseen**
- **Acquire a photographic memory**
- **Communicate with pictures**
- **Give slide presentations**
- **Take notes with your camera**
- **Take your camera shopping**
- **Create records of events and inventories**
- **Play games with your camera**

See the Unseen

Your digital camera allows you to see beyond limits. Have you found that you cannot fit behind a bureau? Do you wish that you had eyes in the back of your head? Let your digital camera come to the rescue. It can help you see things you normally could not. For example, you can finally see a straight-on view of your own ear, as in Figure 9.1.

I am personally incapable of navigating the wobbly ladder that leads to our attic. When I'm searching for a particular box or just want to make a general survey, I send my husband up with the digital camera. By looking at just a few photos, I can tell him exactly what I want and where to find it. No longer do we carry on those insipid conversations. "Which box?" "The brown one, darling." "Which brown box?" "You know, the one with the tape on it, sweetheart." "Which brown box with the tape on it?" Think of your digital camera as a form of marital therapy.

Digital cameras also help when your friend discovers something on your back. "There's something on your back." "What is it?" "I don't know… something." "Does it look bad? Do I have to see a doctor?" "No, it's just a thing." "Well, take it off!" "I'm not sure I should." When your conversation reaches this level of precise description, you'll know that it's time to whip out the digital camera and have your friend take a quick picture of the part in question. (It's usually just a blemish.)

Here are some places you can let your camera do the looking:

Figure 9.1

With a digital camera, you can see your own ear.

Rear views Do you want to know how your hair and dress really look from behind? Don't fuss with mirrors. Set the automatic timer on your camera, pose appropriately, and take a photo of yourself from the rear. Determine for sure if that dress really flatters your figure or if the saleslady is just being kind (and hoping for her commission).

Behind furniture Did you hear something slide down behind the furniture, but you're not sure what it was? You can often use your digital camera to take a downward snapshot (with flash!) at an angle you could never achieve with your head. Use your camera to determine if you've lost another white sock (at least now all the rest are back to being pairs), or if you need to start fishing for your paycheck (how long did they say it would take to reissue it?).

Under furniture Digital cameras do a great job of seeing behind dust ruffles, too. Shoot a flash shot under the bed. See what sort of dust bunnies and third-generation slippers are creating new civilizations in your under-bed netherworld. This method works great for peeking under car seats, too.

New horizons You can open up horizons in other ways, too. Use your digital camera with a magnifying glass, microscope, telescope, or loupe to explore other new worlds. That printed cotton shirt takes on a whole new look under a loupe, as in Figure 9.2.

With instant viewing and no film cost, digital cameras make terrific "take-a-peek" tools for your daily life.

Acquire a Photographic Memory

Who needs to remember when you have a digital camera to remember for you? Your camera expands your personal memory and allows you to recall the most mundane facts without resorting to intensive brainwork.

From the merely informative to the truly treasured, you can snap all sorts of things to remember:

Maps and schedules Has a fixed-in-place map or schedule ever fascinated you? Instead of needing to abandon ready information when your bus or train arrives, snap a photo to study as you travel. Your digital camera can prove an invaluable aid when visiting strange cities and countries.

Parking lot remind e you ever parked at a mall or an airport and forgotten where you left the car? Never for   gain. Take a picture of the section and row sign, as shown in Figure 9.3, and then don'   rry about it. When you're ready to return and look for your car, you'll have the parking   ormation right at hand.

Landmarks for directions Do you need to provide someone with directions to a location, but you're not sure that you remember precisely where the landmarks are? Have a family member or friend drive you to the location from the closest major highway. Take photos of landmarks along the way, and then update your directions to include these pictures. No one will miss the right turnoffs, because they'll recognize them at a glance.

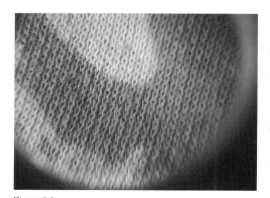

Figure 9.2

A loupe exposes fine detail in a knit cotton shirt.

Figure 9.3

Let your digital camera record your parking location.

Meeting notes Have you ever been to a meeting where you came up with a terrific idea on the white board, but it was one of those old-fashioned boards that didn't make copies? Just pull out your digital camera, snap a photo or two of your notes, and make your copies back at the office. Don't let a good idea go to waste when your camera is on hand.

Shopping lists Are you about to go grocery shopping? Take a quick snapshot of the insides of your pantry and your refrigerator. It can help you remember which items you do and do not have on hand as you're cruising up and down the store aisles.

Where the pieces go Does your child own a toy that looks like (or used to look like) the one shown in Figure 9.4? Before allowing your child to play with a toy with many pieces, take a picture of the box with all the pieces in place. This has saved me many hours of head-scratching and bewilderment when faced with overly complicated toys and poorly labeled boxes.

Fashion help A colleague of mine, away from home for a business trip, snapped a picture of his outfit for "tomorrow." He then e-mailed this photo to his wife, to ask if she thought the shirt went with the trousers. You're never far away from good fashion advice when you own a digital camera.

Figure 9.4

Take a shot of how all the pieces fit in the box.

Last looks Have you ever been to a special place for the last time? Perhaps it will be sold or bulldozed. Maybe you are graduating and moving on, or maybe you're there for a once-in-a-lifetime opportunity. Let your camera capture memories for you.

> Recently, my husband and I visited my mother-in-law's house for the final time after she passed away. We took several photos of the house, in particular the room that my husband grew up in. We knew that we would never again be able to step physically into that spot with the furnishings and memories in place. Instead, we trusted our memories to our handy digital camera so that we could share them with our family and hold onto them for the future.

Communicate with Pictures

Pictures can say a thousand words. This proves especially important when communicating with the preliterate, illiterate, preverbal, and postverbal. Whether dealing with youngsters, stroke patients, foreign nationals, or the senile, a picture can present important information in a way that language cannot. For example, you can use an array of photos on a single display to clearly offer choices to someone, as shown in Figure 9.5.

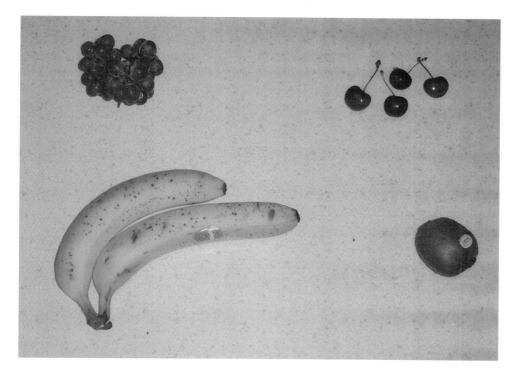

Figure 9.5

Which fruit would you prefer for dessert? When you show photos of the available choices, picking one is as simple as pointing at it.

Digital cameras make it easy to transform everyday objects into visual imagery. Here are some suggestions for successful communication with your photos:

Be concrete Make sure to photograph physical objects or realistic representations. Metaphor and abstractions work poorly in pictorial communication.

Be big Make your pictures large and easy to recognize. Keep physical and optical limitations in mind when snapping your photos.

Be simple Photograph objects on simple backgrounds that do not confuse or overwhelm the subject.

Ignore artistry Communication, not elegance, is the primary motivation for these pictures. Confused tourists will not complain about inartistic snapshots of buses, taxis, and trains when seeking help at an information kiosk. Let your digital camera capture reality exactly as it is.

People pictures are also very helpful for even the most literate and verbal. Mug-shot boards easily allow office visitors to identify department personnel. They're simple to set up, too. Just snap a digital photo of each colleague, add a caption, print it, and pin it onto a bulletin board. These boards really help guests find the person they're looking for without unduly disturbing others.

Give Slide Presentations

With your digital camera or one of the newer digital wallets, you carry a portable presentation tool in your briefcase (or even your pocket). Most people think of digital cameras solely as image-acquisition instruments, without considering their image-display strengths. Most digital cameras can store and present graphs and slides just as easily as they can digitize images. Like personal computers, many digital cameras can connect to a variety of projection devices. Unlike computers, digital cameras and digital wallets are small and light. (See Chapter 2, "Digital Camera Equipment" for information about digital wallets.)

Whether you're on the road or at the office, your digital camera can make giving presentations simple and convenient. If you own a video-capable portable digital storage solution, just follow the included manufacturer's directions. For those of us without portable digital storage solutions, a digital camera alone can often handle the job. This section will describe how.

Are you coordinating a conference or another type of get-together? Don't overlook the photo "Hello My Name Is" badge. Adding digital photos makes it easy for participants to find their own badges. It also allows others time to browse over the badge table and connect names with faces.

Presentation Prerequisites

To give presentations, your digital camera must support both image download and display. Image download involves transferring data from your computer to either the digital camera itself or to its data card. For image display, you need either an LCD screen or a video-out port.

Image Download Support

If you can transfer pictures through a cable or write them onto a memory card and have your camera display them, you're probably set for downloading your presentation images.

Image download by cable is tedious and slow for the most part. In general, this involves hooking up your camera to your computer with a communication cable and downloading pictures one by one using the software included with your camera.

You can bypass the cable download procedure if your camera uses external memory cards or floppy disks. Just insert the cards or disks into your computer and transfer your images directly to these storage media. Make sure to follow your camera's naming protocols. Be aware that some popular digital cameras, such as the Nikon CoolPix series, require special image headers, called EXIF headers. These headers must remain intact and unmodified, just as they were saved by the camera, in order for your camera to "see" them.

Some new PC-based utilities can help you manage your EXIF data. For more information, search for EXIF on Google.com.

Image Display Support

Your camera can support image display in either of two ways: through a built-in LCD monitor or through support for a video-out port. If your camera has either, you can drive a presentation.

LCD monitors provide convenient displays for intimate meetings with one or two others. However, the displays are small, so you'll usually need to pass the camera to each participant for a decent view.

Video-out ports, also called AV or media ports, allow your camera to create a video signal that can be displayed on a television, VCR, projection system, and similar devices. Using the video-out port allows you to present to a much larger audience.

Whichever display solution you choose, it will be energy-intensive. If you intend to give presentations by camera, keep a good supply of power on hand.

Video signals are country dependent. Many cameras support either NTSC or PAL formats, but few support both. That means the camera you use in New York City for a sales presentation may not work with Paris or Rome television sets. The PAL format is used widely in western Europe, Japan, and Australia. Most other countries, including the United States, support NTSC. To paraphrase a government booklet on travel, "Know before you go."

Put Your Presentation Together

Preparing your presentation involves a number of steps:

- Create your show on a personal computer.
- Transfer it to your camera.
- Assemble your presentation materials.
- Practice, practice, practice.

All of these steps can take place before you ever leave your office. Together, they pave the way for smoother and less worrisome presentations.

Create and Transfer Your Slides

Create your slides using your favorite presentation software. Be sure to test your slides fully on your computer before you transfer data. Always assume that transferring the data to your camera will take substantial quantities of time, even when using memory cards. You don't want to do this more than once for your presentation. Adding and reordering slides may involve re-downloading the entire show. An ounce of preparation will save pounds, or at least hours, of downloads.

I like to create my slides in PowerPoint and Excel and save them in JPEG format, which my cameras support. To do this from PowerPoint, I select File → Save As and choose JPEG File Interchange Format (`*.jpg`) from the Save As Type drop-down list. This allows me to save a single slide or an entire presentation as JPEG images. I rename them, copy them to my memory card, and I'm set.

> Do you have several similar but alternative presentations to give? Load each slide show onto a separate memory card. This allows you to choose just the right presentation for each audience while you're on the road.

Create a Checklist

Create a materials checklist to carry with you. This checklist should detail all of the hardware you will need for your presentation. Customize your own presentation "kit," and you will always be ready to go.

The following are some items you might want to include on your checklist:

- A video cable (and, perhaps, an extra one)
- Memory cards containing your presentations
- One or more power sources, such as extra batteries or a power cord

- An extension cord or two
- An alternative presentation (such as transparencies or a PowerPoint show on a floppy) in case of an emergency (like forgetting the last item on this list)
- A laser pointer
- A small, portable television set (with batteries or cord)
- A camera remote control (if available)
- Your digital camera

The contents of a presentation checklist will vary from person to person. Some people may want to travel light; others will want the greater security and reassurance of backup hardware. No matter what your style is, making (and then checking!) a list of needed materials will prevent disaster when you're standing in front of your presentation audience.

> Getting ready to pack? Don't forget your nonphotographic equipment. For example, you might want to bring a laptop computer and a portable printer. These provide you with mass storage, photo editing, communication, and printing capabilities on the road.

Practice!

Practice your presentation in a "safe" environment. You'll be surprised at how many gadgets and buttons there are on your digital camera. The correct power cords and buttons can play hide-and-seek, especially in low-light situations. Practicing with your camera will ensure that you know how to use it for your presentation and will help prevent mishaps.

Make sure to learn how to turn off your camera's image numbering and captions before giving your presentation. Captions—such as the picture number and the time and date the picture was taken—will obscure your pictures and distract your audience. Image numbers cover a large part of the image.

It's surprising how hard it is to gesticulate while holding a digital camera with cords poking out of it in all directions. Your tests may prompt you to use batteries rather than an A/C power cord or encourage you to buy one of the manufacturer's remote-control devices. These free your hands.

Take Notes with Your Camera

Here's a common scenario: You're sitting at a doctor's office reading a magazine, and you come across an item that you want to remember. You consider reaching for your pen and notepad or your PalmPilot to jot it down, but then decide that maybe it isn't worth the effort. Here's where your digital camera can help. Take a picture of that article, quote, Web address, or other item of interest. Let your camera take notes for you. Later, when you're back at the office or at home, use an OCR (Optical Character Recognition) package to recover the text from your photos.

Yes, you can use digital snapshots with OCR. The snapshots will not match the quality of a well-scanned page, but with your digital camera, you can capture a paragraph or two of text.

OCR Test Results

I've tested the OCR method extensively, just to prove it can be done. My goals were to capture one to two paragraphs of text in either a newspaper or a magazine with a hand-held digital camera. I tried to simulate a traveler coming across a particularly interesting article with a few facts or a quote to archive. For my testing, I used a 2.1 megapixel Nikon CoolPix 800 and a copy of Paperport Deluxe 6. Expect to get better results with 3 and 4 megapixel units. After several hours of testing, here's what I found:

Narrow text works better. Newspaper column widths work better than that of magazine formats, such as those used in *Time*, *PC Magazine*, and *Newsweek*. I found it easier to snap close-in photos of a narrow column of newspaper text. Some magazines use whole pages, often spanning from the left to the right margins (this format is typically used for the beginning of articles).

Plain fonts work better. Newspaper fonts prove slightly larger and easier to read than those used in popular magazines. Also, basic text works better with OCR than header material, which usually includes information about the article's author. These headers often use special fonts that OCR software may not understand. Rather than using OCR, you can just look at your photos to recover this information.

Generally, magazine OCR proved a little harder to accomplish because of the small fonts and shiny pages. Newspaper OCR, in contrast, was fairly easy and straightforward.

OCR Tips

Using OCR with your digital camera requires you to master a few techniques. These methods allow you to take clearer and more detailed photos from materials that naturally bend, reflect light, and contain distorting bindings:

- Put your magazine on a table or another flat surface. Do not hold it by hand. Weigh the edges down (you can use a coffee cup) to avoid the natural bend caused by bindings.

- You can hold a newspaper in your hand if you fold it and keep it from bending. However, it, too, may work better on a table.

- Shoot in landscape mode, not portrait. This provides greater pixel coverage for each column. You may need to take extra shots to fully capture the material, but you end up with better source images.

- Hold the camera directly over the center of the text you're capturing. Orient the camera parallel to the page and square to the sides, top, and bottom of the page.

- Magazines are very shiny. Make sure to turn off the flash!

- Try to capture a single paragraph at a time rather than two or three. Less is better when you're working with OCR.

- Don't forget to take a picture of the page number, magazine cover with date, article title, and author name, if you want a complete reference when quoting.

- Turn your camera up to its highest imaging mode. More pixels produce better results.

With good focus, a flat surface, and reasonable lighting, you can easily capture a paragraph or two from a newspaper or magazine for later OCR recovery. I strongly encourage you to experiment with your camera and learn how well it works with this exciting technology.

Take Your Camera Shopping

Whether you're buying or selling, your digital camera can help you. Photos can guide you in making a major purchasing decision. They can also help someone else make the decision to buy one of your possessions.

Comparison Shopping with Your Camera

When you're ready to make an expensive purchase, let your camera do the shopping for you. Slow down and take photos of items before handing over your credit card. Ensure that your choice is the best one possible. Digital images help in several ways. They augment your memory, document an item's condition, and help you build consensus for a purchasing decision.

False Memory

Can you remember exactly what pattern that expensive sofa had? Will it match your curtains and fit into your décor? Take a picture. Then take the image home and compare it directly with the other elements. You've now moved the purchase decision-making process away from the store and into the comfort of your own home.

Like elephants, digital cameras don't forget. They capture important and small details that may sway you one way or another when you leave the showroom floor. And unlike traditional film cameras, you don't need to wait for the film to be processed or pay for prints to be made. Since most digital cameras have built-in LCD screens, you can quickly review your pictures on the spot. The bigger the item you plan to purchase, the more important it becomes to take photos and have them on hand to augment your memory.

For instance, suppose that you're shopping for a new home. You cannot just visit each prospective house on a whim. Make the times you do visit each house count the most by taking a lot of pictures. Then you can review them later. If you're buying a car, you'll improve your negotiating stance if you take pictures and study them rather than returning time and again to the car lot.

Whatever the item, take a lot of pictures. While a single picture will help you remember the general look of the item, the more pictures you take, the more data you will have at hand. Take pictures inside the item and from different vantage points. If you're going to spend money on a big purchase, take the extra time to make sure you have a complete picture—or several complete pictures—of the item you may buy.

Building Consensus

Sharing pictures can help you come to a purchasing decision. Do you need to buy an out-of-state house? Does the sister who has excellent decorating taste live in another city? Do you want to get your friend's opinion before buying that $500 dress? Use digital images to build consensus and draw opinions from a shared pool of expertise.

Unusual Conditions

Use your digital camera to document the condition of an item you are about to purchase. Whether you're shopping for a car, a house, or furniture, once you have settled on a deal, you're entitled to receive the item in the same condition you last saw it. Protect yourself against problems arising from damage or alteration. Here are some examples:

- If furniture arrives with a large new scratch, prove it with pictures.

- If your house contract states that you own all built-in fixtures and the built-in microwave disappears before you move in, a digital image can bring proper compensation for the loss.

- Buying a new boat? You can prove the hull damage occurred after you purchased it (and before you took possession).

The larger the ticket, the more important it becomes to fully inspect and photograph your purchase. This not only protects your investment, but also creates a record trail that you may later need to use for police reports or insurance claims. However, you should be aware that the legal requirements for verifiably unmodified digital pictures are just now becoming established. Consider how easily digital images can be altered and enhanced. You may want to snap a few traditional 35mm pictures instead.

> The United States Department of Justice Web site offers a fuller discussion of the legal issues surrounding the use of digital photography for evidence. Stop by www.usdoj.gov/criminal/cybercrime/search_docs/sect8.htm for additional information.

If you receive damaged goods, take pictures of the carton and the contents to document the situation. Then go directly to the phone and report the damage. Don't just call the store where you bought the item, contact the shipping company, too. Sometimes the delivery service, such as UPS or the post office, is at fault. Each shipper has its own policies for reporting damaged goods, but all of them have one feature in common: They expect you to report the damage immediately! If you cannot arrive at a reasonable accommodation with either the point of sale or the shipper, you may also want to contact your credit card company and contest the charge. No matter which route you take, a digital image taken directly after delivery will help prove your case.

Going Once, Going Twice—Online Auctions and Digital Photos

These days, online auction sites—eBay, Amazon, Yahoo!, and others—are popular. On these auction sites, you can put even the smallest items up for bid and often find a good buyer. You can use your digital camera to engage in selling your excess goods while cleaning up your house and reducing the overall clutter around you.

Most Internet auction sites allow you to include links to pictures of listed items. Take advantage of this opportunity to show your goods to their best advantage. Shoot at least one good, clean picture of your item, showing it in the best possible way. Make sure your image is well illuminated, and let the object fill as much of the frame as you can. The best pictures are the clearest and most depictive ones.

Do not, of course, try to deceive others by covering up flaws, either by taking deceptive photos or editing those photos before uploading them. A good photo will give your purchaser a true view of the condition of the item being offered.

Also, consider taking more than one picture of your lot. You can either post these directly on the auction site or send them to interested parties via e-mail. You may want to take pictures from different angles, show the back as well as the front, or show the object actually being used in different situations. Extra pictures may help to sell your item.

I recommend that you store your auction pictures on a different site than you use for personal ones. For example, if you use Ofoto.com for your family snapshots, consider setting up a Photos.Yahoo.com album for your auction goods. This helps you protect your privacy while allowing others to view your sale items. See the "Field Guide to Online Photo Finishing and Album Sites" appendix for information about Ofoto, Yahoo!, and other sites where you can share your photos.

Create Records of Events and Inventories

Take charge of your property. A digital camera can prove to be a valuable aid when managing moving day, recording an accident, or creating a visual inventory. By creating a visual record, your digital camera helps go beyond lists, descriptions, and other documentation. Instead, you gain better context and instant proof of condition, damage, and more. In this section, you'll see how to use your camera to capture vital visual records.

Moving Day Made Easier

Moving day can prove to be one of the most unpleasant and troubling experiences in a person's life. But your trusty digital camera can help bring a little order into a disordered time. You can use it to create visual inventories and record the condition of your belongings before, during, and after the move. At every stage, your camera can organize, document, and protect your consumer rights.

What's in the Box?

Use your camera to take an inventory of what is in each box. It's always easier to search by looking through pictures than relying on memory or by opening every box. Don't be in the position where you're constantly asking which box some item or another is in. Look through your visual inventory and know right away. Your written inventory might simply say "box of books." Pictures will help you find which box has that all-important cookbook.

> Do not tape your visual inventories to your boxes. It acts as an invitation for theft by advertising the contents. Instead, store your inventories in another location.

Your worst fears may be confirmed when the mover calls and says, "We lost your box, Mrs. Smith. What was in it?" When a box is lost, don't depend on your memory to recall what it contained. Use your pictures to help file insurance claims for missing as well as damaged items.

Hey, Don't Drop That!

If you think your movers are mishandling your possessions, don't hesitate to take out your camera and start taking pictures. At best, the movers will start acting more responsibly. At worst, you'll have valuable evidence of misconduct. And if your boxes arrive at your new location looking as if they've been stomped on, snap a picture, like the one shown in Figure 9.6.

Use your camera to create a record of the conditions of all your belongings. Protect yourself by taking pictures of all your furniture and boxes. When a mover says, "That scratch was there before we moved it," you'll be able to prove that it was not.

Figure 9.6

An actual box from our move to Colorado.

Document Accidents

Taking photos can help enormously in the unpleasant event of an accident. Having personally used my digital camera after I was rear-ended by another car, I can assure you that having pictures is a great help when talking to the insurance agents. (Incidentally, the accident took place just outside my favorite digital camera store.)

Consider these suggestions if you happen to have a camera on hand when an accident occurs:

See the big picture. Take many pictures of the whole accident scene. Capture the positions of the cars. This will help prove who was at fault and protect you against lawsuits.

Take pictures of the participants. Use your camera to document the health and general condition of the other driver and anyone else involved.

Capture document information. Snap a picture of the other driver's license plates, driver's license, and insurance card.

Record damage. Take complete pictures of damage done to the cars involved, as in the example in Figure 9.7. You may also want to take a picture of the VIN plate in the other person's car.

Take pictures of any witnesses. Photograph any people who saw the accident, even if you cannot gather their names and phone numbers. If possible, also capture the license plates of their cars.

Capture dialogue. If your camera has an optional sound-recording feature, this is a great time to use it. Capture the other driver saying, "I'm so sorry. It was all my fault!" before he goes home and changes his mind.

Create an Insurance Inventory

Did you know that your digital camera could help you create a permanent inventory for insurance purposes? You can take pictures of all your possessions and use those images in case of theft, fire, or storm damage.

It's almost impossible to remember what you have stored in each drawer of your house, but a digital camera can remember the important stuff for you. Take your camera for a tour through your house and your belongings. Be sure to cover the following areas:

Drawers Go into every drawer in the house. Even little things cost you money, and you should be covered for them. Consider how much a drawer full of

Figure 9.7

Today's insurance adjusters carry digital cameras to help document auto claims.

socks would cost at the store and multiply that by all the people in your family. Just socks will set you back a bit! Be as thorough as possible and don't forget the closets, toy chests, and storage boxes.

Furnishings Take pictures of the furniture in each room, but also take pictures of your window treatments, ceiling fans, and any other optional extras you have installed in your house. This includes wall treatments and rugs as well.

Garage Don't neglect the garage when performing an inventory of your goods. Take pictures of your lawn mower, bicycles, and even your garden hose. You'll be surprised how many things you keep in your garage.

Outside Take pictures of the home's exterior, including the patio and roof. Make sure to show the condition of any outdoor furniture, awnings, and so forth.

Valuables Take pictures of any keepsakes you have around. You never know when you may lose a valuable piece of jewelry or a precious vase. Use the pictures to help the insurer appraise the true value of your loss. For some precious items, the weight of the item's metal is far less valuable than the craft and skill that went into making it.

Books, CDs, and software Don't forget to photograph shelves of books, CDs, and software. These items are valuable, especially in terms of replacement costs. No matter what sort of collections you have, be sure to take pictures of them.

Once you've created a digital inventory, what do you do with the pictures? My suggestion is to make several copies of your pictures on CD-Rs. If you do not have the CD-burning equipment at your house, you can probably arrange to have it done for a small fee at a local computer store or a friend's house. CDs create a permanent record of your images, invulnerable to magnetic fields. In theory, the life span of a CD should exceed your own.

Store these CDs in a place other than your home. Keep them physically distant enough that damage to your home will not damage the CDs. Put one set in a safe-deposit box. Leave another set at the house of a friend. Just be sure to have more than one copy of your records and to store them in more than one physical location.

Review your possessions with your insurance agent. You might be surprised to discover that you are either over or under insured. Make sure your insurance needs are balanced by the actual value of your house and possessions. Take the time to sit down and discuss your true insurance needs by going through your digital images. You may actually save some money.

Play Games with Your Camera

You've learned about some practical digital camera applications. Now it's time for some fun. Here are some games that you can play with your camera:

Beat the Clock You can use your camera's automatic timer for "beat-the-clock" games. This is probably the silliest of all digital camera tricks. Just set the timer, press the shutter release, and say "Go!" Let the camera be the judge. Determine who built the biggest tower of blocks in the given time, or decide who really had more crackers in their mouths. Your imagination can be your guide.

Scavenger Hunt It's the old classic game, but with a twist. Don't bring a whole lot of junk back to home base; snap pictures of found items instead. Each team gets a list, a digital camera, and then they're off! When time runs out, the team that photographed the most items wins. It's a fun variation of an old-time pleaser.

Catch Me If You Can Have you ever been irritated by your camera's lag time between when you press the shutter release and when the camera actually snaps the photo? You can actually turn this latency into an amusing game. To play, you need a bunch of rambunctious children (family or borrowed kids will do). Set a timer for a minute or two. Say "Go!" and allow the youngsters to run around wildly as you try to snap photos of them. (You may want to play this game outdoors!) After the buzzer sounds, examine the shots you've taken. Any clear photo of a child puts him or her "out" until the next round is over. Incidentally, this game is a terrific way to compare and evaluate cameras for ease of use as well as delay times.

Whose Is That? Here's a fun party game. Take pictures of people's ears, eyes, eyebrows, noses, and so forth. Your guests will guess whose part belongs to whom. Extreme close-up shots may prove harder to identify than you might think. The results can be hilarious, too. Make sure to use a macro lens for close-in photography and carefully label which nose belongs to which person. (It's no fun if after all the guessing, you cannot remember the answer!)

Face Bingo This is one of those icebreaker games that allows near-strangers to meet under the auspices of friendly games. Face bingo works particularly well for large gatherings. Each person receives a "bingo" card with faces rather than numbers, then wanders around the crowd, trying to match the faces with real people. When they find one, they introduce themselves and write down the person's name. It takes five names in a row to win. You can prepare these cards well in advance. Just snap digital photos of the participants and randomly assign them to cards. Print them, bring them along, and you're set. Even if a few people fail to show (and you know that's likely to happen), it won't stop the game. As with traditional bingo, each card allows 12 different ways to win.

Get Lost Have you ever visited a strange city with winding streets and no good map? Use your digital camera to document your turns and provide a digital trail of breadcrumbs to help you find your way back to your hotel. Snap pictures of street signs while your friend or spouse points in the direction you came from. When you're ready to find your way back, view the pictures in reverse order. Each one will provide a visual clue to help you become "unlost."

I'm sure you can come up with variations of these games to suit particular occasions. In fact, you've probably thought of some other original game ideas (but pinning the boss's photo in the middle of the dartboard has been done before).

In This Chapter...

This chapter covered novel and unusual ways to use your camera in your day-to-day life. Here are a few key ideas:

- If you hate dark, dusty, and spider-infested crawlspaces, let your camera make the trip for you.

- Never lose your car again. With a digital camera, you can always remember where you parked.

- Don't depend on memory. Use your digital camera to help you remember all the little details in your life. A snap inside your refrigerator can help you to recall what you need to purchase at the store.

- Never fall into the trap of answering the question "Does this dress make my behind look fat?" Take a picture and let them decide instead.

- Learn to give presentations using your camera. It can prove to be a great sales tool with very little attached baggage.

- Did you read a great review of a recent book? Don't rip the page out of that magazine. Let your camera remember the author and title for you.

- Have fun with your camera. There are a lot of ways you can use digital photography for play and recreation.

CHAPTER 10

Digital Camera Crafts

A digital camera makes the perfect companion for crafts. New and exciting materials, techniques, and equipment offer many ways to combine digital photography with your favorite hobby. Craft projects range from iron-on appliqués to charm bracelets to tattoos. Whatever your area of interest may be, it's likely that you can use digital photography in some way to enhance and enjoy your hobby.

With the supplies for your particular project, your digital camera, and, in some cases, some help from Adobe PhotoDeluxe, you can create truly personalized items. PhotoDeluxe is included on the CD that accompanies this book. See Chapter 3, "An Introduction to PhotoDeluxe" for instructions on using this photo-editing software.

This chapter covers the following topics:

- **Photo fashions**

- **Lamination creations**

- **Greeting cards**

- **Photo labels**

- **Digital photos from old prints**

- **Photo wheels**

- **Novel materials for photo projects**

Photo Fashions

Whether you're making gifts or a fashion statement, personalized accessories are *in!* Now you can plaster the faces of your loved ones on everything from T-shirts to sneakers to handbags. Pick up a pack of photo transfers and see where your imagination leads you.

Photo transfers transform your digital photos into iron-on appliqués. You print on the transfer, as you would print on paper, and then iron the transfer to put your photo onto fabric.

You'll find photo-transfer kits at any office supply store or major family store chain, like Wal-Mart and Target. They're usually called T-Shirt Maker Kits, T-Shirt Transfers, or simply Photo Transfers. Each set usually contains between five and ten transfers and normally costs about a dollar per sheet. You can often find great bargains on these sheets by watching the Sunday newspaper ads.

Pick the Item for the Photo Transfer

A wide variety of materials and fashion-wear will work with appliqués. On a recent visit to a hobby store, I made a quick list of some of the items there that accept iron-on transfers: T-shirts, baseball caps, cooks' aprons and hats, painting smocks, white denim shoes, baby bibs, totes, purses, backpacks, nightgowns, and vests. This list represents just a fraction of the items available in that particular store. The possibilities are nearly endless. And because the transfers are washable, you can include these items in your everyday wardrobe. Just choose, personalize, and wear.

Here are two tips for selecting items for photo transfers:

Look for items with a large, flat ironable area. Remember that you must achieve good contact between the area and your iron. Small, flat portions interspersed among textured fabric may not allow your iron to reach the area fully without damaging the surrounding textures. Then you need to choose between bonding the transfer securely and harming the rest of the item. Try to avoid this situation. Look for materials that contain a large area that easily accepts ironing.

Select light-colored items. Don't attempt to iron a transfer onto a dark-colored background. It will subdue your image and may hide it entirely. Avoid using patterned materials. Unlike traditional iron-on transfers that can be applied to any color surface, ink-jet transfers provide tint without much substance. The hues are very thin and allow a lot of light and color to pass through. If you iron over a bright red T-shirt, you probably won't be able to see your transfer at all. Pick white, beige, or other light colors. And remember that any fabric color, however light, will bleed through your images.

Create the Transfer

Making transfers is simplicity itself. It takes only a few steps:

1. Design your transfer, both text and images.
2. Prepare the transfer using Adobe PhotoDeluxe.
3. Print the transfer on your ink-jet printer. Let PhotoDeluxe's transfer-specific printing routine help you.

Although the process is easy, there are some things you can do to ensure that you're happy with the results.

Design Your Transfer

Transfer material is expensive. Before you print on a transfer, take some time to think about your project and plan. Here are some suggestions:

Plan the image size. Measure your target areas and decide how big your images need to be. Be sure to leave a little extra space around the transfers to allow for complete and effective ironing.

Think about text. PhotoDeluxe makes it easy to add captions. Are you giving a gift to the "Best Grandma in the World"? Plan for caption space as well as image space.

Choose clip art. Small artistic flourishes can enhance your photographic images. You don't need to simply plaster a face on a T-shirt. You can surround it with borders, leaves, angels, and hearts. Survey whatever artistic clip art you have on hand and see how it might soften harsh picture borders and balance your presentation.

Select your photos carefully. Pictures with a lot of background detail may not work well as transfers. Try to select good head shots taken against fairly plain backdrops. Determine in advance how you might want to crop or edit your pictures for your layout.

Use big, simple designs. Fashion items make their statement at a distance. Don't plan on people coming up very close and putting on their reading glasses. Select both text and pictures that can be seen and recognized easily from at least six feet away. For this reason, avoid using group shots for photo transfers. Individual or paired subjects work far better.

Be compact in your layout. Avoid space in your transfer layouts. Extra space wastes precious transfer material. Instead, plan on cutting elements apart with scissors and applying them to different parts of your project as needed. Any un-inked transfer is effectively wasted.

Prepare Your Transfer

Once you've planned your transfer, let PhotoDeluxe help you prepare it. PhotoDeluxe offers many layout and adjustment features you might otherwise overlook.

Use the following PhotoDeluxe techniques to prepare your photo for the transfer:

Create a new image canvas. Select File → New. Make the canvas the exact size you'll be printing, typically 7.5 × 10 inches. (You need to leave room for margins.) Make sure to select a good resolution that matches the capabilities of your printer. If you skimp on resolution, your transfers may look cheesy.

Turn on the rulers. Select View → Show Rulers. The rulers will help you to lay out features more precisely. Use these rulers to determine and plan the size of each iron-on element.

Fix your photo. Use Quality → Instant Fix to enhance your images before adding them to your canvas.

Add captions. Select Tools → Text. Make sure to print large, bold letters using the thickest fonts you can find. The thicker the letters, the better they will look and the easier they will be to read. Arial Black makes a good caption font.

Soften photo edges. Avoid the "block." Rectangular pictures with sharply defined edges generally look awful when transferred to fabric. Instead, soften the edges with feathering (select Effects → Feather) for a smooth transition to the underlying fabric.

Consider using ovals. Rather than having a rectangle as your primary shape, you can make the photo an oval. Use the Oval tool (from the Selections palette or the Select → Selection Tools submenu) to choose part of your photo, and then feather the selection to create a softer, more interesting photo.

Remove backgrounds. Consider using the selection tools to entirely remove the backgrounds from your pictures. Floating heads work much better than full pictures with textured backgrounds.

Add test items. If you have a little leftover space, add a few hearts or flowers that you can use later for testing. These small test features allow you to check for proper iron temperature and give you a way to perfect your transfer technique.

Print Your Transfer

Printing your transfers involves little more than loading your blank sheets and letting PhotoDeluxe handle the rest. Still, there are a few things you must keep in mind:

Print in reverse. When you print on a photo transfer, you're actually printing on the transfer's back. This side will touch the fabric, and a protective coating will cover it. That means you need to reverse your image for it to look right after ironing. Fortunately, PhotoDeluxe makes this a breeze. Click the Get & Fix Photo button next to the activity bar, choose Print → Print T-Shirt Transfer → 1 - T-Shirt, and then click the T-shirt icon. PhotoDeluxe will automatically print a reversed image.

Test first; commit later. Paper is a lot cheaper than a photo transfer is. Print a test run on paper first. This lets you catch mistakes without wasting expensive transfer blanks.

Print on the "fabric" side. When you load your transfers, take note. One side is textured; the other is smooth. The textured side accepts the ink, and the backing side will peel away after ironing. Make sure the textured size faces the ink-jet heads.

Print several on a page. Consider printing several images at once. Because transfer material is expensive, consider loading up your "page" with multiple images and captions. After printing, you can cut the transfers apart and apply them to separate projects or parts of projects.

Ironing Tips

After preparing your transfers, it's time to iron them onto your fabric. Here's the most important thing you should keep in mind: *Follow the manufacturer's instructions!* Transfer material and technology vary by manufacturer. Make sure to read the instructions completely and follow them to the letter. You will achieve the best results when you work with the requirements of each individual transfer type.

Here are a few other tips to keep in mind:

Trim away excess transfer material. Use a pair of scissors to clip out areas that do not contain print. Transfer material is stiff. The less you apply, the better your garments will feel and look.

Prepare the iron. Give your iron time to reach and settle on the right temperature. A few extra minutes will give you consistent and appropriate heat for the transfer process.

Prepare the items. Cut apart individual items and lay them out before committing any item to ironing.

Test your technique. If you've added a few test features to your transfer, now is the time to pull out some scrap material and test your ironing technique. The more you practice, the more likely your transfer will work correctly with your real project. Nothing is more frustrating than a bad transfer using expensive materials. Practice really does make perfect. You may need to adjust the iron's temperature or your timing to get the best result possible.

More Transfer Ideas

Don't think that the digital photo/iron-on transfer story stops at wearables. You can use transfers for all sorts of fabric-based projects. Here are just a few ideas:

Design a quilt. Create a friendship quilt for a pal who is about to move away, go to college, get married, or join the Army. Take a picture of each member of your circle of friends. Sew the photo panels into a quilt, and you'll have made a special treasure that will last for years. And if your friends have access to a computer, they can personalize their panels with their thoughts, memories, and best wishes.

Make a family book. Iron pictures of each family member onto a long strip of cloth. Fold it into a book and run a seam along the binding. It makes a wonderful gift for a toddler.

Personalize sheets and pillowcases. Are you sending little Susie to summer camp? Keep your family as close as her cheek. Iron a picture of the whole clan onto your child's pillowcase. Who needs power heroes when you've got mom, dad, and the dog on your pillowcase?

> The textile fun doesn't end with iron-ons. Many computer-controlled sewing projects (such as knitting machines and embroidery attachments for sewing machines) now allow you to import digital photos into their setup programs. You can embroider your face on Junior's polo shirt—what an idea!

Lamination Creations

With a laminating machine, you can make some very creative gifts. Laminated items are durable, waterproof, and make excellent craft projects. If you don't happen to own a laminating machine, don't despair. Many office supply stores will do the lamination work for you.

Sports Legends

Figure 10.1

Put your favorite sports hero on his own card.

A popular lamination project is sports cards. You can use PhotoDeluxe to create a sports card that turns heads, and then laminate it to create a keepsake. Figure 10.1 shows an example.

Follow these directions to create a sports card of your own:

1. Fire up PhotoDeluxe and click the Cards & More button next to the activity bar. Then click Cards → Sports Cards.

2. Click 1 - Choose Sports Card → Choose Card and select a card (for example, the baseball template) by double-clicking it.

3. Click 2 - Add → Open File. Select an image file from your computer and open it. PhotoDeluxe will automatically add it to your template.

4. Click 3 - Edit and adjust your picture to better fit the sports card.

5. Double-click the default name on the card (for example, Bill Howard on the baseball card) and change it to your subject's name.

6. Double-click the team name and change it to your subject's favorite team.

7. Click 4 - Done.

8. Save and print your picture.

9. Create and print a patterned sheet for the back of the card. Any regular pattern will do. It just looks better than a plain, white back. You may want to print the sports card backing onto standard card stock. This will create a thicker and sturdier lamination.

10. Lay the photo on top of the backing. Make sure the back sheet is face down while the front is face up. Cut out the card, leaving a small border.

11. Take the finished card to your favorite office supply store and have it laminated.

Figure 10.2

You can make terrific coasters using family pictures.

More Lamination Projects

Here's an idea: Laminate photos of your entire family and cut them into circles to use as coasters. Make sure to cut out the photo circles first, as shown in Figure 10.2, before lamination. This prevents the lamination from falling apart. Afterwards you can trim the laminate material into another circle.

Here's another idea: Make an ID badge for your mom (see Figure 10.3), your teacher, your scout troop leader, or some other favorite person in your life. This makes a terrific "thank you" for those who have touched your heart in a special way.

Greeting Cards

PhotoDeluxe makes it easy for you to create memorable, personalized greeting cards with your digital photos. There's probably already a card designed for any occasion you might think of. And if there isn't, you can easily adapt a card template to your needs.

You can pick up good-quality, inexpensive card stock at your local discount store, such as Wal-Mart or Target. (Georgia-Pacific also makes very affordable offerings.) You can use plain card stock or prefolded stock, matte or glossy.

Here's how you can make your own greeting card. For this example, we'll create a "Get Well" card:

1. Start PhotoDeluxe and click the Cards & More button to bring up the correct activity bar. Then select Cards → Greeting Cards.

2. Click 1 - Layout. For this example, select Single Fold Top-Fold. This style allows you to print on both sides of the paper, making a card with a single fold along the top edge.

Figure 10.3

A "Best Mom" ID card makes a wonderful Mother's Day gift.

> Double-fold cards allow you to print on a single side and fold your card into front, back, in, and out sides. I don't really like the results. They don't look quite as nice as single-fold cards, and they can end up pretty thick after all that folding. On the positive side, with a double-fold card you can avoid the hassle of printing twice.

3. Click 2 - Style → Choose Style. Select a style with a double-click. We'll use the Get Well style here.

4. Wait for the card to open. Then click 3 - View. The Views list will appear on the right side of the card window. This allows you to see and edit the front, back, and inside of your card.

5. Click Front in the Views list to edit the front section of your card, as shown in Figure 10.4.

6. Click 4 - Add → Open File. Select a photo and open it. PhotoDeluxe will automatically add it to the front of your card.

7. Click 5 - Edit and adjust your photo to fit the card insertion area, as shown in Figure 10.5.

8. Click Inside in the Views list to edit the inside of the card.

9. Click the Add Text button (labeled with a *T*) at the top of your card window, just under its title bar.

10. Enter your text message in the Text Tool dialog box, as shown in Figure 10.6, and then click OK.

Figure 10.4

The front of your card, ready to be customized

Figure 10.5

The card with the front picture in place

Figure 10.6

Adding the text greeting that makes your card special

11. Drag your text into place.

12. Click 4 - Add → Open File. Select a photo and open it. PhotoDeluxe automatically adds it to the inside of your card.

13. Click 5 - Edit and adjust your photo to fit the card, as shown in Figure 10.7.

14. Click 6 - Done.

You're now ready to print your card. Because you chose a single-fold card in this example, you'll need to print both sides of the card. Remove all paper from your printer and add only one sheet, preferably of good card stock. Select File → Print and print your picture at the highest resolution. After the first side has printed, allow it to dry for a few minutes, and then reinsert it to print the second side. Make sure that you've oriented the card so the second side prints correctly.

Figure 10.7

The finished card interior

Photo Labels

Whether you have an attic, a storeroom, a pantry, or just the natural disorder of kids, finding things you've stored can prove a real headache. Fortunately, digital cameras provide a near-perfect solution for figuring out what's inside boxes, canisters, cartons, and crates with just a glance. Snap a shot of the contents, print it, and tape it on the outside of the container. You'll be able to sort through your things with a quick visual inspection.

Labeling Projects

You can label just about anything around your home or office. Here are some examples of items that could use a photo label:

Toy boxes Everyone knows that storing toys in individual crates helps organize a playroom. But there's one problem: Kids won't play with toys if they don't remember what's in the box. So take a picture of a representative toy and paste it on the end of the box. Now when your children look up and down the toy shelves, they'll be able to tell which box has the Legos, which one contains the Matchbox cars, and which one has the Barbies.

Boxes of clothes If you're like me, you'll have stored a half-dozen boxes, all labeled "Winter Clothes," in the attic. Consider taking a picture of some of the clothes you use the most to help identify the box. Just lay them out on your bed and take a photo. It's easy, and it sure saves time when you're in a hurry to find that one special coat.

Drawers When dealing with the preliterate or foreign-language speakers, it helps to label things with pictures rather than words. Putting a picture of a shirt on a drawer instantly communicates what goes where for your toddler.

Refrigerator magnets Do you want to know what's in the refrigerator and what needs to be bought? Take pictures of your most common staples and attach magnets to the back (also see the "Magnetic Sheets" section later in this chapter). When you run out of an item, move the picture from the front of the refrigerator to the side. Not only do you end up with an instant shopping list, but you also save energy by avoiding opening and closing your refrigerator repeatedly. (And you can always take a digital snapshot of the "things to buy" section and take it with you to the store!)

Folders Do you keep project and art folders for each of your kids? Why not attach a photo of each child to his or her folder? In fact, photos make great "name tags" for many things in a child-friendly household.

Labeling Tips

Picture labels are simple to make and use. Don't try to achieve artistic greatness. Focus on utility instead. Here are some tips to get you started:

Picture quality matters little. You can get by with economy-mode shots and low-resolution prints. Consider printing on a laser printer (if you have one around) to save ink.

Keep things simple. Use plain backgrounds when you shoot pictures. Don't lose information in the confusion of a complicated backdrop. Solid-colored sheets and blankets make excellent backdrops.

Use your flash. You don't need perfect illumination when photographing a can of soup or some Legos. Your camera's flash provides excellent lighting for general-purpose needs.

FROM INSPIRATION TO REAL-LIFE EXPRESSION

Lisa Kmetz read a previous version of this book and became inspired. "I took everything out of my kid's bins, grouped the contents, and took pictures to make labels for the bins," she told me. "It made a huge difference in keeping that toy room clean!" It didn't stop there. She went into her son's preschool co-op and evangelized there. "Cleanup time was a nightmare because none of the bins were labeled. One afternoon, we just did it. It's a simple thing, but it makes such a big difference." It turns out that a local shop was going out of business. Lisa had picked up a box of whole-sheet sticker paper for free (similar to Avery 5165, approximately $15 for a box of a hundred sheets). She printed the pictures on each sheet. Then she peeled the sticker off and applied it directly to the container. "It couldn't be easier," she reported.

Lisa's creativity didn't stop there. She asked her students, special-needs autistic kids, to show her different facial expressions and snapped pictures as they did. She turned these into individual "expression books," one for each kid, and has successfully used these nonverbal reminders for behavior modification. She also plans to create flashcards and labels to use around the house, at work, and in the preschool. She believes that the concrete nature of photos will help connect words with objects for better word-recognition skills.

Digital Photos from Old Prints

A few years ago, I surprised my husband and his brothers by returning home from a trip abroad with pictures of their late father—pictures they had never seen before. Finding these sorts of pictures is always providential. When an opportunity arises, you must seize it. You'll find that a digital camera can help you instantly recapture precious memories.

In this case, I had visited an elderly aunt. During our time together, she took out a large album of photos collected over the years and began to tell me stories about them. Immediately, I took out my digital camera, and as we talked, I began snapping pictures of pictures, like the one shown Figure 10.8.

Unlike a scanner, the camera will not stress the album itself. Unfortunately, the quality of these reproductions cannot match the quality possible with even a halfway decent scanner.

Keys to Capturing Old Photos

Digital cameras are terrific at capturing pictures from old albums, even those faded, brittle pictures fastened to album pages with yellowing tape. You'll need good, diffuse light and your macro lens. A macro lens allows you to shoot pictures from as little as an inch or two away from your subject. Most cameras now come with a built-in macro lens. If your camera doesn't have one, you can buy an external macro lens that will allow you to shoot close-ups with any digital camera. With these two things—light and lens—you can expand your personal albums and spread the wealth of your family's past.

When you work with photo albums, the following tips will help you capture better images and reproduce photos at a higher quality:

If you can, use a scanner. Okay, I know this is a book about digital cameras. But if your goal is to hold onto family treasures, any scanner will produce better results than a snapshot of a snapshot.

Use good, indirect lighting. Many older photos have shiny (not matte) finishes without any surface texture to spread light. Avoid reflections by lighting the photos with a diffuse light source.

Turn off your flash. A flash will produce unwanted reflections and distort your results, if not wash them out entirely. In low-light conditions, you can cover your flash with some tissue paper to create more diffuse lighting.

Figure 10.8

Your digital camera can capture old snapshots to share special memories.

Align your camera with the curve of the page. Pictures shot off-angle will turn out distorted. Although you can partially fix these distortions with certain image-editing software, good alignment will avoid distortions from the outset.

Get in close. Don't waste pixels on the album pages and picture mounts. Use every bit of resolution you have on the pictures themselves.

Take the pictures out of their plastic sleeves. Sleeves cause unnecessary reflections and may actually obscure picture detail. Just remember which sleeve each picture came out of!

Looking for a challenge? How about fixing up old and damaged pictures? You might be surprised by the skills involved. RetouchPRO offers a quasi-monthly game called the Photo Restoration Challenge (it's not a contest—there are no winners) that lets you test your photo-restoration skills and learn from others. Anyone can enter, and there's a chat board that lets participants share techniques. Stop by www.retouchpro.com/challenge to enter. There's a lot you can learn here about retouching and restoring antique images.

Share the Memories

The quality of a "picture of a picture" will never equal that of the original. Still, the emotional impact of looking at dear ones, especially those we have lost, will always be greater than simply knowing that such pictures exist with far-off relatives and friends. Using your camera to copy photos provides an important route toward sharing and spreading the wealth of our past. Consider the following ideas for enjoying and sharing your captured album pictures:

- Collect your pictures on a CD-R. Share copies with family and friends. This makes a marvelous holiday gift.

- Use the pictures for creating computer-generated greeting cards (discussed earlier in this chapter, in the "Greeting Cards" section) and picture calendars (discussed in Chapter 11, "Photo Transformation Projects").

- Upload your pictures to one of the Web album sites listed in this book's appendix and share your family album with the world.

- Print copies of your pictures and send them to your family and friends. You can upload your "pictures of pictures" to a photo-finishing site and create new photos from them. (See Chapter 6, "Digital Photo Printing," for details on creating prints from your digital photos.)

- Make copies for yourself and create your own "new" photo album.

Does grandma have special "pinch-of-this/pinch-of-that" recipes? Use your digital camera to take pictures of the ingredients and amounts as she cooks. Capture secret family recipes so that they'll never get lost.

Photo Wheels

So what's your mood today? You can let the world know in a novel and strangely fun way. Use your digital camera to capture a whole range of your moods and collect them into mood wheel, as shown in Figure 10.9. Pin the wheel outside your office or your room. Let people know what to expect before they face you.

Here's how to create your own mood wheel:

1. Start by taking pictures of a number of expressions: happy, sad, bewildered, angry, and tired. Transfer these pictures to your computer and print them on plain paper.

2. Grab your scissors, a paper plate, and a glue stick. Cut out each expression. Paste the photos around the outside of the plate. Alternatively, create a file in PhotoDeluxe with all the faces on it. Add each face to a different layer in and use the Orientation → Free Rotate command to orient them.

3. Stick a thumbtack through the center of the plate, so you can rotate the plate. Add a down-pointing arrow and an appropriate caption (such as "Mood of the Day") above the plate, and you're set.

The fun doesn't stop with mood wheels. You can create all sorts of wheels. Create a chore wheel to distribute chores. Use your digital camera to shoot pictures of a broom, your toilet, and a feather duster. You'll be set to distribute sweeping, bathroom, and dusting duties to your children. Whose turn is it this week to have a special evening out with Dad? Create a wheel with pictures of your kids, and you'll know who's up next. Do you want to announce the best part of the dinner menu? Snap pictures of your vegetables and make a "wheel of roughage." Let your imagination soar!

Novel Materials for Photo Projects

If you thought that creative ink-jet projects started and ended with glossy half-fold cards, think again. You'll be surprised by the amazing array of materials on which you can print your digital photos. Month by month, this list grows, as major manufacturers debut one new material after another.

> The special materials covered here are available from many craft, office supply, and computer stores. I like to pick up my personal supplies from Michael's, Wal-Mart, Office Depot, Comp-USA, and MicroCenter. Each store offers different vendors and products, so shop around for the best deals.

Window Decals

Are you looking for a novel project that will let you personalize your kitchen windows, bathroom mirrors, or candy jar? Pick up a packet of printable window decal blanks at your local office supply or craft store. This product allows you to print on a transparent, clingy medium that sticks to glass via static electricity. Just print, peel, and stick.

Ink-jet ink is very translucent. It allows light to stream through in beautiful colors. You can instantly transform the glass in your home into "stained glass" masterpieces. I love to use this product with smooth-sided mason jars. It clings like magic and makes a wonderfully unique jar, perfect for gift giving.

> When preparing window decal pictures, you might want to accentuate your photographic subject by minimizing the background. Follow the directions in Chapter 4, "Digital Photo Editing."

TODAY, I FEEL ↓

Figure 10.9

A photo mood wheel alerts the world to your emotional state.

Shrink Material

Shrinky Dinks were popular in the 1970s. You would cut out thin, plastic forms, decorate them with magic markers, and stick them into a toaster oven. The forms would shrink, becoming quite thick. The shrinky days are back! Use your ink-jet printer to print on print-and-shrink material, and then shrink it in your toaster or oven.

You might ask, "What good are they? Why would I want to print and shrink?" Outside the simple "coolness" factor, these shrinking craft sheets will help you make wonderful charm bracelets and necklaces. Just prepare your pictures with PhotoDeluxe, print them onto the sheets, and shrink them. Here's how you can make a collection of your family, your friends, your pets, or any of your favorite items:

1. Open a new 7.5 × 10–inch document in PhotoDeluxe at a resolution that matches the capabilities of your printer.

2. Add pictures of your family or friends, packed tightly onto the sheet, with just enough space for easy trimming and to accommodate a hole on top. Make sure to feather away all backgrounds (select Effects → Feather) to leave just the main figures.

3. To leave space above each picture on your layout, use the Circle tool to add a hole of about ¼-inch diameter. Select Effects → Outline to scribe the circle on your layout. Choose a very thick outline (say 10 or 12 pixels at least) to allow you to trim the outside while leaving space for a good-sized hole.

4. Print your pictures on the shrink material.

5. Cut out the individual pictures, making sure to include the hole on top. Trim as close to your subject's outlines as possible, leaving little extra material.

6. Use a hole puncher to remove the material within the circle to create the hole.

7. Follow the manufacturer's instructions to shrink the printed materials, transforming them into charms.

8. Wait until the shrunken charms have cooled completely before threading them to create your necklace or bracelet.

Jigsaw Puzzles

Did you know that you can print your photos as jigsaw puzzles? Just stick a special sheet into your ink-jet printer, print your photos, and peel the individual pieces away from the backing. You can make prints of the grandkids, the dog, or your close circle of friends.

After you've selected your puzzle photo, print it on the puzzle sheet. Then jumble the pieces up, place them in an envelope, and send them out to grandma or a special friend. They'll be in for a wonderful surprise when their mail arrives.

Adhesive Fabric

Adhesive fabric pages are a fairly new offering that show a lot of promise for crafting. The pages have a peel-and-stick backing. Unlike T-shirt transfers, which print onto stiff, ironable material, these pages allow you to print directly to soft fabric.

You can add artwork to a wide variety of projects, such as mouse pads, clock faces, photo-album covers, and so forth. Unfortunately, the fabric pages can't be laundered (use a damp sponge to clean them), so you cannot apply them to clothes.

Magnetic Sheets

Make your own magnetic art and business cards with printable magnetic sheets. As you might suspect, you just print, cut, and use. You can make all sorts of projects:

Magnetic family Trim magnetic pictures of your family members. Send these as gifts to far-away relatives.

Refrigerator reminders Put a picture of a milk container, egg carton, and other grocery shopping items on magnetic backing.

Your calling card Take a picture of yourself holding a large piece of paper with your phone number printed on it. Print several copies, cut them out, and give them to your neighbors.

Mr. Refrigerator Head Print out family faces, all resized to approximately the same dimensions, cut them into parts—ears, noses, hair, and so forth—and make a magnet game for the young ones (or the young at heart).

Banner Paper

Banner paper allows you to print a several-foot-long sheet of paper with a single Print command. Just create the proper canvas size in PhotoDeluxe (File → New lets you specify the banner size), add your pictures and text, and print. Follow the manufacturer's instructions for loading the banner paper, choosing an appropriate size, and printing.

Here are some ideas for photo banners:

- Print big panoramas. Follow the instructions in Chapter 5, "New Viewpoints: Postprocessing Your Images," to create your panorama.

- Make personalized "Welcome Back" signs. You can add pictures from the whole office.

- Create party greetings. Add photos appropriate to the occasion, along with the "Congratulations!"

- Produce extra-large baby announcements. You're not limited to "It's a girl!"—you can show her, too.

One of my favorite banner projects involves traveling around town with your digital camera. Snap photos of letters on signs wherever you go. Then build a "letter library" from these pictures. Photograph neon letters, slide-on letters, formal letters, and funky letters. When you're ready to make your banner, select individual characters from your library and add an eclectic touch to your artwork. It looks terrific, and once you've built up your collection, takes very little work to assemble.

Stickers

If your kids love stickers, you'll love print-on sticker blanks. These come in a range of sizes and shapes, including circles, rectangles, and full sheets. All you need to do is design your sticker, print to the sheet, and enjoy. Use these stickers to personalize mail, enhance school projects, or whatever else you can think of.

PhotoDeluxe will let you print to most standard sticker-sheet layouts, particularly those made by Avery. Here's how to print stickers on Avery sheets:

1. Open the photo you want to make into a sticker in PhotoDeluxe. Click the Get & Fix Photo button to launch the associated activity bar and select Print → Print Multiple on a Page.

Figure 10.10

PhotoDeluxe can automatically set up your output for Avery brand sticker sheets.

2. The Print Multiple dialog box will appear. Click the Change button.

3. Select Avery from the drop-down menu. Then select the sticker type and size you'll be using, such as 3110 Kids Rectangle Stickers (1.25″ × 2.38″).

4. PhotoDeluxe will automatically resize and arrange your pictures. You'll see a preview of the results, as shown in Figure 10.10. If the preview looks good, click the Print button.

5. Insert your blank sticker sheets into the ink-jet printer. From the Print dialog box, select the Best print quality and click OK to print.

Tattoos

If you're looking for the whole road hog or sideshow tattooed person look, but aren't ready to commit, ink-jet peel-off tattoos may be the answer for you. These print-on tattoo sheets offer skin-art without the risk of hepatitis. And if your children insist on decorating their arms, cheeks, or ankles with strange and exotic art, you can ask them to consider including pictures of you.

Follow these simple steps to make your tattoos:

1. As with all of the other art media, start by preparing your photos and artwork in Photo-Deluxe. Remember to keep your artwork small and sized appropriately to body parts, such as cheeks, ankles, and so forth.

2. Trim away all backgrounds and feather your selections to provide smooth edges. (Select Effects → Feather.)

3. Print to the tattoo sheet and wait for it to dry.

4. Cut out each tattoo, peel it from the backing, and apply.

Wow, instant body art!

In This Chapter...

This chapter barely touched on the many and varied opportunities a digital camera offers hobbyists. There's so much more you can do with a little creativity and a digital camera. Here are a few thoughts to take away with you from this chapter.

- If you want to make a gift that's unique *and* personal, you cannot do better than to combine your digital photos with your crafting.

- New ink-jet friendly materials are constantly arriving on the market. Keep you eyes open to see what new project possibilities are available.

- Thousands of Web sites are dedicated to using digital photography with all the fabric arts. Pop by your favorite search engine to explore them and get inspired. Then follow the directions in this chapter to help get the best results from your fabric transfers.

- Laminated crafts are both waterproof and durable. They offer a great way to make lasting memories with your digital photos. Stop by your local office supply store to get an idea of pricing.

- With your digital photos, you never need to send an impersonal commercial card for special occasions again. Instead, you can add special touches that will transform your greeting card into a keepsake.

- Help your kids clean up after themselves. Photo labels can and do make a difference.

- Give new crafting techniques a try. Whether you build a photo mood wheel, personalized stickers, or customized magnets, remember that there's really no risk involved. If you don't like the results, you can always try something else.

CHAPTER 11

Photo Transformation Projects

Your imagination can transform your pictures into new and innovative possibilities. When you use digital imagery, the results are many and varied. Learn to use bits and parts of your images. See your snapshots as raw material, from which you can select pieces to create fresh and imaginative projects. You might be surprised at what amazing things you can achieve.

In this chapter, you'll learn about original ways to use your digital pictures. You'll see how you can unleash your creativity to bring your images into new expressions—from slide show parades to calendars to animation. You'll discover that taking good pictures is not just an end for digital photography; it can be a beginning as well.

For many of these projects, you'll be using Adobe PhotoDeluxe, included on the CD that accompanies this book. For instructions on using PhotoDeluxe, see Chapter 3, "An Introduction to PhotoDeluxe."

This chapter covers the following topics:

- Launch someone into the clouds
- Animate your slide show with a photo parade
- Create a coloring book from digital photos
- Feature your photos on a calendar
- Add animation to your photos with GIF Animator
- Bring your stills to life with StillMotion Creator

Launch Someone into the Clouds

Do you want to liven up your images? Ask your subject to jump up and down. Perhaps you can capture that moment when both feet are off the ground and the head is tossed back in laughter. You'll be glad you did.

Once you've shot your jumper picture, you can have some fun with it using Adobe Photo-Deluxe. As an example, we'll transform a jumping subject, like the one shown in Figure 11.1, into a super-cloud-jumper.

In these steps, you'll see how to launch your subject.

1. Start PhotoDeluxe, set up power mode (click the Advanced Menus button if the advanced menus are not already displayed and show the Layers and Selection palettes), and open your jumper photo.

2. Choose SmartSelect Tool from the Selections palette and outline your subject.

3. Click the Invert button on the Selections palette to invert your selection. It should now outline every photo element except your subject.

4. Select Effects → Feather and choose a high feathering value, such as 10. Click Delete Selection, and then click OK. This invert-and-feather process creates a feathered selection that eliminates any unwanted background intrusions. In this example, it ensures that no grass, trees, cars, or houses will intrude into your selection.

Figure 11.1

Snap a photo of your subject jumping.

5. On the Layers palette, double-click this layer, label it **Base Image**, and click OK.

6. Drag this layer to the paper icon at the bottom of the Layers palette to create a copy. Rename this copied layer **Blurred Image**.

7. Click the Blurred Image layer to select and display it. Then click the All button on the Selections palette.

8. Select Effects → Blur → Motion Blur. Rotate the blur angle to produce a blur angled along the same general lines as your jumper. Select a large distance, such as 300 to 600, to blur widely, as shown in Figure 11.2.

9. Make sure that both your Base Image and Blurred Image layers are displayed. (To display a layer, click the rectangle to the left of it on the Layers palette until the eye icon appears.) Then click Blurred Image to make it your active layer.

10. Select Trace Tool from the Selections palette. Use this tool to select the blur in front and above your jumping subject, as shown in Figure 11.3.

11. Press the Delete key to remove the excess blur.

12. Drag the Blurred Image layer below the Base Image layer. The blur should now trail behind your subject, as shown in Figure 11.4.

Figure 11.2

Use the Motion Blur effect to create a blur along the lines of the jump.

Figure 11.3

Remove those portions of the blur that go in the wrong direction.

Figure 11.4

Add the blur behind the jumper.

13. Optionally, you can intensify the blurred image by copying it. Just drag it to the paper icon at the bottom of the Layers palette.

14. Select File → Open Special → Get Sample Photo. Choose a scene or background for your subject. In this example, we use the Clouds photo as a background.

15. Drag the background to your picture, resize it to cover the image, and move its layer behind your subject and the motion blur.

16. Click the arrow to the right of the Text layer on the Layers palette and choose Merge Layers to merge the background and jumper into a single layer.

17. Select Effects → Render → Lighting Effects and add some dramatic lighting from the direction of movement. The light source derives from where the line crosses the oval. Drag this intersection to set your light. Drag the oval wider for more light; drag the oval thinner for less light. When you're satisfied with the effect, click OK.

You have now lifted your jumping subject into the clouds, as shown in Figure 11.5.

Figure 11.5

With some Photo-Deluxe help, your subject is jumping into the clouds.

Animate Your Slide Show with a Photo Parade

If you want to create slide shows with your digital images, you don't need to settle for the dull and usual. Photo parades add a whole new twist to your slide shows. With a photo parade, your digital photos appear as part of a high-quality animated cartoon. These aren't clunky just-cute-enough cartoons, but slick, professionally animated work. PhotoDeluxe comes packaged with two sample parades: a Birthday magic-show animation, as shown in Figure 11.6, and a Christmas theme. All the software needed is provided for you, in the Cards & More activities.

If you like these animated presentations, you can accessorize. Stop by www.photoparade.com, where you can purchase additional parade themes that work with your PhotoDeluxe software. You can choose from the Premium pack (9 themes, $29.99) or the Super Pack (41 themes, $39.99). Theme subjects include various holidays, albums, life events, and more.

Create Your Own Photo Parade

After you've decided which pictures you want in your photo parade, you're ready to get them marching. Here's how:

1. Start PhotoDeluxe and click the Cards & More button next to the activity bar. Then select PhotoParade · Create a PhotoParade.

2. Click 1 - Album → Open Album. PhotoDeluxe will open a new PhotoParade album for you. This album allows you to collect a group of pictures in one place to build your photo parade.

3. Click 2 - Photos → Add Photo to add photos to your new PhotoParade album.

4. A file browser window appears. Navigate to your first photo and select it. If you want, add more photos from the folder by Shift+clicking. When you're finished selecting images, click Open. PhotoDeluxe adds the selected images to your album.

5. If desired, repeat steps 3 and 4 to add pictures from other folders.

6. Once you've added all your pictures, click 3 - Captions. If you wish to add a caption to any photo, select its thumbnail in the album, click Add Caption, enter text, and click Apply. Repeat as desired.

Captions and titles do not appear in most photo parades, but they do appear in Carousel mode (which presents a simple slide show). If you plan to present a plain slide show without animation, make sure to properly annotate your images.

7. Click 4 - Theme. Select a theme from the Choose Theme drop-down list. Available themes include Birthday Magic Show and Santa's Little Helper. (The SliderDEMO option allows you to create a slide show without animation.)

8. Click 5 - Build. Leave the Segment Size as Unsegmented and click Build PhotoParade.

9. Navigate to where you wish to save your parade, enter a filename, and click Save. For this example, use the name `MyParade.PhP`.

10. Wait for your parade to build. This may take several minutes. As with other Photo-Deluxe operations, a progress bar appears at the bottom of the screen during the process.

11. When the parade has been built, a confirmation message will appear. Click OK.

12. To see the results, click 6 - Play → Play PhotoParade. Sit back and enjoy the music, pictures, animation, and sound effects.

13. When you're finished watching your photo parade, click 7 - Done.

You can switch from your animated photo parade to a simple slide show at any time. Tap the Escape key, and then click Carousel → Play.

Share Your Photo Parade

Sharing your photo parades with friends is easy. Just place your PhotoParade (`.PhP`) file on a disk along with the player. You will find the player installer file, `PhPSetup.exe`, on the CD in PhotoDeluxe's Extras\PhotoPrd folder. Your friends can then install and run the player and view your parade. You may want to use a Zip disk or a CD-R, because these files can run to multiple megabytes in size.

If you have access to an NTSC scan converter or a video card that produces NTSC output, you can hook up your computer to a VCR and save your parade to video. Make sure to hook up the audio track, too. If you're not sure if your video card supports NTSC output, check to see if it has SVHS or RCA connectors. You can generally buy a video card with RCA output for about $50 at most office supply stores.

Create a Coloring Book from Digital Photos

Do you have a special child in your life? Here's a cute project that you can share: Convert your digital photos into a coloring book. Let your child, or the child in yourself, express his or her artistic side.

For this project, pick a few simple images. The best images will contain strong, clear subjects with few textures and patterns, like the picture shown in Figure 11.7. Then use PhotoDeluxe to transform the images into black-and-white pictures, ready for coloring.

There are two methods you can use to transform your photos into coloring book pages. The simplest way is to use PhotoDeluxe's built-in Coloring Book activity. The alternative is to use some of PhotoDeluxe's advanced features, which give you more control over the results. We'll look at both methods here.

Figure 11.7

A good candidate for coloring book transformation

Use PhotoDeluxe's Coloring Book Activity

After you've selected your coloring book candidates, follow these steps to use PhotoDeluxe's built-in Coloring Book activity:

1. Launch PhotoDeluxe and open your photo.

2. Select Get & Fix Photo → Adjust Quality → Extensis Instant Fix Tools → IntelliFix Instant Fix to automatically enhance the brightness and contrast.

3. Select Get & Fix Photo → Special Effects → Re-color Photo → Coloring Book.

4. Click 1 - To B&W → Color to B&W.

5. Click 2 - Find Edges → Find Edges.

6. Click 4 - Done. PhotoDeluxe creates a line drawing of your photo, as shown in Figure 11.8.

Follow the above directions to create each page of your coloring book. When you're finished, staple the pages together to make a special gift for your little one.

Figure 11.8

The results of Photo-Deluxe's built-in Coloring Book activity

Create Your Own Coloring Book Pages

If you're looking for a little more quality and a little less fuzziness in the open areas, you can use more advanced PhotoDeluxe features to create your coloring book pages. Here's how:

1. Start PhotoDeluxe, set up power mode, and open your photo.

2. Select Get & Fix Photo → Adjust Quality → Extensis Instant Fix Tools → IntelliFix Instant Fix to automatically enhance the brightness and contrast.

3. Click the All button on the Selections palette.

4. To transform this image into a black-and-white picture, select Effects → Color to Black/White.

5. Select Effects → Blur → Blur More. Then select it again to repeat the blurring operation. This will smooth all the fine, noisy textures in your image, while leaving the strong edges untouched. Depending on your photo, you may wish to blur more than twice.

Figure 11.9

With a few extra steps, you can improve on the built-in results for a cleaner final coloring book picture.

6. Select Quality → Brightness/Contrast. Move the contrast up by about 20 and click OK. This will emphasize the image contrast.

7. To transform the image into a line drawing, select Effects → Stylize → Find Edges.

As you can see in Figure 11.9, these extra steps can help you create a smoother and cleaner final product.

Feature Your Photo on a Calendar

If your cutie is a real pinup, why not make a calendar to show him or her off? Let PhotoDeluxe transform your photo into a calendar. It takes only a few steps and produces some great-looking results. Figure 11.10 shows an example. You can use these calendars at your home or office, or even as gifts.

Here's how you can create a (dated) cheesecake of your own:

Figure 11.10

Feature your favorite pinup on her own calendar.

1. Open your snapshot in PhotoDeluxe.

2. Click the Cards & More button next to the activity bar and select Calendars → Monthly Calendars.

3. Click 1 - Month and select a month, such as February. Click OK.

4. Click 2 - Year and select your year, such as 2002. Your version of PhotoDeluxe can make calendars for each year up to 2005.

5. Click 3 - Layout · Choose Layout. Select a nice layout (I like the Tall/Above layout). Double-click the layout and wait for it to load.

6. Click 4 - Style → Choose Style. Pick your style, such as Style 2, and double-click.

7. Click 5 - Add. Double-click your original snapshot. It should be minimized and stored in the Open Photo bin. When you double-click it, PhotoDeluxe automatically adds it to the calendar template.

8. Click 6 - Edit and adjust your picture as needed. Move, resize, and rotate it until everything looks just right.

9. Click 7 - Done.

10. Print and enjoy your calendar page.

Add Animation to Your Photos with GIF Animator

Long ago (in computer terms—the late 1980s), there once was a fairly brilliant person, or to be more accurate, a fairly brilliant committee. This person/committee, almost as an afterthought, decided to include animation in a new graphic file format. This standard came to be known as GIF89a. For a long time, no one could figure out what to do with this ability, so everyone more or less ignored it. Then along came the World Wide Web. Someone remembered that GIF images supported animation. People started building animation support into their Web browsers, and presto—GIF animation took off like wildfire. Everybody wanted Web pages that moved, and GIF gave it to them.

Fast-forward to the present, and we're still using GIF89a animation to add motion and interest to our Web pages. Don't feel left out. You, too, can easily create animations. Between PhotoDeluxe and Ulead's GIF Animator, you have all of the tools that you need (both programs are on the CD that accompanies this book).

Start GIF Animator

After you've installed GIF Animator, you can start the program. Don't be put off by the GIF Animator main window, shown in Figure 11.11. Although the design is a little confusing, the program is powerful, and it's much easier to use than it first appears.

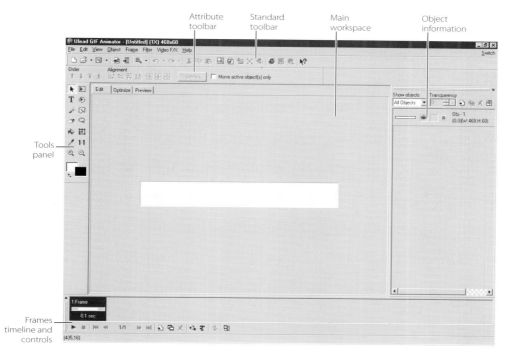

Figure 11.11

The main GIF Animator interface

Look for these key features in the main GIF Animator window:

Main workspace This area contains your GIF image. By default, a white rectangle appears in this space. When you load your image, it replaces the rectangle.

Edit, Optimize, and Preview tabs The three control tabs located directly above the main workspace allow you to select a task. Click the appropriate tab to edit your image, optimize for output, or preview the animation in an uncluttered, full-screen mode.

Frames timeline and controls Animations are composed of a series of frames. The frames timeline appears at the bottom of the window. You can play these frames to view your animation. Simple controls (play and stop, first frame, previous frame, next frame, and final frame) appear just below the timeline.

Object information Each frame is composed of one or more images, called *objects*. Object information is stored to the right of the main workspace and includes all loaded images. The small eye icon indicates which objects are visible for each frame. (If you wish, you can simplify this display by selecting Visible Only from the Show Objects drop-down list.) This window updates as you step through the animation, reflecting all visible images for each frame.

Tools panel This panel provides basic image-editing functions for GIF Animator. It appears to the left of the main workspace. (The examples in this chapter use PhotoDeluxe, rather than GIF Animator, for image-editing tasks.)

Attribute and Standard toolbars The Attribute toolbar, which rests just above the main workspace, allows you to control layout and alignment for frames with multiple objects. The Standard toolbar rests just under the menu. This toolbar includes a series of incomprehensible icons that allow you to perform most of the more common animation functions without going through the menus. To determine what each button does, move the mouse over the icon and wait a second. A helpful pop-up message will appear with a clarifying note.

Create Animations

GIF Animator provides all of the tools you need to create animations. You simply load a single image into GIF Animator and allow the program to add special effects. Save the results, and you're finished—instant animation!

Here's a simple example of how you can animate a photo:

1. Launch GIF Animator. Select File → Open Image and load your picture. GIF Animator will import a wide variety of formats, including BMP and JPEG, among others.

To see the full list, open the Files of Type drop-down list in the Open Image File dialog box.

2. To add a basic video effect, select Video F/X → 3D → Gate-3D. This brings up the Add Effects dialog box, as shown in Figure 11.12. Click OK to apply the default settings for this effect. This will add a series of 15 transitions to your image that make it appear as if the photo were rotating away from the viewer.

Figure 11.12

Choose the effect type.

3. To add a delay to the first image (so there is pause between animation cycles), right-click the first frame and choose Frame Properties from the pop-up menu. In the Frame Properties dialog box, shown in Figure 11.13, set the Delay option to 300 (for a 3-second delay) and click OK.

4. To preview your animation, click the play button (the first one on the left beneath the timeline; it looks like a right-facing triangle.) After viewing, click the stop button (the small square to the right of the play button).

5. To reverse the animation (to make it appear as if the picture were arriving rather than departing), right-click any frame and select Reverse Frame Order from the pop-up menu. In the Reverse Frame Order dialog box, shown in Figure 11.14, confirm that you've selected Reverse the Order of the Entire Animation and click OK.

Figure 11.13

Set the delay in hundredths of a second.

6. Click the play button to view the animation and make sure it works as expected. Then click the stop button to end the preview.

7. Click the Optimize tab. GIF Animator will automatically optimize your animation for output, as shown in Figure 11.15.

8. Click the play button to watch the original and optimized versions play back, side by side, in the main window. Click stop to end the preview.

Figure 11.14

Reverse the order of your animation.

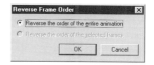

9. Click the Save button in the lower-right corner of the Optimize window. Navigate to where you wish to save your animation, enter a name, and click Save.

10. To view your image, start your Web browser and open the location `file:///C:/`. This corresponds to the top level of your C: disk. Navigate your way down to where you've saved your animation and double-click it.

Figure 11.15

The Optimize window shows the animation before and after the optimization is applied.

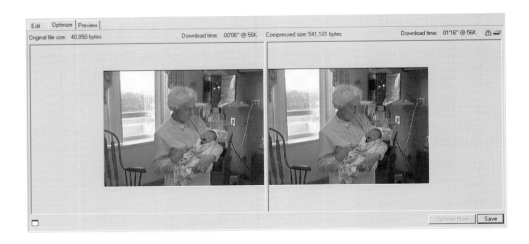

Add Text Effects with GIF Animator

In addition to cool 3D effects, you can add animated banner text to your photos. You can wish someone a happy birthday, identify the image subject, caption the image, and so on. Here's how:

1. In GIF Animator, select File → Open Image and load your image.

2. Select Frame → Add Banner Text to open the Add Banner Text dialog box.

3. Enter the text you want to appear with the animation in the text field, as shown in Figure 11.16. Use the controls in this dialog box to change the text font, size, alignment, and so forth.

Figure 11.16

Place text with the Add Banner Text dialog box.

4. Click the Effect tab below the preview window in the Add Banner Text dialog box. Choose a pair of effects from the two scrolling lists. These options set the way the text enters and leaves the scene. (I'm partial to the Fade effect.) Click the Start Preview button at any time to preview your selections. Click that button again to stop the preview.

5. Click OK and choose Create as Banner Text (Recommended) from the pop-up list. GIF Animator will add the new banner to your image.

6. Click the Optimize tab, and then click the Save button in the lower-right corner of the window. Navigate to where you wish to save your animation and click Save.

7. To view your image, start your Web browser and open the location `file:///C:/`. Navigate your way down to your animation and double-click it.

Export PhotoDeluxe Images to GIF Animator

As you've seen, you can use GIF Animator alone to create animations with special effects and text. But what if you want to take advantage of some of PhotoDeluxe's features for your animations? Simply create your images in PhotoDeluxe, and then export them as GIF89a files. You can open your exported files in GIF Animator, and finish up your animation in that program.

Make an Animation with PhotoDeluxe's Changeables

For our next project, we'll use PhotoDeluxe's Changeables feature to add a happy dog with a wagging tail to a picture. Then we'll move the image into GIF Animator to animate the images.

1. Launch PhotoDeluxe, set up power mode (display the advanced menus, Layers palette, and Selections palette), and load your image.

2. Select File → Open Special → Changeables. Double-click the dog.

3. Start with a minimal tail-wag. (In each successive step, you'll add more wag to your tail.) In the Changeable dialog box, move the Tail Wag slider about two-thirds of the way to the right, as shown in Figure 11.17. Then click OK.

4. Drag the dog into your image to create your first animation layer.

5. Repeat steps 2 through 4 for a series of three or four additional animation cells. Make the tail wag naturally, first up and then down. Figure 11.18 shows an example of the first wag in the series.

6. On the Layers palette, click the eye icon to the left of each layer, except the one that contains your picture with the first dog, to hide all of the layers except that one.

Figure 11.17

Set the amount of tail-wag in the Changeable dialog box.

Figure 11.18

The animated changeable dog placed on the subject.

7. Select File → Export → GIF89a Export and save your image.

8. For each remaining dog, repeat steps 6 and 7 to create an image and save it. Use a different name for each saved image. For example, name them `dogwag1.gif`, `dogwag2.gif`, and so on. You're now ready to create your animation using the "cells" you just produced in PhotoDeluxe.

9. Minimize PhotoDeluxe and open GIF Animator.

10. Select File → Open Image and navigate to your first image. Select it and click Open. Your image will appear in the main workspace and as a frame in the timeline.

11. Right-click in the timeline and select Add Frame from the pop-up menu. GIF Animator will create a new frame and automatically select it. Press the Insert key, navigate to your next image, and click Open. GIF Animator automatically loads it into the selected frame.

12. Repeat steps 10 and 11 until you've added all your photos (in order, please!) to your animation.

13. Click the play button to see your animation in action. Click the stop button to finish the playback.

14. Click the Optimize tab, and then click the Save button in the lower-right corner of the Optimize window.

15. Navigate to where you wish to save your animation and click Save.

16. To view your image, start your Web browser and open the location `file:///C:/`. Navigate your way down to your animation and double-click it.

Add a Wink to Your Animation

Are you feeling a little mischievous? Why not add a little animated wink to your picture? Winks are easy to simulate. Just smudge shut an eye and add the "wink" to your animation for the briefest time possible.

To see how this works, we'll add a wink to a face shot. Here are the steps:

1. In PhotoDeluxe, copy one of your original figures by pulling the layer down to the paper icon on the bottom-left of the Layers palette.

2. Select Tools → Smudge. Choose a brush that approximately matches the size of your subject's iris.

3. From *above* the eye, smudge down the skin onto the eye until you've created a wink, as shown in Figure 11.19. You don't need to create a perfect artistic rendering. Just the suggestion of a wink is all that's necessary for this effect. The animation will display this image very briefly. Do not fret over a slightly sloppy result.

4. Select File → Export → GIF89a Export and save your image.

5. Import both the original and the wink image into GIF Animator, as you did in the previous section.

Figure 11.19

Smudge an eye to create a wink.

6. Right-click your original image and choose Frame Properties from the pop-up menu. Enter 300 for the Delay option. At the end of each 3-second interval, your image will wink—briefly!

7. Click the play button to see your animation in action. Click the stop button to finish the playback.

8. Click the Optimize tab, and then click the Save button in the Optimize window.

9. Navigate to where you wish to save your animation and click Save.

Share Your Animations via E-Mail

You've created some great animations. Why not share them by e-mail? Here's how:

1. With your animation open in GIF Animator, select File → Export → As Animation Package (EXE). This brings up the Export Animation Package dialog box.

2. Choose how many times your image will loop, or select Loop Infinitely.

Figure 11.20

GIF Animator allows you to export your animation for e-mail.

3. Select a message box, such as Memo.emf, from the Message Box Styles list and add a message, as shown in Figure 11.20.

4. Click OK to save your animation.

5. Attach the .exe file you've created to an e-mail message and send it to your friends.

When your friends receive your animation package, they can run it and enjoy your creativity. They do not need any special browser or program. The file you created is a self-contained executable, which means you can just double-click its icon to run it.

Because of concerns about viruses, many people refuse to run executable (.exe) files attached to e-mail messages without prior notification. Make sure to let your recipients know that the .exe file they will receive is legitimate.

Bring Your Stills to Life with StillMotion Creator

Have you ever watched the camera slowly pan across an age-worn civil war picture in a PBS documentary? Along with camera pans, those documentaries use a lot of other nifty camera techniques. Sometimes the camera moves in to focus on a particular small detail. Other times, it zooms out from a single face to reveal more context. Once in a great while, the image seems to rotate away from you.

If you want to create these sort of animations using your own digital pictures, there's an easy-to-use solution. With ImageMatics StillMotion Creator (`www.imagematics.com`, $99 list price, $59 limited-time introductory price), you can build animated sequences that take advantage of these pan, zoom, and rotate techniques. You supply the digital pictures. Still-Motion Creator does the rest. With it, you can build ShockWave Flash animations to upload to your favorite Web site. You can also export your work to a stand-alone AVI movie.

On the CD that accompanies this book, you'll find a fully functional demo of the Still-Motion Creator software. (Until you register, the software adds a large watermark to your animated results). Install and use this demo to explore the features and flexibility of the program.

Digital image with surrounding
yellow-bordered camera box

Viewer preview box

Figure 11.21

**The ImageMatics
StillMotion Creator
interface**

Timeline

Display
zoom for
design
workspace

The following steps show you how to perform a couple of the most basic operations: a zoom and rotate.

1. Install ImageMatics StillMotion Creator on your PC and launch the software.

2. Select File → Load Picture.

3. Navigate to the picture you wish to animate, select it, and click Open.

4. Your picture appears in the center of the workspace grid. Use the magnification radio buttons on the lower-left side of the window to adjust your view size. Allow for space above, below, and to the sides of your picture. In Figure 11.21, I've set the magnification to 25 percent for this 1600 × 1200-pixel image.

5. Locate the floating viewer window at the top-right side of the window and the timeline on the bottom. Take note of the yellow box with the embedded plus sign (+) that appears around your image. This yellow box shows the current virtual camera position. You'll be using all of these features to create your animation.

6. With the Viewer time set at the original 00:00:00.00, move and resize the yellow box to create your first camera angle. This example begins by zooming out from the cheek of the subject. To create this effect, shrink the yellow box by dragging the lower-right corner. Then drag inside the box to move it into place. When set, the yellow box simulates the view that the camera sees.

7. When you've set the camera in position, click the key icon in the lower-right corner of the Viewer, as shown in Figure 11.22. This sets this view as your first keyframe. Notice the new key icon in the timeline.

8. Move your attention to the timeline. Click the timeline at the position you wish to set your second keyframe. In this example, click when the timeline is at around 5 seconds.

Figure 11.22

After setting the camera view, click the key icon to set your keyframe.

9. Resize the yellow camera frame to the full image size and click the key icon in the Viewer. This sets your second keyframe. A second key icon appears in the timeline.

10. Click when the timeline is at approximately 10 seconds. Rotate your image using the rotate handle in the upper-left corner of the yellow camera frame. After rotation, your screen will look like Figure 11.23. Click the key icon to add your final keyframe.

11. Select File → Make Flash SWF Movie. A Make Flash File Options dialog appears. Accept the standard options and click OK.

12. Navigate to where you wish to save your ShockWave Flash movie, enter a name, and click Save. StillMotion Creator reports that your Flash file has been made successfully.

You've created a new ShockWave Flash animation. It will start by zooming out from your subject's cheek over a period of 5 seconds. Then it will rotate for the remaining 5 seconds. To view this animation, just load the file into your favorite Web browser. Make sure you've installed the latest ShockWave Flash plug-in (www.shockwave.com).

This simple example should give you just enough of a flavor of the program to allow you to create animations on your own. As long as you understand how to place the camera and create keyframes, you can design any sort of panning, zooming, and rotating animation you can imagine.

Figure 11.23

When you rotate your yellow camera frame, the original image remains unchanged while the Viewer updates to reflect the camera angle.

In This Chapter...

This chapter explored the ways you can transform your digital photographs to create new and exciting projects. Here are a few key points to keep in mind:

- Once you know how to select and feather in your image-processing program, you can move your subject into nearly any scenario—the clouds, the moon, or wherever you like. You don't need to stick with the original surroundings.

- Slide show parades offer a marvelous way to share special events with friends and family. They add a slick and professional touch without much work on your part.

- Kids love coloring books. A coloring book with people and places you know is just that much more special.

- Personalized calendars make great gifts. Why not give a grandparent a calendar featuring digital photos of the grandkids?

- Animations bring pictures to life, especially when used with good sense, moderation, and style. Use GIF or ShockWave Flash animations to inject fun onto your favorite Web page.

CHAPTER 12

Just for the Fun of It: Digital Photo Projects

Relax already! Digital photography should be fun. Stop sweating about perfect lighting and exact composition. It's time to kick back and start enjoying your pictures.

Digital images have an underlying mathematical representation that allows your computer to manipulate them in ways you might not expect. Your computer can treat images just like any other form of data. You have the power to manipulate, adjust, and enhance your digital images to create really interesting results. In this chapter, you'll have some fun transforming your photo subjects in a variety of ways. The projects presented here involve merging, warping, and blending images.

This chapter covers the following topics:

- **Use special effects from PhotoIsland.com**
- **Transform head shots**
- **Create collage projects with PhotoDeluxe**

Use Special Effects from PhotoIsland.com

Do you remember that old 1970s television show? The one with the old Spanish guy and the short French one? "Zee plane, Boss, Zee plane"? Well, that's not the only Fantasy Island. Stop by ArcSoft's marvelous PhotoIsland Web site (www.photoisland.com) and explore the interactive fantasies you can create with your digital photos.

This free service is based on hope and inspiration. At least, PhotoIsland hopes it will inspire you to purchase a title or two from ArcSoft's software line. For every project on this site, you can buy a similar software package with even more activities and templates. Buying the software also offers a speed advantage. Because the software runs on your own computer, it bypasses variable Internet connection times. Still, the wonderful variety of templates and projects on the PhotoIsland site proves sufficient for most people's needs. From this site, you can turn yourself and your loved ones into astronauts, stretched-out curiosities, freakish animal hybrids, and more.

Go Ape: Merge Your Image with Stock Photography

Figure 12.1

Paste a face onto an ape with PhotoIsland.com's Funhouse service.

Have you ever wanted to make an ape out of yourself? Well, now you can. The PhotoIsland Web site allows you to monkey around with your face and turn yourself into a real animal. Just upload your image and take advantage of the free Funhouse service. You can look forward to pasting your face onto a variety of animals, sports cards, and other novelty fantasies.

The Funhouse service automatically merges your digital images with elements from stock photography. You can transform your subject into a he-man, an astronaut, a star athlete, or, as you will now see, a monkey, as shown in Figure 12.1.

Follow these steps, and you, too, can "go ape":

Photo Island.com | This image was created online at the PhotoIsland Photo WorkShop.

1. Point your Web browser to www.photoisland.com.

2. Click Photo WorkShop to enter the online, interactive photography play center. Then click Funhouse.

3. Click Get a New Template on the left side of the page. As the template-selection page loads, you will find various categories listed. These include Animal Kingdom, Sports, Nostalgia, Babes and Hunks, Trading Cards, and so forth. Each of these categories offers a number of templates.

4. Click Animal Kingdom and wait for the animals to load.

5. Click a dot under an ape picture, and then click Finished in the upper-right corner of the screen. You'll return to the Funhouse page.

6. Click Get a New Photo. This allows you to upload your own image to use with the template.

7. Wait for the photo-selection page to finish loading. Click Browse and select a JPEG image from your computer. Then click Upload and wait for your image to finish uploading.

Smaller pictures will upload faster (and may work better for this service) than large ones.

8. When your photo appears, click your subject's left eye (that is, the one that appears on the left side of the picture), as prompted. Wait for the page to reload, and then click the right eye, again as prompted. This information indicates the size and orientation of your subject's face. The Funhouse service will crop the face from your image and merge it with the template.

9. If you want to experiment, use the tools on the toolbar at the top of your Funhouse image. These tools—zoom, rotate, and so forth—allow you to tweak the way your image merges with the template. You can play with these or stick with the photo as is.

E-Mail Your PhotoIsland Creation

After you create your fantasy, you can choose from a number of PhotoIsland services. You can find these on the lower-left side of the results Web page. I like the e-mail option. This allows me to send my Funhouse photo to friends and family.

Be aware that e-mail can be traced. Some of the more uptight among us might construe as "hostile" a picture of your colleague's face on an ape body.

To use the PhotoIsland e-mail service, follow these simple steps:

1. Click the Send Email button (on the lower-left side of the page where your finished creation appears).

2. Fill in the recipient's e-mail address (Email to:), your e-mail address (Email from:), and an optional subject and message.

3. Click Send. Your photo will be on its way. PhotoIsland will notify you that the e-mail has been sent successfully.

Create a PhotoIsland Postcard

Are you looking for an even more spectacular presentation? Try out PhotoIsland's Postcard feature. This feature allows you to add music, a stamp, and other elements to your shared creation.

Follow these steps to use the PhotoIsland Postcard service:

1. Click the Send Postcard button (on the lower-left side of the page where your finished creation appears).

2. Select a photo to send (by default, it's the one you just created).

3. Select a stamp, music, and a greeting. To skip music, just select None.

4. Fill in the recipient's e-mail address (Email to:), your e-mail address (Email from:), and an optional subject and message.

5. Click Preview to preview your card. The image you created appears on the front of the card. Your message appears on the reverse side, as shown in Figure 12.2. Click View Other Side to see the opposite side of the card.

6. Click Send. A link to your new postcard will be on its way. PhotoIsland notifies you that the card has been sent successfully.

PhotoIsland stores your card for 30 days. Your recipient may visit and view it as often as desired during that time.

Stretch, Tweak, and Wiggle with PhotoIsland's iWarp

Did you ever want to rearrange someone's face? Are you a natural finger-painter? Do you like to stretch, tweak, wiggle, and warp? Well, do I have the place for you! With iWarp, located at the PhotoIsland Web site, you can distort your digital images to your heart's content. Figure 12.3 shows an example.

Figure 12.2

Send your picture on a postcard to add a personalized touch.

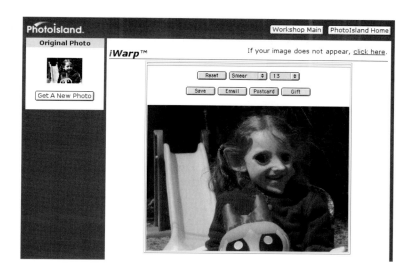

Figure 12.3

iWarp allows you to rearrange your subject's face.

Follow these instructions to use iWarp:

1. Point your Web browser to www.photoisland.com.

2. Click Photo WorkShop to enter the online, interactive photography play center. Then click iWarp.

3. Click Get a New Photo. A new page will load, prompting you with the message "Get My Photo from My Computer." Click Browse and select an image. Then click Upload. Wait for your browser to complete the upload process. You'll automatically return to the iWarp page.

4. Use the iWarp tools to distort the image:

   • Select your brush size at the top of the window. Choose a size between 4 (fine changes) and 37 (big changes). You can change brush sizes at any time.

   • To distort the image, choose Smear, press the mouse button, and drag.

   • To undistort the image, choose Clear, press the mouse button, and drag. As you move over the picture, the original picture will be restored.

   • Click Reset to return the entire image to the original picture.

When you're finished with your iWarp creation, you can click Save to save your image to your PhotoIsland account, click the Email or Postcard buttons to send it to a friend (as described in the previous sections), or click Gift to create a custom gift with this picture on it.

WARPING TIPS

Would you like to increase your photo-warping expertise? The following tips will help you refine your face-squishing skills:

Facial distortions Use a small brush when extending fine facial points like ears and noses. This pulls and extends the desired feature without dragging along and distorting surrounding areas. Use a wide brush to pull out cheeks and foreheads.

Caricatures Extend features along natural lines to exaggerate them and create a caricature without making the subject look unnatural. For example, pull out a strong chin, extend a dimple, or elongate a nose.

Big eyes To create the big-eye look, select the biggest brush and then pull down from just under the eye. Don't start on the eye itself. Repeat from just over the eye, pulling up. You can create fairly natural-looking large eyes in this manner.

Cone heads To create a cone head, use a large brush and start on one side of the head. Move the brush just below the scalp line and push up just a little. Move a little to the side, below the scalp, and push up again. Work your way through an entire layer from one side to another until the whole scalp has been raised just a bit, and then repeat. At each iteration, start your distortion closer to the center.

Blend Images with iMorph

Did you ever feel psychically linked to a special friend? PhotoIsland has just the solution for those who need to merge with a special someone. It can help you create your own separated-at-birth soul mate and provide the photographic proof that the two of you really share a special relationship.

PhotoIsland Web site's iMorph service will automatically combine facial features for you. Just upload two images and point to common features—like eyes, ears, and noses—and let iMorph do the work. You'll create a blended image that combines the best features from both subjects, merging them through the magic of video.

Follow these steps to create a merged image:

1. Point your Web browser to `www.photoisland.com`.

2. Click Photo WorkShop to enter the online, interactive photography play center. Then click iMorph.

3. To make this project work, you need to upload two photos. These photos should show faces with fairly similar sizes and shapes. Click Get Photo 1. On the upload page, click Browse. Select your first photo from your computer and click Upload. As prompted, click the eye on the left and then the right.

4. To get the second photo, click Get Photo 2. On the upload page, click Browse. Select your second photo and click Upload. Once again, click the left eye and then the right as prompted.

5. You are now ready to add points of similarity. Start by clicking a feature on Photo 1. For example, you could click the left corner of the mouth, the tip of the nose, or the base of the right ear. Two red points will appear, one at your click on Photo 1 and one on Photo 2. Drag the red point on Photo 1 to the *same* feature on Photo 2.

6. Repeat step 5 for up to a dozen or so other features, as in the example shown in Figure 12.4. When you're finished selecting points, click Morph.

7. On the morph page, you can click a level between 0 and 10 to preview the transformation frames. When you're finished exploring, click the Click Here link to create and download your video.

8. Wait for the video to finish downloading, and then click the Play button. Your morph movie will thrill and astound you. (Okay, it's not a Michael Jackson video, but it's pretty good for something you can do on your home computer, right?)

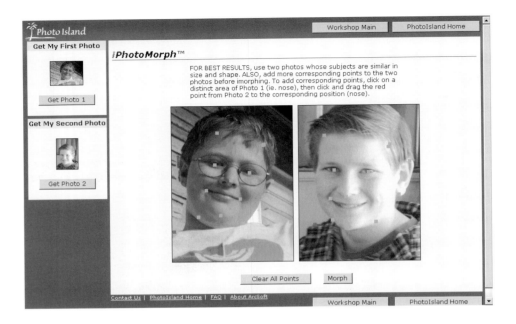

Figure 12.4

Select corresponding points on your two subjects to create the morphing boundaries.

Create a Montage with iMontage

A few years ago, I saw the most incredible movie poster. From a few feet away, it just looked like a picture of the main actor. But as I moved closer, I realized the picture was made up of thousands and thousands of smaller pictures. Now you can do the same thing with one of your own digital images. The iMontage service at the PhotoIsland Web site will transform your image into a montage of many, many tiny photos in exactly the same way!

Here are the steps for creating your own photomontage:

1. Point your Web browser to www.photoisland.com.

2. Click Photo WorkShop to enter the online, interactive photography play center. Then click iMontage.

3. Click Change Picture to upload your own digital photo.

4. Wait for the upload page to appear, and then click Browse. Select your photo, and then click Upload. Wait for your browser to finish uploading your image.

5. Click Make Me a Montage.

6. While you sit back and wait, PhotoIsland will attempt to entertain you (whether it suc-
ceeds is another story).

7. After the montage is finished, you can click anywhere on your image to zoom in for more
detail. Figure 12.5 shows an example of a completed montage. Remember that you're
dealing with a very small image on the Web site with the free interactive version. Don't
expect the crisp detail you get with the purchased software.

8. If you like, click Order a PhotoMontage Poster to purchase a copy for yourself.

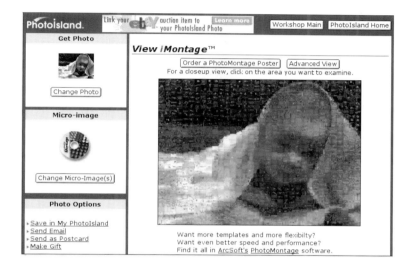

Figure 12.5

**This montage is
composed of a series
of tiny photos.**

Transform Head Shots

Are you surrounded by grumps and sourpusses, frowners and grouches, or soreheads and
grousers? If it's your job to make them smile, the projects in this section are for you. You can
bring joy and silliness into their drab and dreary lives. You can amuse, entertain, and enliven
with your digital camera and a few special Adobe PhotoDeluxe tricks hidden up your sleeve.
Think of the good deeds you'll be doing!

For instructions on using Adobe PhotoDeluxe, including how to open photos, access the
advanced features of power mode, and use the selection tools, see Chapter 3, "An Introduction
to PhotoDeluxe."

Bozo-in-a-Can

Clown noses are easy to create and can prove enormously amusing when done with a good heart and righteous intentions. When you digitally place a clown nose on an ill-tempered friend, you are actually making the world a nicer place to live. Good for you!

Here's how to add a bit of merriment to your digital photos:

1. Launch PhotoDeluxe and set up power mode (display the advanced menus and Layers and Selection palettes).

2. Open your picture. Pick a photo with a good head shot, facing forward. Try to select a picture with a large, clear head (or two, as shown in Figure 12.6) that a big, red nose won't obscure.

3. Choose Circle Tool from the Selections palette and select a circle around your subject's nose. Keep the circle fairly small—less is better in this case. Do not overwhelm your subject's face.

4. Select Effects → Selection Fill. Click Color, and then click the button just beneath it. This opens the color swatch selection dialog box. Choose a red swatch and click OK to return to the Selection Fill dialog box. Click Selection, and then click OK. A large, red circle will appear.

Figure 12.6

Choose a picture with clear, front-on head shots for this project.

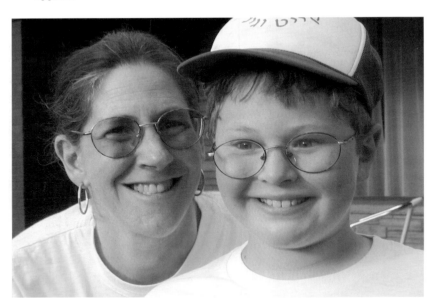

5. Select Effects → Render → Lighting Effects. In the Lighting Effects dialog box, move the light bulb (where the line crosses the circle) to roughly approximate the natural source of light in your picture, as shown in Figure 12.7. You can increase the light intensity by widening the circle or by moving the light bulb closer to the red circle. When you've created a three-dimensional-looking sphere, click OK.

6. Choose Tools → Brush. Click the Color square, select a white swatch from the color swatch selection dialog box, and click OK. Then click a fuzzy brush. I like the one on the second row, third from the left.

7. Paint a small, white highlight at about one-third of the way in from the top left of your red circle (per the light direction you selected in step 4). This creates the illusion of shininess on your clown nose.

8. Select Tools → Smudge. Choose a large smudge brush, such as the 45 brush. Now nudge up the ends of your subject's face to create a more clown-worthy smile, as in the example in Figure 12.8. Turn the least-amused subject into a smiling clown. This feature proves especially important when altering pictures of your boss.

Enjoy your newly clowned friend.

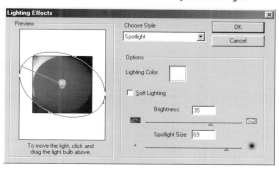

Figure 12.7

The Lighting Effects dialog box sets the direction, style, and color of your added light.

Figure 12.8

A bulbous clown nose adds that certain *je ne sais quoi* **to your portraits.**

Instant Brainiac

Do people say you have a swelled head? Do you say that other people have swelled heads? Now you can have actual photographic proof! If you're in the mood for a mind-blowing experience, this project is for you.

With just a digital photo of your subject and PhotoDeluxe, you can transform anyone into an instant brainiac. Here's how:

1. Launch PhotoDeluxe, set up power mode, and open your picture.

2. Create a copy of your subject's head. Choose Select → All, then Edit → Copy, and then Edit → Paste. This creates a new layer on top of your original photo. You'll edit this copy.

3. Choose Polygon Tool from the Selections palette and select your subject's forehead and hair, as shown in Figure 12.9. (For polygon selection, click at each point and double-click the final point.) Avoid selecting your subject's eyes, eyebrows, and ears.

4. Select Size → Perspective. Pull the upper-right handle first to the right and, only then, up to distort and magnify the head.

5. Now clean up your image. Select Tools → Smudge and smudge away any awkward transitions. See Figure 12.10 for an example of the results.

Figure 12.9

Select the portion of the head you intend to expand.

Whose Head Is It Anyway?

Have you ever dreamed of creating Frankenstein's monster? Have you wondered how you, too, might become a head-relocation specialist? Now you can. With PhotoDeluxe, you can enter the demanding and challenging world of cerebral translocation. Figure 12.11 shows an example of the process.

Select a photo with two good head shots. Both subjects should face fully forward, but it's okay if they have different head orientations and sizes. Then just follow these simple instructions:

1. Launch PhotoDeluxe, set up power mode, and open your picture.

2. Make two copies of the original picture. Choose Select → All, then Edit → Copy, and then Edit → Paste. Then repeat the process to create another copy.

3. Select your first copy by clicking Layer 1 on the Layers palette.

4. Choose SmartSelect Tool on the Selections palette and outline the first head.

5. Remove the entire picture except for the head. Select Effects → Feather. Specify to feather the edge of the selection to 4 pixels, click Delete Background, and then click OK.

6. You're now ready to work on the second head. Click Layer 2 and repeat steps 4 and 5 for the second head. At this point, your picture should contain three layers: Layer 0 will hold the original picture, and Layers 1 and 2 should each contain one head.

7. Hide Layer 2 by clicking the rectangle (the one with the eye icon) to the left of its name.

8. Choose Object Selection Tool from the Selections palette, click Layer 1, and then click the first head.

9. Now you'll transplant the first head onto the second body. Use PhotoDeluxe's move, resize, and rotate features to move the first head into the second one's position. In general, you will need to resize the head to slightly larger than life in order to fully cover both the head area and any small artifacts around it.

10. You're ready to work on the second head. To hide Layer 1 and redisplay Layer 2, click the square to the left of Layer 1. The eye icon should disappear from Layer 1 and reappear next to Layer 2. Now click Layer 2.

Figure 12.10

After resizing with Perspective, your subject's head expands into true "brainiac" proportions.

11. Ready for another head transplant? Click the second head and move it into place on the first body. Once again, use PhotoDeluxe's move, resize, and rotate features to place the new head.

12. Click the square next to Layer 1 to bring back the first head.

    Congratulations, Dr. Frankenstein. Your next patient is waiting.

The Mona You

Has anyone ever called you a classic beauty? Do poets write odes to your eyes? Now you can emphasize your timeless splendor with just a few image-processing steps. Here's how to celebrate yourself with a fine portrait:

1. Launch PhotoDeluxe, set up power mode, and open your picture.

2. Find an archetypal picture and load it into PhotoDeluxe. In this example, we'll use Da Vinci's *La Gioconda*, better known as the Mona Lisa.

3. Follow the instructions for the previous head-swapping project to extract your subject's face and paste it into a layer over the Mona Lisa background. Replace her face by moving, rotating, and resizing your selection.

4. To adjust the new face to match the tones and colors of the underlying picture, select Quality → Variations. For the Mona Lisa, progressively add more yellow and red to your subject's face. Just click More Yellow and More Red until you're satisfied that your picture matches the original's tones. Then click OK.

Kick back and enjoy your "original" artwork. Figure 12.12 shows an example.

Create Collage Projects with PhotoDeluxe

Adobe PhotoDeluxe comes packed with special goodies. These include stock photography, clip art, and other props to play with. The activities you'll find under Get & Fix Photo → Special Effects → Collage guide you through fun projects using those props.

Go "Undercover"

Here's how you can create a silly disguise starring your digital photo:

1. Launch PhotoDeluxe and open your picture.

2. Click the Get & Fix Photo button next to the activity bar at the top of the screen.

3. Click Special Effects → Collage → Disguise Your Face

4. Click 1 - Disguise → Get Clip Art. Then click the Photo Disguises tab and scroll through the available disguises.

5. Select the disguise you wish to work with and double-click it.

6. When the art opens, select the art, drag it from its window into your main picture, and move it roughly into place.

7. Use the resizing handles to adjust your art overlay until it works with your picture. Figure 12.13 shows an example using the beanie hat and mustache art.

8. Click 2 - Done and enjoy your disguise.

Figure 12.12

My next-door neighbor Ruth Lubliner, recast as the Mona Lisa

Figure 12.13

Transform your subjects with Photo-Deluxe's photo disguises.

SILLY HEAD TRICKS

Do you like "using your head"? Here are a few more ideas:

Cartoons Replace the faces in your favorite cartoon with heads extracted from photos of your friends and family. If you can get a few pictures of your colleagues, Dilbert cartoons work particularly well. (Just remember about fair use and copyright issues.)

Body switches Place a favorite pet's head on a supermodel's body. Better yet, stick your *own* head on the body of the aerobics instructor whose picture can be found in the PhotoDeluxe sample photos.

The unexpected Stick your head in unlikely places. Let your head peek out of a coffee mug, from behind a door, or in a famous news photo. You, too, can be a "Forrest Gump," appearing in famous historical scenes.

Create Travel Photos without Leaving Home

Have you ever wanted to visit the Eiffel Tower, the Taj Mahal, or even Mars? When you're stuck with a limited travel budget, Adobe PhotoDeluxe will leap to the rescue. Not only can you visit places you've never been, you'll bring back pictures as evidence!

Follow these steps to be on your virtual way to exotic locales:

1. Start PhotoDeluxe and open your picture.

2. Click the Get & Fix Photo button next to the activity bar.

3. Select Special Effects → Collage → Change Background.

4. Click 1 - Select → SmartSelect. Use the SmartSelect tool to extract your subject from the picture. When you're finished, click Delete Background. Use the Eraser tool as necessary to clean up any spare bits and pieces.

5. Click 2 - Add Background → Sample Photos. In the Samples window, click the Scenes tab and double-click one of the photos. (You'll find the best travel photos on your CD in PDART/PHOTOS/TRAVFOOD). Close the Samples window.

6. Click 3 - Resize. Adjust the size of your subject. Figure 12.14 shows an example using the Taj Mahal background.

7. Click 4 - Done.

In these few steps, you've created travel memories to last a lifetime. If only you could remember having been there in the first place.

In This Chapter...

This chapter explored some ways that you can use your photos for fun and amusement. Here are a few tips to keep in mind:

- Digital photography does not force you to use your pictures in constructive and meaningful ways. There's no harm in playing with your images and using them to have silly fun.

- For interactive play value with your digital snaps, there's no better place on the Web than PhotoIsland.com. Stop by and spend a few minutes or hours amusing yourself with the free tools found there.

- When you need to create a greeting card or gift item, consider using the techniques covered in this chapter to combine a portrait you snap with a classic work of art.

- Consider transplanting heads in a formal group picture before judiciously posting the results in a public place. It provides an interesting way to confuse people.

- For those who toil day to day, and cannot keep the pace, consider planting a clown nose on the boss's face.

Figure 12.14

Transport your subject to an exotic location.

Field Guide to Online Photo Finishing and Album Sites

SERVICE	URL	CONTACT	WHAT'S OFFERED
Altiplano	www.altiplano.com	support@altiplano.com	Albums and finishing; membership (Europe)
Bignose	www.bignose.com	1-877-672-4466, info@bignose.com	Poster processing, both digital and film
Black's	www.blackphoto.com	1-800-668-3826 (toll free in Canada only), smile.centre@blackphoto.com	Finishing; delivery to any Black's store
HP Photo Cartogra	www.cartogra.com	www.cartogra.com/home/contactus.asp	Hewlett-Packard's photo sharing site
Club Photo	www.clubphoto.com	1-408-557-6740, support@clubphoto.com	Albums and finishing; membership
ColourMailer	www.colormailer.com.au	info@colormailer.com	Finishing (Australia)
Digitaalfoto.nl	www.digitaalfoto.nl		Albums and prints (Netherlands)
dotPhoto	www.dotPhoto.com	http://dotphoto.custhelp.com/cgi-bin/dotphoto/people	Finishing; accepts CD, Zip, Superdisk, and Orb.formats
eFrames	www.eframes.com	1-877-370-7000, 1-415-401-9211, customerservice@eframes.com	Finishing, albums, and framed prints
ez prints	www.ezprints.com	1-888-584-7040, ezprints@ezprints.com	Finishing, including panoramic and large (20 × 30) prints; accepts CDs
EZShots	www.ezshots.com	email@ezshots.com	Albums
Fotango	www.fotango.com	+44 20 7251 7920, 9am-6pm, M-F, help@fotango.com	Finishing, reprints, and gifts (Europe)
Fotofun	www.fotofun.be		Finishing (Belgium)
FotoTime	www.fototime.com	support@fototime.com, feedback@fototime.com	Albums and finishing
Future Shop	www.futureshop.ca	1-888-785-8384, service@futureshop.ca	Finishing (Canada)
ImageStation	www.imagestation.com	1-877-488-2880, support@imagestation.com	Sony's storage, sharing, and prints site
IPrint.com	www.iprint.com	1-650-298-8500, Customer_Service@iprint.com, Customer_Support@iprint.com	Business and gift production
Michael's Camera, Video & Digital	www.michaels.com.au	(03) 9672 2224	Finishing (Australia)
MotoPhoto	www.motophoto.com	1-800-733-6686	Finishing
MyPhotosNow	www.myphotosnow.com		35mm to online photos
Mystic Color Lab	www.mysticcolorlab.com	1-800-367-6061, cservice@mysticcolorlab.com	Finishing
Ofoto	www.ofoto.com	1-877-986-3686, support@ofoto.com	Finishing (subsidiary of Kodak)

Continues

Continued

SERVICE	URL	CONTACT	WHAT'S OFFERED
PhotoAccess	www.photoaccess.com	1-206-264-2488, then push 0, support@photoaccess.com, info@photoaccess.com	Finishing
PhotoBox	www.photobox.co.uk www.photobox.ie	020 7691 1208, info@photobox.co.uk	Finishing and gifts (UK and Ireland)
PhotoChannel	www.photochannel.com	1-604-893-8955, support@photochannel.com, info@photochannel.com	Finishing
PhotoIsland	www.photoisland.com	1-800-762-8657, support@photoisland.com	Albums and image-processing fun
PhotoPoint	www.photopoint.com	help@photopoint.com	Albums; membership
PhotoWorks	www.photoworks.com	1-800-445-3348, 1-800-FILMWORKS, info@filmworks.com	Finishing (formerly Seattle Filmworks)
Printroom	www.printroom.com	1-510-413-1200, support@printroom.com	Lexar's albums and finishing site (partnered with the excellent digital photography tip site, www.saycheese.com)
Shutterfly	www.shutterfly.com	customerservice@shutterfly.com	Finishing
Signature Color	www.signaturecolor.com	1-512-445-0256, cs@signaturecolor.com	Finishing
Snapfish	www.snapfish.com	1-304-420-5615, service@snapfish.com	Finishing
Wal-Mart	www.walmart.com		Finishing; store pickup available
Wolf Camera	www.wolfcamera.com	1-800-643-9653, wolfstore@wolfcamera.com	Finishing, including panoramic prints
Yahoo	http://photos.yahoo.com	yahoo-photos@shutterfly.com	Albums and finishing

Glossary

A/C adapter A power adapter that allows you to plug your camera into a wall outlet. Your camera's manufacturer usually provides this adapter at an additional cost.

aliasing The jagged effect produced on lines, characters, and so forth when the resolution of the display is not sufficient to capture fine image detail.

alkaline battery A type of non-rechargeable battery that can be used in your digital camera. Alkaline batteries drain very quickly under the demands of most digital cameras.

anti-aliasing The technique that smoothes jagged effects in images caused by aliasing. Anti-aliasing combines image data from a higher-resolution image or model into adjacent pixels and produces cleaner, more natural lines.

aperture The size of the camera's lens opening. A small aperture provides a larger depth of field while letting in less light. A large aperture lets in more light at the cost of a narrower range of focus.

artifact An unintentional image element produced in error by an imaging device or as a byproduct of software or algorithms.

aspect ratio The ratio between an image's width and height. Typical ratios include 3:2, 4:3, and so forth. The first number refers to the image's width and the second refers to its height. As in mathematics, an aspect ratio of 1.5:1 is identical to 3:2.

ATA adapter A type of adapter that allows you to read data from a digital camera using the computer's PCMCIA ports. You insert your memory card into the ATA adapter and place the adapter into your port. It appears on your computer just like any other hard drive, ready to be read and provide rapid data transfer.

auto-focus lens A camera lens that automatically chooses the proper settings to create a sharp picture.

AV port See *video-out port.*

backlight An image effect that occurs when the sun or another light source shines too close to your subject's back. Backlight tricks your camera into thinking it is taking a picture of a very bright object. Your camera adjusts its light levels too high. Instead of picking up the light levels from your subject, it picks them up from the background.

banding The "layered" effect produced in images when smooth gradients are displayed or printed with a smaller number of hues than demanded by the image. Similar hues are printed with different colors because they fall to either side of a threshold and produce a visual discontinuity.

barrel distortion Image distortion that spreads the center of the image.

bitmap Strictly speaking, a black-and-white image constructed of arrays of black-and-white pixels. However, in common usage, the term *bitmap* (incorrectly) refers to arrays of pixels of any colors.

blooming Image distortion caused by overexposing a charge couple device (CCD) camera to light. A white area will appear to bleed from light sources such as a window or lamp.

BlueTooth standard A proposed wireless standard that allows electronic devices to communicate with each other using radio frequencies.

blurring A loss of image detail caused by incorrect focus or camera motion. Blurry pictures can be partially corrected with sharpening filters and deconvolution techniques.

BMP A graphic file format for Windows systems. It stores images as an uncompressed matrix of pixels.

brightness The amount of light detected at each picture element by the camera's charge couple device (CCD).

capture To acquire digital data through a camera or other scanning device.

CCD See *charge couple device.*

CF See *compact flash.*

charge couple device (CCD) A light sensor used in digital cameras to sample light intensity for gathering image data. CCD sensors produce more accurate images than CMOS sensors. A CCD array consists of a series of CCD sensors arranged in the digital camera to capture many points of light at once.

cloning In photo-editing software, a feature that allows you to copy a part of a photo and use that copy to replace another part of the photo. Cloning is typically used to hide flaws and undesirable features.

CMOS See *complementary metal-oxide semiconductor.*

CMYK The color standard for professional printing services. Instead of printing in red, green, and blue, this standard uses cyan (C), magenta (M), yellow (Y), and black (K) ink.

color temperature The temperature, in Kelvin, of a light source. The lower the temperature, the redder the light. The higher the temperature, the more blue. Candlelight clocks in at about 2,000° Kelvin and sunset at 3,000° Kelvin. Daylight and flash photography both register at about 5,000° Kelvin.

compact flash (CF) A type of removable media used in some digital cameras. Compact flash cards are built from banks of flash memory and a controller embedded in thin plastic.

complementary metal-oxide semiconductor (CMOS) A light sensor used in digital cameras to sample light intensity for gathering image data. CMOS sensors produce images with more noise and errors than do CCD sensors. However, CMOS sensors are available at a lower price than CCD sensors.

compression Techniques used to reduce the amount of space used to store image data. GIF and JPEG images both use image compression.

continuous tones Arbitrary image tones. Digital cameras cannot produce continuous tone because they must approximate colors and shades within fixed-byte values.

contrast The ratio in brightness between the darkest and lightest elements of an image. Natural scenes should contain moderate contrast, unlike printed text, which should be highly contrasted.

depth of field The area in front of the camera that appears in sharp focus within a scene.

digital Made up of binary information, readable by a computer.

digital accuracy How close pixel values match the colors and shades of the physical qualities of the item being imaged.

digital camera A film-free camera that uses a CCD array or CMOS sensors to capture images in digital form.

digital camera speed The time during which light is allowed through the digital camera's lens to fall upon the sensor. The faster the speed, the less likely the image will be subject to motion blur. Digital camera speed is analogous to traditional shutter speed, although some digital cameras do not come equipped with true shutters.

digital film See *removable media.*

digital zoom Magnification of an image by means of software within a digital camera. Digital zoom does not increase resolution and creates a lower-quality image by interpolating between pixel values.

digitization Conversion of analog "real-world" data into digital form.

dithering The technique of placing a series of monochromatic dots in a small area to simulate a range of tones and colors.

dye-sublimation printer A type of printer in which a thermal print head transfers ink from a roll or ribbon onto paper. The color intensity of the dye is controlled by the heat level of the print head. Dye sublimation produces the best quality prints for home use, but at a substantial cost.

dynamic range The difference between the darkest and brightest light that a digital camera can capture and reproduce.

equalization A technique for distributing image data across a greater range of pixel values. Typical equalization techniques include gamma correction and adaptive histogram equalization.

exposure compensation The mechanism that overrides a camera's automatic exposure sensors to manually select a longer or slower exposure.

exposure meter The system that sets the speed and aperture of a camera. Using the segment-metering system, the image is divided into segments, each of which is evaluated by the camera's light meter. With the center-weighted-metering system, the meter gives greater importance to the light values at the center of the image.

feathering In photo-editing software, a feature that allows you to soften the edges of a selected area so you can gently blend it with other picture elements.

fill-in flash See *forced flash.*

filter A camera accessory that allows you to customize the light entering your camera. You can accessorize your digital camera with optical filters to create a variety of special effects. In photo-editing software, a feature that allows you to alter image quality. Software filters can produce artistic, distorted, blurred, sharper, and many other versions of an image.

FireWire See *IEEE-1394.*

first-curtain flash A camera mode in which the flash fires at the moment the shutter opens.

fish-eye lens A lens that produces a distinctive distorted view. Elements at the center of a fish-eye view occupy proportionately greater space than elements that lie towards its edges.

fixed-focus lens A wide-angle lens that provides good focus over a wide range of distances from the camera. Fixed-focus lenses do not require your camera to provide auto-focusing.

FlashPath A type of adapter that allows you to transfer data from a digital camera into your computer. A FlashPath adapter looks like a 3.5-inch floppy disk. FlashPath systems transfer data from 2 to 15 times faster than serial cable connections.

focal length The distance between the lens and the point where light rays focus behind the lens when light enters the lens in parallel lines. The longer the focal length, the greater the magnification that the lens will provide.

forced flash Forcing the flash to fire when the camera does not sense that it is required. Also called fill-in flash.

fractals Mathematical representation of images. An image converted into fractal representation is resolution-independent. Fractals are composed of scalable textures rather than pixels, so you can create images ten times as large as the original or bigger, without blocky or jagged artifacts.

gamma correction The distribution of image data to match the mathematical gamma curve that enhances details and generally lightens the image in a visually "natural" manner.

GIF See *Graphics Image Format.*

GIF89a The standard for GIF image support for animation.

Graphics Image Format (GIF) One of the two most common formats of digital pictures. The GIF format was copyrighted by CompuServe. GIF pictures store images in a lossless format, using at most 256 colors.

grayscale A colorless image consisting of black, white, and gray elements. Grayscale images are similar to black-and-white photos.

horizontal resolution The greatest possible number of pixels that a digital camera can produce along the width of an image.

hue The color (as opposed to the brightness) of a pixel.

IEEE-1394 A high-speed, serial data-transfer standard that offers rates of 400Mbps. The Apple version of this technology is known as FireWire; the Sony version is called iLink.

iLink See *IEEE-1394.*

infrared-block filter A type of camera filter that reduces some of the infrared light entering your camera, while allowing regular visible light to pass through.

ink-jet printer A printer in which colored dyes are squirted from cartridges onto paper. Ink-jet printers create color intensity by dithering.

IR-block filter See *infrared-block filter.*

Joint Photographic Experts Group (JPEG) An image format for digital pictures. JPEG pictures use efficient (but lossy) compression algorithms and averaging techniques to minimize image size at a slight accuracy cost. JPEG pictures can capture an arbitrary number of colors, providing greater color sensitivity than GIFs.

JPEG See *Joint Photographic Experts Group.*

JPEG-2000 A new standard for storing digital pictures that extends the JPEG standard to include lossless compression, transparency, and other features.

Kelvin A temperature measurement system used for light sources. See also *color temperature.*

landscape A digital picture whose width exceeds its height. Landscape is also a paper-orientation option for printing.

laser printer A type of printer that uses a laser to set electrical charges along a print drum. Toner (an ink mixture) is drawn to the charged areas of the drum, and a heating element fuses the toner from the drum to paper.

layer In photo-editing software, a feature that allows you to isolate your picture elements so you can work on each one individually.

LCD See *liquid crystal display.*

lenticular print A printing technology that uses small prisms above the print surface to direct light, creating a pseudo three-dimensional effect.

liquid crystal display (LCD) A display made of a liquid crystal material sandwiched between transparent sheets. Typically, an LCD on the back of a digital camera allows the photographer to preview and review digital images. LCDs consume a large percentage of the battery's power. New advances in LCD technology, particularly in passive-matrix LCD displays known as DSTN, produce brighter screens with sharper colors. Many cameras support two types of LCD displays: one icon/character-based for displaying camera status and one pixel-based for use as a viewfinder.

lithium battery A type of one-time-use battery that provides greater power and endurance than alkaline batteries. Some new lithium batteries can be recharged.

lossless compression Any compression scheme that produces a decompressed image that is identical to the original. For example, TIFF compression is lossless.

lossy compression Any compression scheme that produces a decompressed image that is not identical to the original, usually manifested in a loss of detail or color and the addition of artifacts that may appear blocky or jagged. Usually, colors have been blended, averaged, or estimated in the decompressed version. For example, JPEG compression is lossy. Each time you load and resave a JPEG image, you may lose valuable image information.

luminance The intensity (as opposed to the color) of a pixel.

macro lens A camera lens that allows you to shoot pictures from as little as an inch or two away from your subject.

media port See *video-out port*.

megapixel camera A digital camera that produces images of at least one million pixels.

memory card A type of removable media used in digital cameras. Flash memory cards include compact flash, smart media, and stick memory. They use solid-state memory chips to store your pictures indefinitely and without power.

Memory Stick See *stick memory*.

MMC See *MultiMedia Card*.

moiré A photo artifact consisting of bands of diagonal distortions. These distortions arise from interference between two geometrically regular patterns.

MultiMedia Card (MMC) A type of solid-state memory card.

National Television Standards Committee (NTSC) Refers to the video standard for television signals used in the United States, American Samoa, Barbados, Bermuda, Bolivia, Canada, Chile, Columbia, Costa Rica, Cuba, Democratic People's Republic of Korea, Dominica, El Salvador, Equador, Guam, Guatemala, Haiti, Honduras, Mexico, Micronesia, Myanmar, Nicaragua, Panama, Peru, Philippines, Puerto Rico, Suriname, Taiwan, Trinidad, Tobago, and Venezuela.

NiCd battery See *Nickel-Cadmium (NiCd) battery*.

Nickel-Cadmium (NiCd) battery A type of rechargeable battery that provides excellent camera operation. Because NiCds (pronounced "nigh-cads") contain the heavy metal cadmium, they promote concerns about proper disposal.

Nickel-Metal Hydride (NiMH) battery A type of rechargeable battery that provides excellent camera operation, long effective life, and fewer environmental concerns than alkaline or NiCd batteries. NiMHs (pronounced "nimms") also have fewer "memory effects" than NiCd batteries do. You do not need to drain them each time before recharging.

noise Random, unintended image values added to and distributed across a digital picture. See also *artifact*.

NTSC See *National Television Standards Committee*.

OCR See *Optical Character Recognition*.

Optical Character Recognition (OCR) A technology that allows a computer to recognize printed or typed characters. It's possible to use OCR packages with digital camera images.

optical zoom Magnification of an image by means of an optical zoom lens. Optical zoom does not lower resolution and creates the same quality image as an image taken without optical zoom.

PAL See *Phase Alternation Line*.

panorama A series of images joined together to produce a composite image of arbitrary size.

PC card Any media you can insert in a PCMCIA slot in your computer. A few digital cameras use PC cards to store photos.

PDD Adobe PhotoDeluxe's proprietary format for image files.

Phase Alternation Line (PAL) The video standard for television signals used in Western Europe, Australia, Japan, and other countries that do not specifically support the NTSC standard.

photographic-quality paper Printer paper that is very stiff, or photo weight, and very bright. It is designed to avoid spreading ink and to produce a glossy finish after printing.

PICT A file format for storing uncompressed pictures.

pixel A picture element. A pixel is the smallest part of an image, which when placed into a two-dimensional array with other pixels forms a picture.

polarizing filter A type of camera filter that uses circular polarization to allow or deny access to certain types of light.

portrait A digital picture whose height exceeds its width. Portrait is also a paper-orientation option for printing.

quilt A two-dimensional panorama. Quilts are made up of photos snapped in two dimensions, both rows and columns.

red-eye An effect that appears to make a person's eyes glow red in an image. Red-eye occurs when light from flash photography reflects from the blood-vessels (or *choroids*) directly behind a person's retina. Animal retinas reflect light, too. However, many animals have an extra layer inside their eyes (known as a *tapetum lucidum*). Unlike humans, this layer is not composed of black pigment but some other color and can produce all sorts of red-eye variations, including green-eye.

red-eye reduction mode A solution for red-eye built into some digital cameras. In this mode, the camera flashes twice. The first flash causes people's pupils to quickly contract. This allows less light into the eye, and thus produces less reflection when the light flashes a second time to actually take the picture.

removable media Any of the many types of storage devices that can be inserted into your camera and read from your computer. Removable media are often called "digital film." Media include floppy disks, compact flash cards, smart media cards, and Clik! disks among others. Removable media allow you to transfer pictures to your personal computer without using cables. Using removable media, you can expand your camera's memory by replacing a full card or disk with a fresh one when needed.

resolution The number of pixels that a display or printing device can control. Each pixel must be "addressed" for writing or reading. Resolution also refers to the pixel density.

RGB The standard set of colors used by computer monitors to create images on your screen. RGB stands for red, green, and blue.

second-curtain flash A camera mode in which the flash fires just before the shutter closes.

serial cable transfer A method used to transfer images from a digital camera to a computer. This method uses software packaged with the camera and serial cable plugged into the camera and the computer's serial port. Serial cable transfer is very slow. Speedier transfer methods are available for cameras that use removable media.

silver-halide paper Traditional photo-quality paper, typically used by photo finishers for prints.

slow-synch flash A camera mode that captures both a dark background as well as a well-illuminated foreground. This technique combines a long exposure with a short flash. This allows the camera to create a well-exposed image of the background and add it to the flash photography of the foreground.

smart media A type of removable media used in some digital cameras. The actual name for this type of memory is Solid-State Floppy Disk Card (SSFDC). These cards consist of a flash memory chip embedded in thin plastic.

solar power pack A type of power supply for digital cameras that uses the sun as its energy source.

Solid-State Floppy Disk Card (SSFDC) See *smart media*.

stereo images A pair of images that, when viewed through a special viewer, produce a three-dimensional effect. The two photos approximate the location of our eyes. The left image and right images are taken at exactly the same height and orientation, but offset horizontally by about 2.5 inches.

stick memory A type of removable media used in digital cameras. The Memory Stick product, developed by Sony, is a form of flash memory that shares many of the same features of compact flash cards.

streaming video A video-delivery system in which an Internet connection is established between a video data server and a viewing program. Streaming video provides controlled, on-demand delivery of both real-time (live event) and previously recorded data.

Tagged Image File Format (TIFF) An image format used to store high-resolution images. Although TIFF images are often uncompressed, this format does support some proprietary compression algorithms. TIFF images are lossless. This makes TIFF a good choice for storing your pictures while you are working on them.

telephoto lens A magnifying lens with a very high focal length. The opposite of wide-angle lenses, telephoto lenses provide images with a narrow angle of view. Telephoto lenses take pictures of a smaller area of the scene. Use a telephoto lens when you cannot get close to your subject, such as in wildlife photography.

TV-out port A connection port that allows you to connect your computer to a television, mirroring the contents of your monitor.

ultraviolet (UV) filter A type of camera filter that helps cut through fog and creates clearer pictures in misty conditions.

Universal Serial Bus (USB) A cable connection standard that provides quick and efficient data transfer. Most newer computers provide USB ports. Some digital cameras have started to support USB transfer in place of, or in addition to, the more traditional serial cable transfers.

USB See *Universal Serial Bus.*

UV filter See *ultraviolet (UV) filter.*

vertical resolution The greatest possible number of pixels that a digital camera can produce across the height of an image.

video CD (VCD) A standard established to record MPEG-1 video data onto a compact disc (CD). Also called White Book.

video-out port A port on a digital camera that allows you to create a video signal that can be displayed on a television, a VCR, a projection system, and similar devices. Also called an AV or media port, this port typically creates NTSC or PAL signals, or sometimes both.

vista A type of panorama that shows images aligned in a row. To produce a simple vista, you stitch together a linear series of pictures.

watermark A visual mark that overlays your images to protect them from illegal copying. A nonvisual digital version (called digital watermarking) adds invisible author copyright information into a picture, without noticeably altering the image.

white balance A feature that allows you to manually adjust how your camera reacts to different light sources with differing color temperatures. When a camera is balanced for one temperature of light and used to photograph another temperature, it creates colors that are not true.

White Book See *video CD.*

wide-angle lens A lens that allows your camera to capture a wider image. The opposite of telephoto lenses, wide-angle lenses provide greater depth of field. Wide-angle lenses take pictures of a larger part of the scene.

Wi-Fi standard A new and popular standard for transmitting information between electronic devices without using a wired connection.

zoom See *digital zoom; optical zoom.*

zoom lens A lens that provides a magnification effect by changing your camera's focal length.

Index

Note to the Reader: Throughout this index **boldfaced** page numbers indicate primary discussions of a topic. *Italicized* page numbers indicate illustrations.

Get *Savvy*™

Sybex introduces Savvy,™ a new series of in-depth, premium graphics and web books. Savvy books turn beginning and intermediate level graphics professionals into experts, and give advanced users a meaningful edge in this competitive climate.

In-Depth Coverage. Each book contains compelling, professional examples and illustrations to demonstrate the use of the program in a working environment.

Proven Authors. Savvy authors have the first-hand knowledge and experience to deliver useful insights, making even the most advanced discussions accessible.

Sophisticated Package. Savvy titles have a striking interior design, enhanced by high-quality, coated paper for crisp graphic reproduction.

SYBEX®
www.sybex.com

Flash™ MX Savvy
by Ethan Watrall
and Norbert Herber
ISBN: 0-7821-4108-0
US $50

Photoshop® 7 Savvy
by Steve Romaniello
ISBN: 0-7821-4110-2
US $50

Maya™ 4.5 Savvy™
by John Kundert-Gibbs
and Peter Lee
ISBN: 0-7821-4109-9
US $60

**Dreamweaver™
Fireworks™ Savvy**
by Christian Crumlish
ISBN: 0-7821-4111-0
US $50

Style. Substance. Sybex.